Starting with the Spirit

At last, a systematic treatment of Third Article Theology! Such a volume was overdue, and Myk Habets and Gregory Liston's book does not disappoint. This solid groundwork will give others confidence to explore the ramifications of "starting with the Spirit" in every aspect of theology. Arguably, beginning with the third article of the creed is the most natural entry to theology because it is through the work of the Holy Spirit in the world (and in the church) that we come to know God and get connected with Christians globally.

Kirsteen Kim, Fuller Theological Seminary, USA

Myk Habets and Gregory J. Liston have made a significant contribution to the theology of the Holy Spirit. Their exposition and promotion of Third Article Theology is both novel and visionary. In two parts, the book first examines the ground and grammar of Third Article Theology and then the content and consequences of Third Article Theology, treating such issues as Christology, Trinity, Ecclesiology, Soteriology, Anthropology, Missiology, and Eschatology. All are reconceived and recrafted in the light of the Holy Spirit. For anyone interested in Pneumatology, this book is a must read.

Thomas G. Weinandy, OFM, Cap. Washington, DC.
Former member of the Vatican's International Theological Commission

This wonderful work is an academically rigorous yet pastorally accessible invitation to look afresh at the mystery of God and all of life in view of God through the lens of the Holy Spirit. Habets and Liston argue convincingly for the methodological incorporation of Third Article Theology into our theological toolbox. But as seasoned teachers with a commitment to spiritual formation, they also show us many biblically sound and theologically practical examples of what it actually looks like to practice becoming a TAT theologian! Highly recommended!

Leopoldo A. Sánchez M., Concordia Seminary, USA

Third Article Theology captures in a theological movement the impetus that theology has found in recent years in taking seriously the ongoing activity of the Spirit in leading the church and humanity into all truth. This book offers a rigorous, comprehensive, systematic, and practical account of Third Article Theology; but—even more than that—it offers fascinating and rich insights into the breadth and depth of the very person and work of the Holy Spirit and into the benefits of prioritizing pneumatology in theological discourse. Theologians and church people alike would do well to read and understand this important book.

Tom Greggs, University of Aberdeen, UK

This new book on Third Article Theology provides a very clear and systematic account of the movement to prioritize the Spirit in systematic theology, and the historical and contemporary reasons to think this is not only important, but indeed transformative, for spiritual life today. There is a wealth of bibliographic allusion in the text, making it a perfect volume for teaching.

Sarah Coakley, University of Cambridge, UK

Habets and Liston have given us without question the standard work on Third Article Theology. Their basic idea is both simple and revolutionary. Since all of God's works occur in the Holy Spirit, all areas of theology are to be viewed through the lens of pneumatology. I know of no other work that makes this case as clearly, thoroughly, and compellingly as this one.

Frank D. Macchia, Bangor University, UK

Starting with the Spirit

The T&T Clark Introduction to Third Article Theology

Myk Habets and Gregory J. Liston

t&tclark
LONDON • NEW YORK • OXFORD • NEW DELHI • SYDNEY

T&T CLARK
Bloomsbury Publishing Plc
50 Bedford Square, London, WC1B 3DP, UK
1385 Broadway, New York, NY 10018, USA
29 Earlsfort Terrace, Dublin 2, Ireland

BLOOMSBURY, T&T CLARK and the T&T Clark logo are trademarks
of Bloomsbury Publishing Plc

First published in Great Britain in 2024

Copyright © Myk Habets and Gregory J. Liston, 2024

Myk Habets and Gregory J. Liston have asserted their right under the Copyright, Designs and Patents Act, 1988, to be identified as Authors of this work.

For legal purposes the Acknowledgments on p. xii constitute an extension
of this copyright page.

Cover image © Bim / Getty Images

Excerpts from *The Mysteries of Christianity* by Matthias J. Scheeben, copyright © 2006. Used by permission of Crossroad Publishing Company.

Excerpts from *An Unconventional God* by Jack Levison, copyright © 2020. Used by permission of Baker Academic, a division of Baker Publishing Group.

All rights reserved. No part of this publication may be reproduced or transmitted in any form or by any means, electronic or mechanical, including photocopying, recording, or any information storage or retrieval system, without prior permission in writing from the publishers.

Bloomsbury Publishing Plc does not have any control over, or responsibility for, any third-party websites referred to or in this book. All internet addresses given in this book were correct at the time of going to press. The author and publisher regret any inconvenience caused if addresses have changed or sites have ceased to exist, but can accept no responsibility for any such changes.

A catalogue record for this book is available from the British Library.

A catalog record for this book is available from the Library of Congress.

ISBN HB: 978-0-5677-0861-8
PB: 978-0-5677-0860-1
ePDF: 978-0-5677-0863-2
ePUB: 978-0-5677-0862-5

Typeset by Newgen KnowledgeWorks Pvt. Ltd., Chennai, India
Printed and bound in Great Britain

To find out more about our authors and books visit www.bloomsbury.com
and sign up for our newsletters.

To Paul Molnar, Ivor Davidson, and other theological mentors, who tried their best to educate me; I appreciate you and dedicate this work to you in respect.
Myk Habets

To my wife Diane, for her unwavering kindness, enthusiasm, and support.
Gregory J. Liston

Contents

Acknowledgments xii
Note to the Reader xiii

Part I The Ground and Grammar of Third Article Theology

1 Introduction 3
  1.1 What Is Third Article Theology 3
  1.2 Why Do Third Article Theology 14
  1.3 The Grammar and Content of a TAT 20

2 Spirit Christology as Entry to TAT 24
  2.1 Introduction: Why Start a TAT with Christology 24
  2.2 Defining Spirit Christology 30
  2.3 Establishing a Spirit Christology from the Messianic *kairoi* 35
  2.4 Conclusion 43

3 The Methodology of Third Article Theology 45
  3.1 Introduction 45
  3.2 The Methodology of TAT 45
  3.3 The Method of TAT 55
  3.4 Conclusion 65

4 Critiques and Questions 66
  4.1 How Has TAT Been Received? 66
  4.2 Addressing the Main Critiques of Spirit Christology 67

- 4.3 Addressing the Main Critiques of TAT 75
- 4.4 Conclusion 81

5 Third Article Theology Applied 83

- 5.1 Introduction 83
- 5.2 Conciliar and Ecumenical Theology 83
- 5.3 Systematic Theology 86
- 5.4 Practical Theology 90
- 5.5 Conclusion 91

Part II The Content and Consequence of Third Article Theology

6 Trinity: Viewing God through a Pneumatological Lens 95

- 6.1 Introduction 95
- 6.2 Inseparable Operations 97
- 6.3 Reciprocal Relations 101
- 6.4 On Learning to Pray "Our Father" 110
- 6.5 Conclusion 113

7 Ecclesiology: The Church as a Community of the Spirit 115

- 7.1 Introduction 115
- 7.2 The Church as a Sequel to the Incarnation 116
- 7.3 The Church as a Participant in Trinitarian Life 123
- 7.4 A TAT Understanding of Worship 131

8 Soteriology: Pneumatological Participation in the Life of God 135

- 8.1 Introduction: Salvation Today 135
- 8.2 The Spirit and Salvation 136
- 8.3 The Spirit and Atonement 142
- 8.4 The Weight of Our Neighbor's Glory 149

9 Anthropology: The Spirit Reveals and Releases Our True Humanity 152

9.1 Introduction 152
9.2 What Anthropology 153
9.3 Sanctification: Or, toward Becoming a *soma pneumatikon* 158
9.4 Identity and the Spirit: Me, Myself, and the Spirit 161

10 Missiology: The Spirit as Present and Active in the World 168

10.1 Introduction 168
10.2 Andrew Lord's *Spirit-Shaped Mission* 170
10.3 Pneumato-Ecclesiology and Pneumato-Missiology 177

11 Eschatology: The Spirit as Transforming and Perfecting Presence 189

11.1 Introduction 189
11.2 Developing a Spirit Eschatology 191
11.3 Applying a Spirit Eschatology to Ecclesiology 197
11.4 Application to Communion 202

12 Conclusion 211

Suggested Further Reading 215
Bibliography 217
Author Index 233
Subject Index 237

Acknowledgments

Thanks go to our families, Odele, Sydney, and Liam (Myk), and Diane, Emily, and James (Greg) for cheering us on from the sidelines and for being partners in ministry in every sense of the word. To Albany Baptist Church (Myk) and Mt. Albert Baptist Church (Greg) for being homes and extended families of faith, thank you for your ongoing support. To Laidlaw College, its staff and faculty, for being a place to teach and research, serve and minister, thank you. And to the many students who have been the laboratory of learning for the genesis of this book, thank you for your critical questions, your enthusiasm, and your application of the truths contemplated in these pages. Our thanks to Tim Walker for compiling the index. Finally, our thanks and appreciation goes to the staff of Bloomsbury T&T Clark—Anna Turton, Jack Curtin, Sam Augustin, and the rest of the crew—thank you.

Myk Habets *Greg Liston*
Doctor Serviens Ecclesiae *Soli Deo Gloria*

Note to the Reader

To help readers navigate what is to follow, our approach in writing the text of this volume was that each chapter was initially written by an individual author, and then edited by the other author to ensure consistency and coherence. No attempt, however, was made to try to imitate one another's writing styles to achieve a third voice, as it were. Those who wish to engage in source criticism to determine which author initially wrote which chapter will not find it a difficult task. It would be claiming too much to say this dual authorship approach resembles the two hands of God at work in the economy, but two people working on one document in real time may be as close to *perichoresis* as it gets in academia. Our prayer is that you enjoy reading this as much as we enjoyed writing it.

Part I

The Ground and Grammar of Third Article Theology

1

Introduction

1.1 What Is Third Article Theology

In the hours immediately before Jesus was arrested, he comforted his followers with the promise of the coming Holy Spirit. This Spirit would work in the world, Jesus said, convicting of sin, promoting righteousness, and making known God's future judgment (John 16:5–11). But, even more reassuringly, the Spirit would also work in the minds and hearts of the disciples, and in the church they would eventually form. To a frightened group who were beyond overwhelmed at the thought of Jesus leaving, and who struggled to understand even a fraction of what was being said to them, Jesus specifically and clearly promised that the coming Spirit would lead them into all truth.

> There is so much more I want to tell you, but you can't bear it now. When the Spirit of truth comes, he will guide you into all truth. He will not speak on his own but will tell you what he has heard. He will tell you about the future. He will bring me glory by telling you whatever he receives from me. All that belongs to the Father is mine; this is why I said, "The Spirit will tell you whatever he receives from me." (John 16:12–15, NLT)

Third Article Theology (TAT) launches from this promise. Deriving its name from the *Third Article* of the Niceno-Constantinopolitan Creed, "[We believe] in the Spirit,"[1] TAT builds explicitly and directly upon the faith-inspired conviction that Jesus has sent the Spirit to reveal to his church the truth about God. TAT is thus pneumatological in impetus (intentionally

---

[1] Jaroslov Pelikan and Valerie Hotchkiss, eds., *Creeds and Confessions of Faith in the Christian Tradition: Early, Eastern and Medieval* (New Haven, CT: Yale University Press, 2003), 169.

prioritizing the Spirit in the theological task), Trinitarian in foundation (affirming that all theological truth is located in God's united being and work), and comprehensive in scope (focusing on the entire spectrum of theological doctrines, and even beyond these).

TAT is pneumatological in impetus. It starts with the Spirit.[2] Rather than delaying or downplaying pneumatological considerations, as if the Spirit can be tacked on after other theological truths have already been determined, TAT intentionally prioritizes pneumatology, putting it front and center in the theological task. So, for example, in the study of Christology, a TAT approach follows Pinnock's guidance, who suggests: "Let us see what results from viewing Christ as an aspect of the Spirit's mission, instead of (as is more usual) viewing Spirit as a function of Christ's."[3] Given that it is the Spirit who leads us into all truth, prioritizing the Spirit in our theological method aligns our epistemological approach with our existential reality. As a result, it leads us more directly and clearly to a theological understanding closely aligned with the full truth of God's revelation.

TAT is Trinitarian in foundation. Prioritizing the Spirit does not imply minimizing the person or work of the Father or Son. In contrast, TAT locates itself within the broader category of intentionally Trinitarian methodologies. Indeed, some theologians suggest that adopting a pneumatological priority provides a surer route to a fully rounded Trinitarian understanding than many alternative approaches. As Dabney argues, "Christian theology has never come to grips with the fact that relationship to God through Jesus Christ starts with the Spirit. There may have been good reasons for that in the past. But now, a host of voices suggest, there are good reasons for beginning our theologizing where we begin our discipleship."[4]

Finally, TAT is comprehensive in scope. It is not just pneumatology. The objective of TAT is not merely to look at the Spirit, or to focus on just that individual theological doctrine (pneumatology) as an isolated reality. Rather, TAT looks through the Spirit, examining every theological doctrine and even beyond that to all of reality. Consequently, the most common image used to describe TAT is that of the Spirit as a lens. A lens is transparent and difficult to focus on in and of itself, but when it is looked through, the

---

[2] D. Lyle Dabney, "Starting with the Spirit: Why the Last Should Now Be First," in *Starting with the Spirit* (ed. Stephen Pickard and Gordon Preece; Hindmarsh: Australian Theological Forum, 2001), 3–27.
[3] Clark H. Pinnock, *Flame of Love: A Theology of the Holy Spirit* (Downers Grove, IL: IVP Academic, 1996), 80.
[4] Dabney, "Starting with the Spirit," 27.

object being examined comes into perspective. Similarly, TAT looks through the lens of the Spirit in order to see other realities more clearly. It views pneumatology not just as the starting point, but as the connecting link that binds all the different theological doctrines together. "Pneumatology is not so much one specific chapter of Christian theology as an essential dimension of every theological view of the church and of its spirituality and liturgical and sacramental life."[5]

"Third Article Theology is a new, exciting, and ambitious project."[6] Indeed, the aim of TAT is nothing less than to re-envisage the whole of theology through intentionally starting with the Spirit. Consequently, the phrase TAT is utilized in two senses. First, it refers to a specific theological methodology that intentionally prioritizes pneumatology. Second, it is also used to indicate the theological understanding that emerges when this methodology is adopted. It is one of the core convictions of those theologians pursuing a TAT that an intentionally pneumatological perspective has been an unfortunate omission from theological investigation in the past, and that the time is ripe for such an approach. This book is an invitation to join in this journey of discerning what light is shed on our central Christian doctrines when they are considered from the standpoint of the Spirit. And this introductory chapter begins that journey by exploring exactly what TAT is and why it matters, before outlining the structure of the chapters to come.

1.1.1 Three Characterizations of Third Article Theology

What does it mean to start with the Spirit? Proponents of TAT most often describe this theological method by contrasting it with alternative approaches. This section describes three characterizations, two that intentionally contrast it with other theological methods, and a third that positively situates TAT within the broader suite of Trinitarian theological approaches. While the contrasting descriptions are helpful and illustrative, this new methodological approach should primarily be understood in the latter manner. In other words, TAT should be seen as an important and

---

[5]Boris Bobrinskoy, "Holy Spirit," in *Dictionary of the Ecumenical Movement* (ed. Nicholas Lossky, José Miguez Bonino, John S. Pobee, Tom F. Stransky, Geoffrey Wainwright, and Pauline Webb; Grand Rapids, MI: Eerdmans, 1991), 470.
[6]Kirsteen Kim, "Foreword," in *Third Article Theology: A Pneumatological Dynamics* (ed. Myk Habets; Minneapolis, MN: Fortress Press, 2016).

necessary subset of the Trinitarian renaissance that has fueled much of twentieth-century theology.

i) First, Second, and Third Article Theologies

The first and most common characterization used to locate and describe TAT, and the one from which its name is originally derived, was proposed by the United Methodist theologian, D. Lyle Dabney. Dabney characterizes TAT by contrasting it with two alternative theological strategies that have dominated Western Christian thought, namely First and Second Article theologies.[7] The comparisons he outlines are helpful if seen as broad generalizations rather than detailed historical critiques.

The first article of the Niceno-Constantinopolitan Creed states, "We believe in one God the Father, all-powerful, Maker of heaven and of earth."[8] So, First Article theologies start with the Father. Utilizing this lens, their focus is initially on God's creation—our innate God-given abilities and capabilities—and from this starting point, they trace a continuous path from nature through to grace. First Article theologies argue that there is a universal, inbuilt, human capacity for and tendency toward God. So, grace fills out and purifies what is already in us and in all of creation—that which has been tarnished and diminished by sin—and brings it to perfection and completion. First Article theologies are most clearly evidenced in medieval scholasticism.

The second article of the Niceno-Constantinopolitan Creed states, "[We believe] in one Lord Jesus Christ, the only begotten Son of God."[9] Second Article theologies thus start with the Son, and view reality through the lens of Christ and his redemptive work. They focus on humanity's universal rejection of God, the darkly impenetrable divide between humanity and God, and a God who miraculously makes his way down to fallen humanity. Second Article theologies consequently interpret reality through discontinuity— through contrast and contradiction. God is pure; humanity depraved. God

---

[7]The following subsection is based on D. Lyle Dabney, "Why Should the First Be Last? The Priority of Pneumatology in Recent Theological Discussion," in *Advents of the Spirit: An Introduction to the Current Study of Pneumatology* (ed. Bradford E. Hinze and D. Lyle Dabney; Milwaukee, WI: Marquette University Press, 2005), 240–61. See also Dabney, "Starting with the Spirit," 3–27; and D. Lyle Dabney, "Saul's Armour: The Problem and Promise of Pentecostal Theology," *Pneuma* 23 (2001): 126–31.

[8]Pelikan and Hotchkiss, eds., *Creeds and Confessions: Early, Eastern and Medieval*, 169.

[9]Pelikan and Hotchkiss, eds., *Creeds and Confessions: Early, Eastern and Medieval*, 169.

is powerful; humanity impotent. Second Article theologies are most clearly evident in the theological work emerging from the Protestant Reformation.

The third article of the Niceno-Constantinopolitan Creed states, "[We believe] in the Spirit, the holy, the lordly, and life giving one."[10] So, TAT starts with the Spirit and his transformative work. Where First and Second Article theologies focus on universals (either our *universal* tendency toward, or *universal* rejection of, God), TAT focuses on the *particular*—the specific reality of the Spirit in communities and relationships, and most specifically on the reality of *transformation*. Consequently, TAT balances and affirms both the continuity and discontinuity of nature with grace, of time with eternity, and ultimately of humanity with divinity. For First Article theologies, the key concept is the *beatific vision*—the perfection and completion of humanity. For Second Article theologies, the key concept is *justification*—the restoring of a right standing. But for Third Article theologies, the key concept is *participation*—the drawing of individuals and communities into the life of God.

There is no claim that a TAT as represented here is entirely novel or unique. Irenaeus in the patristic period,[11] John Owen[12] or Jonathan Edwards[13] after the Reformation, or Edward Irving in the Enlightenment[14] are just a small sample of those who developed components of a TAT. Moreover, theologians who focus primarily on other approaches certainly do not neglect pneumatology, often using the lens of the Spirit to complement and balance the views they gain in developing First or Second Article theologies. Medieval scholarship is not entirely based on the first article, nor is Reformation theology entirely based on the second. Further, there is no implication that Third Article theologies should *replace* First and Second Article theologies. The methodological portraits above

---

[10] Pelikan and Hotchkiss, eds., *Creeds and Confessions: Early, Eastern and Medieval*, 169.
[11] See, for example, Anthony Briggman, *Irenaeus of Lyons and the Theology of the Holy Spirit* (Oxford: Oxford University Press, 2012).
[12] See, for example, Kelly M. Kapic, "The Spirit as Gift: Explorations in John Owen's Pneumatology," in *The Ashgate Research Companion to John Owen's Theology* (ed. K. M. Kapic and M. Jones; Surrey: Ashgate, 2012), 113–40. Also Alan Spence, "The Significance of John Owen for Modern Christology," in *The Ashgate Research Companion to John Owen's Theology* (ed. K. M. Kapic and M. Jones; Surrey: Ashgate, 2012), 171–84. And Colin Gunton, "John Owen and John Zizioulas on the Church," in *Theology through the Theologians: Selected Essays (1972–1995)* (London: T&T Clark, 1996), 187–205.
[13] See, for example, Myk Habets, "The Surprising Third Article Theology of Jonathan Edwards," in *The Ecumenical Edwards: Jonathan Edwards and the Theologians* (ed. Kyle Strobel; Farnham: Ashgate, 2014), 195–211.
[14] See, for example, Colin Gunton, "Two Dogma's Revisited: Edward Irving's Christology" in *Theology through the Theologians: Selected Essays (1972–1995)* (London: T&T Clark, 1996), 151–68.

are stylized caricatures, not detailed, historically accurate photographs.[15] Nevertheless, the claim of those promoting Third Article theologies is that the lens of the Spirit as a theological starting point provides a profound perspective that has not been comprehensively pursued with depth and rigor. "Such a theology of the third article is still truly in its infancy," writes Amos Yong, one prominent advocate of this perspective.[16] Although it has been hinted at, the development of a thorough, complete, and systematic TAT still lies in front of Christian endeavor. It promises a significant and valuable complement to the already well-developed First and Second Article theologies.

ii) Theologies from Above and Below

A second common characterization locating TAT and distinguishing it from other approaches is that it is a theology "from below" and not "from above." Unlike some other theological methodologies, TAT has its epistemic foundation in Spiritual experience rather than Trinitarian ontology. It focuses first on the Spirit-empowered works of God *ad extra* rather than the internal makeup of his being *ad intra*. It starts from below and works upwards, rather than starting from above and working downwards. TAT is an *a posteriori* scientific approach, not an *a priori* one.

A distinction needs to be made here between ontology and epistemology. Ontologically, TAT affirms a top-down understanding. All that we are is because God has reached down to us, and humanity does not, cannot, and will not ever be able to work its way up to God. Epistemologically, though, we start from where we are. For TAT, our understanding of who God is and what he has done is based on genuine reflection on the work that he is doing in our lives. In adopting a methodological approach that intentionally moves from below to above, then, our theological reflection matches our discipleship. As we are drawn by the Spirit from our current fallen state into participation in the Godhead, our theological reflections start from our current experience and knowledge (limited and tainted

---

[15] Regarding the challenges of applying a "Kuhnian" paradigmatic approach in a complex theological and cultural landscape, see Martin Sutherland, "Pine Trees and Paradigms: Rethinking Mission in the West," in *Mission Without Christendom: Exploring the Site* (ed. Martin Sutherland; Auckland: Carey Baptist College, 2000), 132–6. Sutherland's work applies particularly to missiological categories, but has broader relevance.

[16] Amos Yong, "Introduction: Pentecostalism and a Theology of the Third Article," in *Toward a Pneumatological Theology: Pentecostal and Ecumenical Perspectives on Ecclesiology, Soteriology, and Theology of Mission* (ed. Amos Yong; Lanham, MD: University Press of America, 2002), xvii.

by our creaturely mortality and sinfulness) and move upwards toward reflections on the nature and existence of God. Consequently, a key feature of Third Article theologies is the assumption of movement. Although the starting point for Third Article theologies is from *below*, this is merely the epistemic starting point *from* which movement occurs. The intent is to move upwards. As Gunton has written specifically of a Christology from below, "there is every intention and indeed expectation to leave the ground, to speak theologically as well as anthropologically, and not to remain stranded on the earth."[17]

Note that Third Article theologies, as theologies from below, are intended to complement and not replace theological methods that start from above. While some argue for such replacement,[18] and there are even discussions about whether the top-down or bottom-up epistemologies are preferable,[19] the two approaches are best seen as complementary. The value of TAT and its bottom-up approach is that it fills out and corrects some of the over- or underemphases, the intractabilities, and particularly the dichotomies of other theological methodologies. As Dabney writes, a TAT may "bring together what we have so often let slip apart: worship and theology, service to God and service to God's world, the honouring of God's creation and the proclamation of God's redemption."[20]

iii) A Trinitarian Theological Approach

More than the perceived inadequacies of other theological approaches, though, TAT finds its positive justification and impetus as a subset of twentieth-century theology's Trinitarian renaissance. Stanley Grenz, writing in 2004, comments that "whenever the story of the last hundred years is told, the rediscovery of the Trinity that sprouted and then came to full bloom during the eight decades following the First World War must be given centre stage, and the rebirth of Trinitarian theology must be presented as one of the most far-reaching theological developments of the century."[21] This renewed

---

[17]Colin Gunton, *Yesterday and Today: A Study of Continuities in Christology* (London: Dartman, Longman and Todd, 1983), 11.
[18]For example, those Spirit Christologies that attempt to replace Logos Christology. See Section 2.2 of this volume for further discussion of such proposals.
[19]See, for example, Myk Habets, *The Anointed Son: A Trinitarian Spirit Christology* (Eugene, OR: Pickwick Publications, 2010), 50–1.
[20]Dabney, "Starting with the Spirit," 27.
[21]Stanley J. Grenz, *Rediscovering the Triune God: The Trinity in Contemporary Theology* (Minneapolis, MN: Fortress Press, 2004), 1. Not all see the direction this Trinitarian renaissance has taken as

interest has extended well beyond an investigation of the Trinity as a lone subject, to the impact that these newly derived or rediscovered Trinitarian understandings have on other theological doctrines. As Gunton famously remarked, "In the light of the theology of the Trinity, everything looks different."[22] Significant numbers of theologians are following the Trinitarian renaissance by reexamining soteriology, ecclesiology, Christology, and other theological aspects through interpretational grids developed from a Trinitarian starting point.

One pertinent insight that has emerged from this explosion of interest in the Trinity is the relative underemphasis historically on pneumatology—an oversight that is rapidly being redressed. McGrath's often quoted witticism is that "the Holy Spirit has long been the Cinderella of the Trinity. The other two sisters may have gone to the theological ball; the Holy Spirit got left behind every time. But not now."[23] Yong comments similarly that "the resurgence of thinking about the Holy Spirit, long recognized as the shy, silent, or even forgotten member of the Trinity—has been underway at least since the middle of the twentieth century."[24] But just as a renewed interest in the doctrine of the Trinity led to a viewing of other theological doctrines through a Trinitarian lens, a renewed interest in pneumatology has led to the similar desire to view other theological doctrines through the lens of the Spirit. While such an approach fits within the subset of broader Trinitarian approaches to theology, it has shown great potential for theological insight. Theologians across the denominational spectrum are adopting this new and fruitful methodology. The following subsection outlines some of the key voices and streams that are emerging.

1.1.2 Key Streams within Third Article Theology

Theologians pursuing a TAT approach are cautiously hopeful that starting with the Spirit has significant ecumenical potential. While there are various

---

positive, however. See, for example, Stephen R. Holmes, *The Quest for the Trinity: The Doctrine of God in Scripture, History and Modernity* (Downers Grove, IL: IVP Academic, 2012), 198–200.
[22] Colin Gunton, *The Promise of Trinitarian Theology* (Edinburgh: T&T Clark, 1997), 7.
[23] Alister E. McGrath, *Christian Theology* (Malden, MA: Blackwell, 1994), 279. The nomenclature of the Spirit as a Trinitarian Cinderella can be traced back to (at least) G. J. Sirks, "The Cinderella of Theology: The Doctrine of the Holy Spirit," *Harvard Theological Review* 50 (1957): 77–89.
[24] Yong, "Introduction," xvi.

reasons for this optimism, primary among them is that its starting point of particularity enables the contextual distinctiveness of each position and community to be acknowledged up front, while also affirming the common and shared reality of the Spirit within each expression.[25] Perhaps the key empirical evidence undergirding this hope, though, is that theologians from many different traditions have begun to explore TAT. With no attempt to be comprehensive, this section briefly outlines these streams and some representative voices within each.[26] The core recognition emerging from this survey is the sheer range of voices contributing to this new theological endeavor.

Following on from Yves Congar's voluminous and magisterial survey of pneumatology originally published in 1979,[27] together with calls from Pope John Paul II and Pope Francis to pursue an understanding and practice of Christian living from an intentionally pneumatological perspective,[28] a raft of Roman Catholic scholars began exploring the benefits of giving the Spirit priority in the theological task. They often build on the work of an early forbear, Heribert Mühlen, who in the 1960s argued that the Spirit is "one person in many persons" and that through the Spirit, Christ and the church together form a single personality.[29] Sometime later, Thomas Weinandy was perhaps the first to intentionally use the bottom-up nature of a pneumatologically derived Christology to reconceive the nature of the Trinity, arguing for an understanding where the Father begets the Son in or by the Spirit.[30] Following this same trajectory, although coming to slightly different conclusions, Ralph Del Colle and David Coffey, colleagues at Marquette University together with D. Lyle Dabney, have "forged a formidable contribution to Spirit Christology and, by means of such,

---

[25]For a further exploration of the ecumenical potential of Third Article Theology, see Gregory J. Liston, *The Anointed Church: Toward a Third Article Ecclesiology* (Minneapolis, MN: Fortress Press, 2015), 21–3, 32–3.
[26]For more detail on these streams, see Myk Habets, "Prolegomenon: On Starting with the Spirit," in *Third Article Theology: A Pneumatological Dogmatics* (ed. Myk Habets; Minneapolis, MN: Fortress Press, 2016), 3–14.
[27]Yves Congar, *I Believe in the Holy Spirit* (3 vols; New York: Crossroad, 1997).
[28]See Habets, "Prolegomenon: On Starting with the Spirit," 5.
[29]See Heribert Mühlen, *Una Mystica Persona. Die Kirche als das Mysterium der heilsgeschichtlichen Identität des Heiligen Geistes in Christus und den Christen: Eine Person in vielen Personen* (Paderborn: Ferdinand Schöningh, 1967). For an English explanation of his work, see Wolfgang Vondey, *Heribert Mühlen: His Theology and Praxis* (Dallas, TX: University Press of America, 2004).
[30]Thomas Weinandy, *The Father's Spirit of Sonship: Reconceiving the Trinity* (Edinburgh: T&T Clark, 1995).

a reevaluation of how to conceive the doctrine of the Trinity along more relational and pneumatological lines."[31]

Perhaps unsurprisingly, given the movement's strong pneumatological focus, theologians from within Pentecostalism have also contributed significantly to the emergence and development of TAT. Key voices here include James K. A. Smith, whose *Thinking in Tongues* and the more recent *The Nicene Option* provide a solid philosophical and epistemological grounding for adopting an intentionally pneumatological approach.[32] Significant contributions have also come from Amos Yong and Veli-Matti Kärkkäinen, two colleagues at Fuller Theological Seminary, whose prodigious output intentionally builds on a strong pneumatological priority.[33] And particularly pertinent in this stream is Frank Macchia, whose many works build on a central theme of characterizing baptism of the Spirit as the defining metaphor for Pentecostalism.[34] While Pentecostal scholars (among others) are still debating whether giving priority to the Spirit necessarily means abandoning a Christocentric understanding, their contribution to TAT is extremely significant.

Beyond the Pentecostal movement, Protestants of various affiliations are also adopting a TAT approach. Among the many examples that could be mentioned, perhaps the most famous progenitor of the movement is the Reformed theologian, Karl Barth, who foreshadowed the entire movement of TAT by arguing that his entire Christologically focused work could be replicated from a pneumatological perspective. In an often mentioned quote, he alludes to "the possibility of a theology of the third article, in other words, a theology predominantly and decisively of the Holy Spirit. Everything that needs to be said, considered, and believed about God the Father and God the Son in an understanding of the first and second articles

---

[31] See Habets, "Prolegomenon: On Starting with the Spirit," 6. The question of precisely which understanding of the Trinity most naturally flows from looking through a pneumatological lens is a question addressed in Chapter 6.

[32] See James K. A. Smith, *Thinking in Tongues: Pentecostal Contributions to Christian Philosophy* (Grand Rapids, MI: Eerdmans, 2010). Also, James K. A. Smith, *The Nicene Option: An Incarnational Phenomenology* (Waco, TX: Baylor University Press, 2021).

[33] For Yong, see, for example, his recent examination of mission from a pneumatological perspective: Amos Yong, *Mission after Pentecost: The Witness of the Spirit from Genesis to Revelation* (Grand Rapids, MI: Baker Academic, 2019). And for Kärkkäinen, see the collection of papers gathered in Veli-Matti Kärkkäinen, *Toward a Pneumatological Theology: Pentecostal and Ecumenical Perspectives on Ecclesiology, Soteriology, and Theology of Mission* (Lanham, MD: University Press of America, 2002).

[34] See, for example, Frank D. Macchia, *Baptized in the Spirit: A Global Pentecostal Theology* (Grand Rapids, MI: Zondervan, 2006). Or more recently, Frank D. Macchia, *The Spirit-Baptized Church: A Dogmatic Inquiry* (London: T&T Clark, 2020).

might be shown and illuminated in its foundations through God the Holy Spirit."[35] Sometime later, Baptist theologian Clark Pinnock completed the first intentional survey of theology from a pneumatological perspective in 1996.[36] His work, like Barth's, foreshadowed the explosion of interest among Protestant theologians that has emerged in the early decades of the twenty-first century. Two examples of this interest will suffice. First, an American based Lutheran theologian, Leopoldo Sánchez has recently explored the implications of Spirit Christology on transformation in a book that is both rigorous and strongly pastoral.[37] And the New Zealand Reformed and Baptist theologian Myk Habets, in addition to his own contributions to TAT, has intentionally gathered together theologians from all streams to produce the most definitive and complete volume on this methodology and theology to date.[38]

Other denominational streams and theological movements could equally be considered in this brief survey. Liberation theology has embraced TAT as an approach, as have other contextual theologies, including feminist theology. For example, Sarah Coakley writes at the end of the first volume of her *God, Sexuality and the Self* that "it has been the daring invitation of this book to make the problematic 'third' in God the 'first' in human encounter … If finally, we make this mind shift, everything changes."[39] Indeed, the list of streams and movements embracing the approach of TAT could go on and on. But perhaps the primary other grouping deserving mention before this overview concludes is the Eastern Orthodox. This tradition deserves special mention as while much of the Western church is (re)discovering the value of starting with the Spirit, the Orthodox have always included a strong pneumatological element within their theological explorations. In particular, the Basilian theme of the creating and perfecting Spirit is present throughout the Orthodox vision, and the Orthodox doctrine of *theosis* provides one of the clearest examples of the Spirit being constitutive across the entire theological exercise.

---

[35] Karl Barth, "Concluding Unscientific Postscript on Schleiermacher," in *The Theology of Schleiermacher* (ed. D. Ritschl; Grand Rapids, MI: Eerdmans, 1982), 278.
[36] Pinnock, *Flame of Love*. The ongoing influence of this work is shown in its republication in 2022.
[37] Leopoldo A. Sánchez M., *Sculptor Spirit: Models of Sanctification from Spirit Christology* (Downers Grove, IL: IVP Academic, 2019). This work builds on the foundation of Spirit Christology he laid in an earlier volume. See Leopoldo A. Sánchez M., *Receiver, Bearer, and Giver of God's Spirit: Jesus' Life in the Spirit as a Lens for Theology and Life* (Eugene, OR: Pickwick Publications, 2015).
[38] Myk Habets, ed., *Third Article Theology: A Pneumatological Dogmatics* (Minneapolis, MN: Fortress Press, 2016).
[39] Sarah Coakley, *God, Sexuality, and the Self* (Cambridge: Cambridge University Press, 2013), 333–4.

Even from such a high-level summary, then, it is evident that across virtually the full breadth of the Christian church, and in a variety of different ways, the theological approach of giving pneumatology priority is being fruitfully adopted. As Habets summarizes, "Each of these moves is conducive to a TAT, offering insights from across the broad range of the tradition that today are being adopted, adapted, and … being recommended to the theological community as a constructive dogmatics for our time. Slowly but doggedly the foundations for TAT are being developed across the ecclesiological spectrum."[40]

Such a broad range of theologians are being drawn to this new theological approach primarily because of the new way of seeing the world that it offers, a way that is entirely appropriate for the time and space we are currently living in. "Theologically, we must act our age," says Dabney. "That does not mean conforming the faith to the age, it means proclaiming that faith in a manner that is appropriate to the age, in a way that is both faithful to God and authentic to God's world today."[41] TAT offers a theological approach that sees past the dichotomies and discontinuities of previous approaches. It gives theologians a way of doing theology that starts from where they are—the reality of the Spirit at work in their specific lives and communities—but does not stay where they are—outlining a vision of a world infused with the power, presence, and potential of the Holy Spirit. This book is an invitation to adopt this vision, to see the world through a pneumatological lens, to start with the Spirit. The next section outlines five key reasons why such a vision is appropriate, accurate, and timely.

1.2 Why Do Third Article Theology

What is to be gained by giving pneumatology priority in theological investigations? What imperatives imply that starting with the Spirit will complement other more established theological approaches and yield valuable theological insight? The following discussion considers five overlapping imperatives that point to TAT as an appropriate, accurate, and timely theological method.

---

[40] Habets, "Prolegomenon: On Starting with the Spirit," 13.
[41] Dabney, "Starting with the Spirit," 26.

1.2.1 The Biblical Imperative

The first imperative is biblical. God's word reveals the Spirit as God's transcendent immanence. God is present to us by his Spirit in an immediate and not mediated sense.[42] This recognition allows us, and even encourages us to view God's other activity in the world as an aspect of the Spirit's mission, rather than the Spirit as an aspect of God's other activity. So, for example, the fact that the Bible speaks of the incarnation being facilitated through the Spirit (Matt 1:18, 20) leads naturally to seeing the Son's mission as an aspect of the Spirit's, rather than the reverse.[43] The realization that God regularly initiates his action in the world through the Spirit suggests a theological approach that views God's work in the world through a pneumatological lens.

There are multiple biblical examples of God initiating his action through the Spirit. In creation, even before the word of God was spoken, the Spirit hovered over the waters (Gen 1:2). The Spirit or breath of God is viewed as both life's animator (Gen 2:7; Job 27:3) and its *re*-animator (Ezek 37:1–14). The nation of Israel was established through the Spirit (Exod 15:8,10; Isa 63:11–14), and her prophets, priests, and kings were chosen and empowered through the Spirit (Zech 7:11–12; 2 Chr 24:20; 1 Sam 16:13–14). Turning to the New Testament, Jesus' birth was facilitated by the Holy Spirit (Luke 1:35), his ministry was initiated by the Spirit (Mark 1:9–12), he was led to the cross by the Spirit (Heb 9:14), and he was resurrected by the power of the Spirit (Rom 1:4). The church similarly was born of the Spirit (Acts 2:1–41). Indeed, all our Christian life is enabled by the Spirit: our conversion (John 3:5–8), our prayers (Jude 21), and our final resurrection (Rom 8:11). The Spirit is the first fruit of God's life in us and our life in him (2 Cor 1:22). Even the very Bible that conveys these truths was inspired by the Spirit (2 Pet 1:20–21).

Given that God, according to the clear biblical witness, so often initiates his work through the Spirit, there is motivation for adopting a theological approach that reflects this revealed reality—an approach that intentionally views God's activity through the lens of the Spirit. There is, of course, no definitive, logical link from "God works this way" to "We should learn of God this way." But it is nevertheless suggestive. At the very least, it implies

---

[42]See, for example, Steven M. Studebaker, *The Trinitarian Vision of Jonathan Edwards and David Coffey* (New York: Cambria, 2011), 164–5.
[43]See particularly Pinnock, *Flame of Love*, 80.

that a theological methodology that starts with the Spirit is congruent with Scripture and is well worth pursuing.

1.2.2 The Theological Imperative

A second imperative is theological. It is through the Spirit that we are united to Christ and increasingly conform to his image. By starting with the Spirit, then, our theological method matches our discipleship.

Analyzing the Spirit is difficult. "Understanding is often more incomplete and confused here than with most of the other doctrines."[44] There is less explicit revelation in the Bible concerning the Spirit than the other two persons of the Godhead.[45] While the Father and the Son have images enabling us to conceptualize them (however inaccurately), the Spirit is intangible and difficult to apprehend. When we turn from looking *at* the Spirit to looking *through* the Spirit, however, the picture quality changes dramatically.[46] It is only *through the Spirit* that we are convicted of our sinfulness (John 16:8-11), recognize Jesus as the Son of God (John 15:26), or approach the Father (Rom 8:14–17; Eph 2:18). It is *through the Spirit*, however implicitly, that we know about God and approach him in relationship. The approach of TAT, then, is to make explicit what is implicit; using TAT means we intentionally begin our theological examinations by looking *through the Spirit*. In this way, our theological method matches our reality, our experience, and our discipleship.

The image of the Spirit acting as a lens mentioned earlier is helpful here. When we look *at* a lens—particularly a high-quality lens—it is transparent and difficult to focus on. When we look *through* a lens, the object in view comes into perspective. Third Article theologies aim to use the Spirit as a God-given lens through which we can conduct theological inquiry. As Mühlen writes, "The doctrine and person of the Holy Spirit is not one doctrine among others, but a fundamental doctrine and reality in the

---

[44] Millard Erickson, *Christian Theology*, 3rd ed. (Grand Rapids, MI: BakerAcademic, 2013), 773.
[45] Erickson, *Christian Theology*, 773-4. See also Killian McDonnell, "The Determinative Doctrine of the Holy Spirit," *Theology Today* 39 (1982): 142–5.
[46] This echoes a distinction made by C. S. Lewis of looking *along* something rather than merely looking *at* it. See Clive S. Lewis, "Meditation in a Toolshed," in *Compelling Reason: Essays on Ethics and Theology* (ed. W. Hooper; London: Fount, 1998), 52–5. It also echoes the idea of tacit knowledge introduced by Polanyi. See, for example, Michael Polanyi, *Personal Knowledge: Towards a Post-Critical Philosophy* (London: Routledge & Kegan Paul, 1969).

Church."[47] Third Article theologies explicitly aim to allow the Spirit to guide us into all truth (John 16:13).

1.2.3 The Philosophical Imperative

A third imperative is philosophical. The nature of created reality is irreducibly plural, and hence our theological examinations benefit from starting with the intrinsically relational category of Spirit.[48]

According to Steven Smith, twentieth-century philosophy has moved past classical ontology (which starts with the abstract concept of existence) and postfoundationalism (which starts with the limits of human capacity) and now begins its examination of reality through the medium of language and speech.[49] But language and speech are essentially interpersonal. Relationship undergirds and intrinsically indwells language. So, before anything else, claims Smith, relationship must be the starting point of any examination of reality. But, as theologian Welker notes, accepting this starting point of relationship and the irreducible plurality of our reality inevitably brings pneumatology to theology's forefront because it is through the Spirit that we relate to God and others.[50] Pneumatology thus becomes the primary lens through which we examine reality. As McDonnell writes, "Pneumatology is to theology what epistemology is to philosophy. Pneumatology determines the 'rules' for speaking about God."[51]

1.2.4 The Cultural Imperative

A fourth imperative is cultural. TAT, with its emphases on particularity and relationality, has significant potential to speak with relevance to contemporary society in a way that can be heard.

---

[47]Mühlen, *Una Mystica Persona*, 5. As translated by Vondey, *Heribert Mühlen*, xv.
[48]See Dabney, "Starting with the Spirit," 5–11.
[49]See Steven G. Smith, *The Concept of the Spiritual: An Essay in First Philosophy* (Philadelphia: Temple University Press, 1988). Particularly pp. 3–5.
[50]See Michael Welker, *God the Spirit* (trans. J. F. Hoffmeyer; Minneapolis, MN: Fortress Press, 1994). Particularly pages ix–xiii. Note that it is the Holy Spirit and not a generalized notion of human spirit that is being referred to here. These two concepts need to be carefully distinguished.
[51]Killian McDonnell, "A Response to D. Lyle Dabney," in *Advents of the Spirit: An Introduction to the Current Study of Pneumatology* (ed. Bradford E. Hinze and D. Lyle Dabney; Milwaukee, WI: Marquette University Press, 2005), 264. See also Killian McDonnell, "A Trinitarian Theology of the Holy Spirit," *Theological Studies* 46 (1985): 214–18.

Although the claims of cataclysmic shifts in cultural perception are exaggerated, there is nevertheless genuine validity in the notion of postmodernism. The way people view and understand the world around them has altered. Historical "givens" such as human rationality and the inevitability of progress are increasingly questioned. But if there is scant acknowledgment of human rationality or any Godward tendency in today's world, the potential for a First Article Theology to be heard is significantly diminished. Similarly, the claims of Second Article Theology can sound negative, and appear, at least initially, to offer little hope in a world that is already broadly acknowledged as chaotic and disintegrating. These theological approaches, quite appropriate to their time, have decreasing connection with a postmodern mindset.

In contrast, the themes of TAT—particularity, relationality, and transformation—closely align with the leitmotifs of postmodernism. Good theology will always teach the church how to proclaim and live the truths we believe in a manner that is appropriate and understandable to our age. In a world that has rejected the universal for the particular, TAT begins with the localized claim that in *this* people, at *this* time, the Spirit is present and drawing us as a community toward redemption with God. In a world that values community,[52] a TAT begins with the Spirit that draws us *together* to God. In a world where good and evil dwell side by side, a TAT that focuses neither on universal continuity or discontinuity can "enable the Christian community both to socially and intellectually affirm some and yet contradict other aspects of the age we live."[53] Through its theme of transformation, it can speak hope to a world whose fundamental fabric is threatening to unravel.

1.2.5 The Ecumenical Imperative

A fifth imperative is ecumenical. A TAT has the potential to speak with relevance not just to contemporary society but also to the current church. Naturally, no single methodology will result in practical unity, but if hopes are realized, starting with the Spirit will provide an approach that begins to cross theological spectra and draws diverging groups together.[54]

---

[52] Even if that community is a pale imitation of true Christian communion.
[53] Dabney, "Starting with the Spirit," 25–6.
[54] See Kärkkäinen, *Toward a Pneumatological Theology*, 65–79. This article outlines ways the ecumenical imperative is being fulfilled through Third Article Theology.

If the world is changing, the church is changing too. First, Christianity's influence is rapidly declining as Christendom "collapses." Religion is increasingly privatized and Christianity is seen as just one choice among many. Second, the sociological and historical barriers that separate us from our Christian brothers and sisters are diminishing. In many cases, the major remaining causes of division between distinctive Christian groupings are theological dichotomies that the vast majority even within those groups neither recognize nor understand. Third, and most significantly, Christianity has spread globally. The Western missionary endeavor, for all its failings, has been immensely successful. Christianity exists and thrives in an increasingly vast variety of contexts. Furthermore, not just the sociological and historical barriers, but the practical barriers of distance and communication with other believers are diminishing.

In this changing context, what is needed is an ecumenical way of doing theology—a methodology that stretches wide to embrace different aspects of Christian diversity, drawing them into an emerging and common doctrinal unity.[55] In addition to the empirical reality mentioned in the previous section that broad swathes of theologians across the denominations are adopting this approach, Third Article Theologians claim there are also several theoretical reasons to be hopeful that starting with the Spirit has ecumenical potential. First, pneumatology as a relatively unexamined theological subject allows Christian groups a new meeting place for dialogue, which can be approached without too many preconceived opinions and agendas.[56] Second, the starting point of particularity as opposed to universality enables the contextual distinctiveness of each position and community to be acknowledged up front, while also affirming the common reality of the Spirit in each particular expression. Third, there is hope that the both/and approach of TAT (rather than First and Second Article Theology's emphasis on discontinuities) will enable new ways to resolve or minimize long-standing internal disputes and dichotomies. Fourth, a TAT may be able to redefine what ecumenism means altogether, enabling a meaningful "unity within diversity" framework applied not just to individuals within local churches but to groups and traditions within the global Christian community. Fifth, TAT as a method invites, and in many ways requires, a strong integration of spirituality and

---

[55]For a lucid summary of the aims and limitations of an ecumenical theology, see George Hunsinger, *The Eucharist and Ecumenism* (Cambridge: Cambridge University Press, 2008), 1–18. Particularly insightful is the list of seven guidelines on pages 9–10.

[56]See, for example, Philip J. Rosato, "Called by God, in the Holy Spirit: Pneumatological Insights into Ecumenism," *Ecumenical Review* 30 (1978): 110–26. Particularly pages 110–11.

intellectualism.[57] Given that the Spirit has always been understood as the binding factor, not just within the Trinity but historically within the church, it does not seem a vain hope that by starting with the Spirit we may find means to develop an emerging commonality not just in our thinking, but in our practice.

1.3 The Grammar and Content of a TAT

As explained earlier in this chapter, TAT is both a method and a theology. As a method, TAT intentionally views all of reality through the lens of the Spirit. As a theology, the insights that arise from an approach that prioritizes pneumatology are deep and rich, offering a penetrating vision into the central and defining theological issues of today. Over recent decades, many theologians spanning multiple denominations and varying cultural backgrounds have adopted a TAT approach and used it to great effect. The objective of this volume is to introduce both the methodology of TAT and some of the many theological insights that have arisen from its utilization. Further, it provides the tools and techniques inviting readers to participate in the immensely practical and pastoral exercise of viewing reality from a pneumatological perspective, to catch a vision of the world as infused with the power, presence, and potential of the Spirit, and to lead their lives accordingly.

The book thus serves as a practical introduction to the topic of TAT and an invitation to further research in this burgeoning field. It consists of two sections. The first section—the ground and grammar of TAT—introduces the methodological distinctives of the approach. Divided into five chapters, this first chapter has introduced and described TAT, explaining what it is and why it is of value, before outlining the structure of the book.

Rather than jumping directly to the intricate details of the methodology of TAT, Chapter Two utilizes Spirit Christology as an illustrative example of the approach and value that arises from starting with the Spirit. As noted earlier, a TAT approach to Christology views Christ as an aspect of the Spirit's mission, rather than the more common approach that reverses this order. This chapter explores the biblical justification for adopting this perspective,

---

[57]See, for example, Kärkkäinen, *Toward a Pneumatological Theology*, 78–9.

the relationship between the two approaches (Logos and Spirit Christology), and new insights arising from viewing Christ through the lens of the Spirit's mission. It also explores the practical implications these insights have for Christian living.

Building on the illustrative example of Spirit Christology explored in Chapter 2, Chapter 3 then proceeds to outline the key methodological criteria that distinguish TAT, explaining each in detail. It explores how these nuanced criteria distinguish TAT from the theological caricatures that often are used to critique it. And it introduces the methodical approach of Wolterstorff and its application to TAT, explaining how TAT can be extended beyond a merely Christological focus.

Chapter 4 intentionally addresses some of the common critiques made, and questions asked, of TAT (and Spirit Christology). In addition to dispelling false notions that arise, responding to these criticisms allows for a deeper appreciation of what TAT is and how it is conducted. Interacting with critics brings a clear focus to the field of TAT and its position within the overall vista of theological endeavor.

Left as a merely theoretical exercise, theology can often be impractical or disembodied. Considering the claims that TAT is both a grounded theology from below and that it has existential viability, the final chapter in this first section of the book sketches how TAT recognizes and incorporates faith and experience, grace and nature, and how it is compatible with a range of methodologies from the humanities, especially critically realist approaches and qualitative methodologies. Dogmatics and practical theology are brought together in this chapter in a theological-applied synthesis.

Having explored the ground and grammar of TAT in the first part of the book, the second major section explores its content and consequence. These chapters work through each major theological doctrine in turn, exploring the insights that arise when a particular theological *locus* is viewed from a pneumatological perspective. Each chapter also applies the insights gained to an issue of practical importance to the church today. So, for each doctrine considered, the chapter both outlines the theological implications of prioritizing a pneumatological perspective and illustrates the practical relevance of adopting this approach.

Chapter 6 addresses the Trinity. It begins by making the case that Spirit Christology provides the best mode of access to an accurate, detailed, and practical understanding of the immanent (and consequently the economic) Trinity. It then goes on to explore the immanent Trinitarian understanding that most naturally emerges when viewed from the perspective (or control belief) of Spirit Christology, and its implications for understanding the working of the economic Trinity. Particular focus is given to the personal nature of the Spirit within the Trinity, and the repeated and reprising roles (inseparable operations) that each of the persons of the Trinity plays within eternity, time, the church, and beyond.

Starting with the understandings of Christology and the Trinity that have already been developed through a TAT approach, Chapter 7 uses these perspectives as vantage points from which to look through the lens of the Spirit to determine the features of the church. Here it is argued that the church is a sequel to the incarnation, and a meditation on worship in the Spirit is offered. The next chapter views the topic of salvation through a pneumatological lens, which brings the theme of union with Christ to the forefront. Indeed, from a pneumatological perspective, *theosis* is God's ultimate goal and intent for humanity. Viewing soteriology through the lens of the Spirit, perhaps even more than other doctrines, illustrates how each of the theological *loci* are intricately and intimately pneumatologically intertwined.

Chapter 9 explores theological anthropology from a pneumatological perspective, and following on from the insight that Christ is the clearest revelation to us of what it means to be truly human, this chapter argues that just as it was through the Spirit that Christ's true humanity was both revealed and released, so it is with our humanity. Indeed, the claim of TAT is that our humanity can be precisely understood as a pneumatological participation in Christ's humanity. Chapter 10 extends this understanding to the topic of missiology. While the trinitarian renaissance of the twentieth century has had a significant missiological impact in its recognition that the church is involved in the Trinity's ongoing mission in the world, this chapter explores what refinements to this understanding a specifically pneumatological approach to mission can bring.

Chapter 11, quite appropriately, develops a TAT of eschatology. It argues that a Spirit eschatology complements more Christologically focused eschatologies in a similar fashion to the way a Spirit Christology complements a Logos Christology. Consequently, this chapter explores the intrinsically pneumatological relationship between the church and the kingdom, drawing insights about the nature of time, the reality of ecclesial transformation, and how practically we can partner with the Spirit in his present and ongoing transforming and perfecting ecclesial role.

Having explored the ground and grammar of TAT in the first section, and its content and consequence in the second, the final chapter in this volume summarizes the key theological and practical insights that have emerged, gives advice for pursuing research in this subject area, and suggests relevant topics within the field that remain to be researched and could profitably be pursued. As an introduction to TAT, it is hoped this volume provides the necessary insights and impetus for others to build upon what is established here.

2

Spirit Christology as Entry to TAT

2.1 Introduction: Why Start a TAT with Christology

In Chapter 1, we argued for three characteristics of a Third Article Theology (TAT): it starts with the Spirit, it is Trinitarian, and it is comprehensive, serving as an architectonic structure for the task of theology as a whole. In this chapter, we illustrate this claim by considering one central aspect of theology—Christology—specifically a Spirit Christology. This chapter introduces and describes Spirit Christology, offering the rationale for starting a work on TAT with Christology, followed by a description of Spirit Christology. Key Messianic *kairoi* (moments or episodes) will be discussed to make a case for Spirit Christology, along with the theological appropriateness of this approach and its practical implications.

We start this work on TAT with Christology for several reasons. First, Christology is one of the central mysteries of the faith, along with the Trinity, and Christ forms the centerpiece of the drama of redemption. Second, systematic theology has the unenviable reputation of being irrelevant, esoteric, and impractical. No doubt these may be true of some theology, but they are certainly not constitutive of theology itself. Assuming the traditional posture of theological enquiry as "faith seeking understanding" (*fides quarens intellectum*) we wanted to start not with methodology or prolegomena, but with Christ, the author and perfector of our faith (Heb 12:2). Readers of this work are interested in Christ already (otherwise why would you be reading this book!), and many will have a faith commitment of some sort. Many will also be familiar with the Holy Spirit and so, to start with Christ and to illustrate what a TAT looks like in Christology, the central and defining doctrine of the faith, seems the most intuitive and helpful place to start. Third, as Christology is constitutive for the task of theology, so a Spirit Christology is constitutive for a TAT. Finally, Spirit Christology is the area that has garnered the most attention to date from advocates of a TAT, and so it seems an obvious place to start this work. So, before we define in detail the methodology of TAT and then examine various doctrines, Christology is our first port of call.

Spirit Christology is relatively simple to summarize: to properly understand the identity and mission of Jesus, we must understand him in relation to the Holy Spirit (and through him with the Father). Extending this most basic definition, we argue that the Gospels present Jesus in relation to the Holy Spirit, and that the work of Christ is understood and enriched by seeing it through the lens of the Spirit. As Catholic pneumatologist Yves Congar famously quipped, "No Christology without pneumatology and no pneumatology without Christology."[1] What Congar knew well was that Christ and the Spirit go together and, thus, so should Christology and pneumatology. A Spirit Christology is one way to make good on that affirmation.

We have further suggested that Clark Pinnock's insight is useful: "Let us see what results from viewing Christ as an aspect of the Spirit's mission, instead of (as is more usual) viewing Spirit as a function of Christ's."[2] What we take this to mean is that in the history of redemption, God's missions in the world take a threefold form corresponding to a united work of the Father, Son, and the Holy Spirit. From the beginning the triune God has been working all things together for the great consummation whereby "in everything Christ might have the supremacy" (Col 1:18). The Son, however, did not assume human nature until around 4 BC when the Holy Spirit overshadowed Mary and she was with child (Luke 1:35). The Holy Spirit's mission precedes that of the incarnate Son in this respect and thus we should, as Pinnock suggests, see Christ as a function of the Spirit's prior mission. This in no way diminishes or decentralizes Christ from the history of redemption. Rather, it puts Jesus Christ and his mission into the very center of the great drama of redemption and asks us to see the

---

[1] Yves Congar, *The Word and the Spirit* (trans. David Smith; San Francisco: Harper & Row, 1986), 1.
[2] Pinnock, *Flame of Love*, 80.

contexts—theological and cultural—into which Jesus was born in order to rightly understand who he is and what he did. Without this pneumatological pre-mission we could misunderstand Christ and his mission along similar lines to some of the religious leaders of Jesus' own day, and other observers of his ministry, who merely saw a unique man but could not see the Messiah. As John declared, "The Light shines in the darkness, and the darkness did not comprehend it" (John 1:5).

All orthodox accounts of trinitarian agency affirm what are called the inseparable operations of the persons of the Trinity. Simply put, this affirms that because God is one being, all external works of God are works of the undivided Trinity. This is a helpful doctrine and one we uphold. A doctrine of inseparable operations also argues, however, for the appropriateness of ascribing economic action to one or other of the triune persons (Augustine termed this a doctrine of divine appropriations).[3] There are many ways to do this. The easiest way is to follow the clear lead of Holy Scripture, which ascribes work to one or other of the divine persons.[4] As long as this theological tool is not used to separate the persons or to divide the work of God in a partitive way, it is a time-honored and useful way to tell the drama of redemption in a trinitarian key.[5] When we ask about the mission of the Spirit, we see an active ministry throughout the Old Testament preparing the way for the coming of Christ in the Gospels.[6] Jack Levison writes, "Trying to understand the spirit as if the word *rûah* did not occur 389 times in the Jewish Bible makes no sense."[7] And further, "New Testament authors did in fact cull from the Jewish Scriptures in order to clarify their own understanding of the spirit, and it is essential for

---

[3] For a detailed account, see Adonis Vidu, *The Same God Who Works All Things: Inseparable Operations in Trinitarian Theology* (Grand Rapids, MI: Eerdmans, 2021). See Torey J. S. Teer, "The Perfector of All Divine Acts: The Holy Spirit and the Providence of God," *Bibliotheca Sacra* 177 (2020): 402–21.

[4] See Torey J. S. Teer, "Inseparable Operations, Trinitarian Missions, and the Necessity of a Christological Pneumatology," *Journal of Theological Studies* 72 (2021): 337–61. Teer argues for the complementarity of Spirit Christology (seeing Christ by means of his relationship with the Spirit) with a Christological pneumatology (seeing the Spirit by means of his relationship with Christ).

[5] On the unity of God's operations in the Spirit-filled life and ministry of Jesus, see Steven J. Duby, *Jesus and the God of Classical Theism: Biblical Christianity in Light of the Doctrine of God* (Grand Rapids, MI: Baker Academic, 2022), 209–29.

[6] For a detailed survey, see Myk Habets, *The Progressive Mystery: Tracing the Elusive Spirit in Scripture and Tradition* (Bellingham, WA: Lexham Press, 2019). I draw on this material in this section.

[7] Jack Levison, *A Boundless God: The Spirit according to the Old Testament* (Grand Rapids, MI: Baker Academic, 2020), 4.

Christians to consider the influence the Jewish Scriptures had on the New Testament."[8]

The Old Testament antecedents to the coming of Christ are too numerous to mention but three interrelated themes are worth commenting on to highlight how the mission of Christ should be read as an aspect of the Spirit's prior mission, and how this leads to a fully-fledged Spirit Christology. We can look at the creation, the community, and the consummation in Christ.[9]

When we look at the creation accounts in the Old Testament, we clearly see the ordered work of the triune God whereby the mission of the Spirit is initiated as the executive of the Godhead, the perfector of creation, and God's empowering presence. In Genesis 1:2, the Spirit is portrayed as the one who brings order out of chaos, inaugurating the perfecting work of the Spirit that is to be a theme across the drama of Scripture. As I have written elsewhere,

> What is clearly stated in Genesis is that God's presence is active in the *ruach* and that the *ruach ᵉlōhîm* is superintending the work of creation and, linked to verse 3, bringing creation about through the Word, the Logos of John 1:1. As Hildebrandt states, "The passage is emphasizing the actual, powerful presence of God, who brings the spoken word into reality by the Spirit."[10]

Many more texts and episodes from the Old Testament could be drawn upon to highlight the Spirit's creative and perfecting work, not only of the cosmos, but of all humankind and all people groups, especially the chosen people of God (Pss 71:6; 89:48; 94:9; 100:3; 139:13; 149:2; Deut 32:6). "The sphere of the Spirit's operations is only limited by our lack of comprehension."[11]

In the various texts indicating the work of the Spirit in creation, the Old Testament presents the efficacy of the Spirit's activity.[12] It is both creation and preservation that is the direct result of the Spirit of God. It is important to notice the creative work of the Spirit as this is a theme that redounds throughout Scripture and will be important to bear in mind when we come to consider the way in which the Son enters the world as Jesus Christ (Luke

---

[8] Levison, *A Boundless God*, 7.
[9] For detailed commentary on each theme see Habets, *The Progressive Mystery*, 23–41.
[10] Habets, *The Progressive Mystery*, 25, slightly adapted. Citing Wilf Hildebrandt, *On Old Testament Theology of the Spirit of God* (Peabody, MA: Hendrickson, 1995), 35.
[11] Habets, *The Progressive Mystery*, 26.
[12] Cf., Job 26:13; 27:3; 33:4; 34:14; 59:19; 40:7; Pss 36:9; 104:30.

1:35) and the way in which believers are born from above (John 3:3) in an act of new creation and the Spirit's work of ushering creation to its perfection.

Second, the Spirit is also active in the community of believers in the Old Testament: active in establishing, protecting, judging, and restoring the people of God. The Exodus provides the paradigm for this activity. The Exodus deliverance becomes the ultimate paradigm of deliverance for Israel in the Hebrew canon that, from the beginning, is associated with the *ruach*/Spirit. From that time on, the people of God experienced the preservation of God via his *ruach*/Spirit (cf., 2 Sam 22:16; Ps 18:15; especially Isa 31:3; 63:7–14).

The Spirit is the active agent in the establishment of the community of Israel, her ordered life, and her theocratic government. As part of the Spirit's Old Testament ministry, he bestows gifts upon certain members of the community, enabling them to accomplish God's purposes on earth. These theocratic gifts include strength, energy, courage, and wisdom.[13] In all these instances, the *ruach* fills people, comes from outside with often violent force, and enables them with skill, wisdom, and the ability to perform their tasks.[14]

More specifically, the work of the Spirit within the ancient community concerned the calling and equipping of leaders for ministry and filling prophets so they could bear true testimony to God. The majority of references in the Pentateuch to *ruach* deal with some kind of leadership ability.[15] From the period of the judges through to monarchy, the activity of the Spirit continues to be evident; 1 Sam 10:6, 10, 11:6. The equipping of Saul is paradigmatic; Saul is successful as long as the *ruach* is on him. When it departs, he becomes unable to lead. The Spirit is then transferred to David (16:13, cf., Ps 51). Clearly from the leadership narratives of the kings, it is necessary for the king to be anointed and receive the Spirit of God, empowering him to rule in God's kingdom, if he is to be successful.[16] As I have pointed out elsewhere,

---

[13] A sample includes the following. Judges 3:10; 6:34; 11:29; 13:25; 14:6, 19; 15:14. Kings, Saul: 1 Sam 11:6, David: 1 Sam 16:13, clothed Amasai: 1 Chron 12:18. Craftsmen, Exod 28:3; Bezalel and Oholiab: Exod 31:3 cf., 35:31, to David: 1 Chron 28:12. The many Administrators, Moses: Num 11:17, 25; Joshua: Num 27:18; Deut 34:9. And most prominently in the office of the Prophets, Ezek 3:12, 14, 24; 8:3; 11:1, 5, 24; 37:1; Balaam: Num 24:2; Saul: 1 Sam 10:6; David: 1 Sam 16:13; Zechariah: 2 Chron 20:14; Hosea 9:7; and so on.

[14] Habets, *The Progressive Mystery*, 30–1.

[15] This leadership includes the practical leadership of building and teaching others to build the temple (Exod 35:34; 36:1). We clearly see leadership and the Spirit of God in the ministry of Joshua (Deut 34:9), Moses (Isa 63:11, 14), and the Judges—the abilities exhibited by a judge are attributed to the coming of the *ruach* that makes the judge "charismatic" and gives the judge power to mediate Yahweh's deliverance (Othniel, Judg 3:10; Gideon, 6:34; Jepthah, 11:29; Samson, 13:25; etc.). Habets, *The Progressive Mystery*, 31.

[16] Habets, *The Progressive Mystery*, 32.

In the Prophets the Spirit and prophecy are closely related (Saul, 1 Sam 10:6, the ecstatic outbursts, etc.). The various manifestations of having the Spirit serve as public indicators that the person has received the *ruach* and is designated leader or spokesman. Prophetic inspiration, visionary or auditory, is attributed to the Spirit, as is true from false prophecy; 2 Sam 23:2, Zech 7:12, 1 Kings 22:24 cf., Mic 2:7. Prophecy through the Spirit comes on the priests in 1 and 2 Chronicles (1 Chron 12:18, 2 Chron 15:1; 18:23, etc.). The prophets, then, become the mediators of God's revelation to Israel.[17]

Once more, it is important to take note of this activity of the Spirit as the background to the formation of the Church on the day of Pentecost (Acts 2) and the subsequent gifting of the people of God for ministry.

The Spirit is active in creation, the community, and finally for our survey, the consummation of God's work, which culminates in the coming of Jesus the Messiah. As argued previously,

> Against the backdrop of the failure of the people of Israel to fulfil the high calling of God, to rule the nation in righteousness and with justice, and to be a light to the nations, the prophets look beyond the exile and into the future when the perfect ruler would sit on David's throne and fulfil the plans and design of God. This ruler would be exceptional in many respects, but the most exceptional element being his special endowment and association with the divine Spirit of God. The classic promise of a future ruler endowed with God's Spirit is Isa 11:1–5, 10. This Messianic, Davidic king would be specially endowed with the divine Spirit in unequalled measure. The same theme is pursued in Isa 42:1–4. The sense of these passages intensified as the people considered the Spirit of God to have departed from Israel, and so they fixed their hopes on the coming Messiah in whom the Spirit would completely fill. Because of the failure of the judges, the kings, and the people of Israel; a future coming servant and Messiah was the only hope for the nation. Yahweh would select this person, anoint, and send him in the power of the Spirit for the express purpose of establishing a righteous rule as the example of the original expectations and plan of God for his people. The nature of the servant's work is manifold and at times unexpected. It includes the aspects of humility, suffering, lament, alongside exaltation, and victory. The ministry of the servant will open blind eyes, heal the sick, reconcile the wayward, judge the wicked, and bring peace to all people.[18]

---

[17]Habets, *The Progressive Mystery*, 34.
[18]Habets, *The Progressive Mystery*, 37–8.

This brings us to the Incarnation. The Gospels were written after the Epistles, a detail often lost on Christian readers, and this is an important insight. As Jack Levison reminds us,

> as they remember his story, the authors of the four Gospels recollect that the uncommon presence of the Holy Spirit spanned Jesus's life. The Spirit is, in a real sense, the tensive presence that holds together their narratives. Before Jesus even takes a step, some recall that the Holy Spirit inspired Elizabeth, Mary, Zechariah, and John the Baptist (still in Elizabeth's belly) to pray or praise or find themselves—Mary, at least—pregnant. They remember the descent of the Holy Spirit at Jesus's baptism, the force of the Holy Spirit in the wilderness, Jesus's dire warning about blasphemy against the Holy Spirit, his assurance of the Holy Spirit for martyrs, and even the promise of the Holy Spirit after his death. ... The presence of the Spirit with Jesus is decisive in all four Gospels.[19]

Jesus steps into history as one who is already stamped with the Holy Spirit, as it were. He comes clothed in the Spirit of Israel, the Spirit of God. The cloak of the Spirit is worn by Jesus throughout the incarnation and without this background information, his actions, words, and accomplishments would be incomprehensible. A Spirit Christology is a formal way to represent this biblical account of the Christ who comes as an aspect of the Spirit's prior mission.[20] But what is Spirit Christology, what forms does it take, and what does it consist of?

2.2 Defining Spirit Christology

2.2.1 Types of Spirit Christology

A persistent misconception dogs contemporary Spirit Christology: many scholars unfamiliar with the area automatically rule it out as being

---

[19] Jack Levison, *An Unconventional God: The Spirit according to Jesus* (Grand Rapids, MI: Baker Academic, 2021), 2.

[20] What we are trying to avoid are two extremes. On the one hand is the extreme that says Jesus acts immediately as the Divine Son on the human nature *simpliciter*, effectively bypassing the human nature and, in so doing, having no need of the Spirit. On the other hand is the extreme that the Son is passive in the incarnation and the Holy Spirit is the singular acting subject. Both positions are wrong. As Duby writes, "the biblical description of the Spirit's acting upon the Son's humanity does not negate the Son's divine acting upon and by his own humanity. For whenever the Spirit is acting, he is acting from the Son. And whenever the Son according to his divinity is acting, he is acting with and through the Spirit," Duby, *Jesus and the God of Classical Theism*, 227. And later, "while Jesus is endowed with habitual graces, he nevertheless has to look to the Spirit for the sustenance, movement, and evocation of these graces and for strength and comfort in his application of them," 241.

unorthodox, thinking it succumbs to one or another ancient heresy.[21] It is true that in the history of the church, there have been those types of Spirit Christologies that are expressly unorthodox.[22] One thinks here of Paul of Samosata or Apollinaris in the early church, or Geoffrey Lampe and Roger Haight in our own time. But many more, the majority in fact, are orthodox accounts of Jesus Christ that conform to the biblical testimony and work within the conciliar tradition.[23] This has led those writing on Spirit Christology to construct various suggestions for how to categorize proposals for a Spirit Christology. Bryant suggests a three-phase taxonomy for modern Spirit Christologies.[24] Bryant characterizes the first revisionist phase as classically liberal as they each "significantly revised the Chalcedonian christological confession and triune theology."[25] A second, trinitarian phase followed and "the contours of the second phase were shaped by attempts to formulate trinitarian Spirit Christologies which complement Logos Christology."[26] A third phase is identified by Bryant as Pentecostal contributions. Bryant notes that "Contributions by Pentecostal scholars to the modern discussion … do not attempt to construct Spirit Christology; rather, focusing on Pentecostal issues, these scholars integrate Spirit Christology into Pentecostal theology."[27] Bryant believes this third phase, Pentecostals, are in fact, leading the way.[28] That is a point of some dispute, of course.[29]

---

[21] Writing on Spirit Christology in 2003, I noted various authors of the time who did this. Since 2003, many more names could be added to this list.
[22] The most comprehensive historical survey of Spirit Christology is Herschel O. Bryant, *Spirit Christology in the Christian Tradition: From the Patristic Period to the Rise of Pentecostalism in the Twentieth Century* (Cleveland, OH: CPT Press, 2014). For a theological survey see Myk Habets, "Spirit Christology: Seeing in Stereo," *Journal of Pentecostal Theology* 11 (2003): 199–235.
[23] On criteria for Christology within which our own version of Spirit Christology fits, see Habets, "Spirit Christology," 200–3.
[24] Bryant, *Spirit Christology*, 2–38.
[25] Bryant, *Spirit Christology*, 16.
[26] Bryant, *Spirit Christology*, 33.
[27] Bryant, *Spirit Christology*, 37.
[28] Bryant, *Spirit Christology*, 38.
[29] While Pentecostals have contributed significantly to the development of Spirit Christology, to my mind (Habets) the most important Spirit Christologists to date are Ralph del Colle, Myk Habets, and Leo Sánchez. Del Colle is a Catholic, Habets a Baptist, and Sánchez a Lutheran. Del Colle produced one of the first modern treatments of Spirit Christology and retrieved the topic for others to follow, especially focusing on Roman Catholic writers and theology; see *Christ and the Spirit: Spirit-Christology in Trinitarian Perspective* (Oxford: Oxford University Press, 1994). In addition, he has contributed other essays to the topic. Habets has written extensively on Spirit Christology including the influential *The Anointed Son*, "Spirit Christology: Seeing in Stereo," "Spirit Christology: The Future of Christology?" in *Third Article Theology: A Pneumatological Dogmatics*

Leo Sánchez is another prominent contributor to Spirit Christology, and he suggests a three-tier typology also, but this time dividing contributions up into Pre-Nicene, Nicene, and Post-Nicene theology.[30] Sánchez is especially interested in the identity of the Spirit within each tradition, and he sees this as a way to define how each group develops a Spirit Christology. Pre-Nicene Spirit Christology refers to those who define spirit as simply a synonym for divinity or the divine, hence when applied to Christ, it merely means the presence of God in the life of Christ. Nicene scholars include those who accept and work within the conciliar tradition, and hence their Spirit Christology complements Logos Christology as the Spirit is identified as the third person of the Holy Trinity. Post-Nicene Spirit Christology works consciously after or well beyond the bounds of Chalcedon and rejects its two-nature Christology, positing spirit as a metaphor or symbol best suited to speak of how God is present in Jesus. "Post-Nicene Spirit Christology essentially replaces Nicene (Trinitarian, Chalcedonian) Logos Christology."[31] This is not an unhelpful taxonomy, but it does seem too convoluted and finds more discontinuity between Pre- and post-Nicene theology than the evidence might suggest.

By far the easiest taxonomy, and one that seems to more clearly account for the various groups discussed above, is that of Habets (and Del Colle before him) who identifies two groups, those that want to complement Logos Christology, and those that want to replace it.[32] The first is thoroughly trinitarian and conciliar, the second is post-trinitarian in that it self-consciously rejects any traditional doctrine of the Trinity.[33]

(ed. Myk Habets; Minneapolis, MN: Fortress Press, 2016), 207–31, and "Spirit Christology and the Power of Jesus," in *T&T Clark Handbook of Christology* (ed. Chris Tilling and Darren Sumner; London: Bloomsbury T&T Clark, forthcoming). In addition to *Receiver, Bearer, and Giver of God's Spirit* and *T&T Clark Introduction to Spirit Christology* (London: T&T Clark, 2022), Leopoldo A. Sánchez, M. has produced the fruits of his application of Spirit Christology to sanctification in *Sculptor Spirit* and other essays. Sánchez and Habets also coedited a special volume of the *Journal of Theological Interpretation*; see Myk Habets and Leopoldo A. Sánchez, M., "Introduction: Spirit Christology and the Theological Interpretation of Scripture," *Journal of Theological Interpretation* 12 (2018): 1–2. In addition to Pentecostalism, Roman Catholics contribute a significant amount to Spirit Christology, including but not limited to the work of Del Colle, Raniero Cantalamessa, David Coffey, Joseph Ratzinger (Pope Benedict XVI), and others. In short, there is no third phase of Spirit Christology that belongs to one group over another, hence, the twofold taxonomy used here.

[30] Sánchez, *T&T Clark Introduction to Spirit Christology*, 5–17. For his full account of Spirit Christology, see *Receiver, Bearer, and Giver of God's Spirit*.
[31] Sánchez, *T&T Clark Introduction to Spirit Christology*, 14.
[32] Habets, "Spirit Christology," 203–28.
[33] See Habets, *The Anointed Son*, 53–88.

Within the Fathers, we find a variety of approaches to Christology, and trying to level that bumpy terrain would be facile.[34] However, it is a fact that both Logos and Spirit Christologies happily coexisted within this period, even if Logos Christology did gain the ascendancy. Logos Christologies are those explanations of the identity and mission of Jesus Christ that start with the presupposition of his divinity and work to account for his humanity. These approaches have canonical support (including John 1:1–18; Col 1:15–20; Phil 2:5–11; and Heb 1–2 among others), and have been especially helpful at presenting a pro-Chalcedonian picture of who Jesus is.[35] Logos Christology is characterized by a method from above to below, hence it is a descending Christology, emphasizes ontology over function, dogma over experience, and begins with the divinity of Christ only to then problematize his humanity. Chalcedon's two-nature Christology is clearly important here. Spirit Christology as we use it here, by contrast, is characterized by a method from below to above, hence it is an ascending Christology, emphasizes function over ontology, and experience over dogma.[36] Here the strict imaging of the two Christologies ends.[37] Spirit Christology does not begin with the humanity of Christ only to then problematize his divinity; rather, Spirit Christology begins with the *person* of Jesus the Messiah and through his life and work comes to see him as the God-man, the person of the eternal Son incarnate as Jesus of Nazareth. Nicaea's *homoousion* is clearly important here.

Hopefully, it is clear that these two approaches to Christology are complementary; each is an attempt to read with the grain of Scripture and see who Jesus is as the Messiah and what he has done and is doing for us and our salvation. Liston clearly shows that "applying a TAT method to Christology has enabled two 'Chalcedonian propositions' to be affirmed. First, that Jesus Christ our Lord is fully and uniquely the person of the

---

[34]One of the best treatments of Christological perspectives of the period is that of Brian E. Daley, *God Visible: Patristic Christology Revisited* (Oxford: Oxford University Press, 2018).
[35]A definition, history, and explanation for the eventual dominance of Logos Christology can be found in Habets, *Anointed Son*, 53–88.
[36]See the helpful table charting the two Christologies in Sánchez, *Receiver, Bearer, and Giver of God's Spirit*, 241–2.
[37]See Gregory J. Liston, *The Anointed Church: Toward a Third Article Ecclesiology* (Minneapolis, MN: Fortress Press, 2015), 35–64, for a detailed overview of what a "Chalcedonian" Spirit Christology looks like, but one that applies the methodology of TAT to the discussion. As Liston concludes, "Applying a Third Article Theology approach to Christology suggests this dualistic distinction of natures is no longer adequate, and that not only should the relationship between the Son's divine nature and human nature be examined, but also the way the Son and Spirit relate to each other within the incarnation," 63.

Son and fully and uniquely anointed by the Spirit. Second, that within the incarnation the identity and missions of the Son and the Spirit are logically and chronologically synchronous (without priority), distinct (without confusion), and interdependent (without separation)."[38]

The contention of Spirit Christology is that without an explicit focus on the Spirit in Jesus's life, we will not fully recognize him as the Messiah, the Spirit endowed One sent on his mission to be our Prophet, Priest, and King, Lord, Master, and the author and perfector of our faith. As Bryant remarked, "Spirit Christology is very fluid in nature and transcends rigid boundaries, so several paradigms are necessary to account for its presence in the Christian tradition."[39] We have only canvassed a few varieties here. What is now required is a more technical definition of the Spirit Christology adopted in this work before discussing the contours of what this entails.

2.2.2 A Trinitarian Pneumatic Christology

Spirit Christology as used in this work may be defined as a Christology that takes its impetus from the mission of the Spirit in the life of Christ; hence it is a form of inspirational Christology, but one that reads the Scriptures to the end and acknowledges that Jesus the Messiah cannot be appropriately acknowledged without due reference to his divine nature. Hence, it is a form of inspirational incarnational Christology: Jesus the Messiah is the eternal Son incarnate. Hence, a trinitarian pneumatic Christology is the content of the Spirit Christology we develop. A Spirit Christology of this sort provides the lenses required to see who Jesus is as the Messiah and the eternal Son in the one person. By focusing on the life of Christ from a Spirit-oriented direction, we see that Jesus is defined, as it were, by the Spirit. The life of Christ without the Spirit would be incomprehensible, and so we start with this affirmation: Jesus is who he is on the basis of the revealing work of the Holy Spirit in the life of the incarnate Son. We endorse the words of Del Colle:

> Spirit Christology is an attempt to account for the identity and mission of Jesus Christ from a pneumatic viewpoint, but not exclusively so. It seeks to build a Trinitarian construction from the pneumatological and Christological

---

[38]Liston, *The Anointed Church*, 64.
[39]Bryant, *Spirit Christology*, 42.

reciprocity to the Father. Anything less than a mutual reciprocity between Christology and pneumatology in the articulation of what Christians mean by God, revelation, and redemption, results in a diminution of the full deposit of the faith.[40]

2.3 Establishing a Spirit Christology from the Messianic *kairoi*

2.3.1 What Are Messianic *kairoi* and How Do They Function?

Jesus is repeatedly addressed as, referred to, and called attention to his status as the Messiah, the Spirit anointed Son of Man. Jesus is framed as the one who comes in the power of the Spirit and achieves his ministry in cooperation with the Spirit. The Spirit is so all-encompassing a presence on Jesus that he is called The Anointed One, The Messiah/Christ. This use of Messiah is more than a titular nod at his function; rather, it is an attempt to say not only is this man, Jesus of Nazareth, special and marked out for a particular office, he actually embodies such offices. For instance, Jesus is not simply a great prophet come to give a word from God, he is *the Logos*, the Word of God eternal. Christ is the Messiah and the Messianic ministry defines who Jesus is.

The Gospels are consistent in presenting Jesus as the Messiah. "If we look at Jesus' identity through the lens of *anointing* language, a link between Jesus and the Spirit of God emerges."[41] I call these episodes in the life of Christ Messianic *kairoi*, or disclosure episodes: windows into a revelation of who Jesus Christ is made possible via his relationship with the Spirit. There are many Messianic *kairoi* in the Scriptures, but for our purposes we will use three headings to illustrate the contents of a Spirit Christology and we will focus on the Gospels: Preparation, Ministry, and Current Session.[42]

---

[40] Del Colle, *Christ and the Spirit*, 4. The Pro-Chalcedonian stance of our Spirit Christology is further developed in Liston, *The Anointed Church*, 35–64.
[41] Sánchez, *Receiver, Bearer, and Giver of God's Spirit*, ix.
[42] A comprehensive commentary on the Messianic *kairoi* can be found in Habets, *The Anointed Son*, 118–87, including a discussion of the Pauline corpus.

2.3.2 Preparation: Conception, Birth, Baptism

The first phase of the Gospel accounts of Jesus the Messiah coalesces around his preparation for Messianic ministry, specifically here we see a focus on the virgin conception and birth of Jesus, followed by his baptism in the Jordan. Levison puts it well:

> Luke's Gospel begins with an infinity of grace, Matthew's with the calculus of hope. At the center of both sets of stories—Matthew's measured five and Luke's rush of canticles—lies an uncannily similar perspective. Not just the baby Jesus, whose birth is the glue. There is also a hue, an atmosphere, an ambience. For both Matthew and Luke, the Jewish Scriptures are essential, indispensable for grasping what went on in these early days. They are the leaven, the bread that is baking in the oven. They are a background scent, yes, rich and undeniable and welcoming. Yet there is something more to these stories. The Holy Spirit is also essential, indispensable for grasping what went on with the first glimmer of inspiration. And here is the rub: the Spirit is essential not because something altogether *new* was happening—the birth of Christianity, let's say—but because something *old*, ancient, yet timeless was coming to fruition. The Holy Spirit is central to the birth of Jesus not so much to spawn something new as to spark something old, not so much to invent as to ignite.[43]

There is too much going on in the Gospel accounts of Jesus' conception, birth, and baptism to comment on in detail, suffice to say that Jesus is presented as the fulfillment of Israel's hopes and prophecies. The coming of the Son into the world is saturated in Spirit talk just as the Son is saturated with the Spirit. Both Matthew and Luke make it clear that Jesus is born of the Spirit (Matt 1–2; Luke 1–2). Matthew speaks of Mary's conception "from holy spirit." Levison argues that by missing out the definite article either or both of the two references to holy spirit in the Old Testament are being referred to, Isaiah 63 and Psalm 51. The first seems to fit the evidence more clearly.[44] Isaiah 63 speaks of the Holy Spirit being put within Israel to lead her out from Egyptian tyranny and bondage and into the freedom of the

---

[43] Levison, *An Unconventional God*, 9.
[44] If Psalm 51 is in view, then "Mary would be pregnant because of the sanctity of *her* spirit," Levison, *An Unconventional God*, 12. Levison believes this is a possibility on linguistic grounds, I rule it out on theological grounds.

Holy land, memorably in the form of pillars of cloud and fire (both symbols of the Spirit).

> From the vantage point of Isaiah 63, the birth of Jesus occasioned by the Holy Spirit within Mary, is the culmination of a long story of leading, designing, and delivering. Is it too much to say, in light of Isaiah 63, that the water of Mary's womb, awake now with the Holy Spirit, is like a latter-day red Sea, through which Israel, alert to the Holy Spirit within them, can be liberated? This is a great deal to invest in a single birth, but this is the birth of the Messiah.[45]

In Luke's more lively account, we have Jesus' conception and then birth surrounded with prophetic activity, "this is no pedestrian drama. In this Gospel the Holy Spirit is hard at work before Jesus's birth, inspiring pregnancy, praise, and promise."[46] And why? To mark Jesus out as unique, as the Messiah, the last Adam, the Coming One. Jesus is the Davidic King, the High Priest, and the Prophet of God. Through the Spirit, Jesus is revealing himself as the Messiah.

There is much more going on in the infancy narratives, of course, but we shall have to pass over that for sake of time.[47] "When the time was right" and to "fulfil all righteousness" (Matt 3:15) Jesus is baptized by John in the Jordan and the heavens open, the Father speaks, and the Holy Spirit rests on Jesus in an act of anointing for further ministry (Mark 1:9–11; Matt 3:17; Luke 3:22; John 19–34).[48] Cyril of Alexandria beautifully described the import of this occasion as follows:

> He knew no sin at all so that, just as through the disobedience of the first we came under God's wrath, so through the obedience of the second, we might escape the curse and its evils might come to nothing. ... The Spirit flew away because of sin, but the one who knew no sin became one of us so that the Spirit might become accustomed to remain in us.[49]

---

[45] Levison, *An Unconventional God*, 11.
[46] Levison, *An Unconventional God*, 14.
[47] See Habets, *The Anointed Son*, 123–31, where Jesus' contrast with John the Baptist is noted along with other key Messianic indicators in the text.
[48] "The contours of Jesus's sonship are multifaceted, at once communicating Jesus's ontological filial relationship to his Father, announcing Jesus's messiahship (Pss 2:7; 89:27; 2 Sam 7:14), evoking corporate Israel (Exod. 4:22–23), and recalling Adam's royal-filial sonship," Brandon D. Crowe, *The Last Adam: A Theology of the Obedient Life of Jesus in the Gospels* (Grand Rapids, MI: Baker Academic, 2017), 70.
[49] Cyril of Alexandria, *Commentary on John* 184, cited in Crowe, *The Last Adam*, 9.

What began at conception extends to ministry; the Spirit accompanies Jesus to the far country and Jesus makes room for the indwelling Spirit in his human life. Culminating at Golgotha, the Spirit is forming Christ as the Messianic obedient Son and at the same time the Son is molding the Spirit into a Christological form. At Pentecost this Holy Spirit, the Spirit of Christ, will be given to Christ's disciples—given with the biography of the obedient Son imprinted all over it in order to conform us to the image of the incarnate Son.

"The Son obeys the Father's will; the Spirit drives him forward. The two statements describe the same inward compulsion that found expression in Jesus's deeds and words."[50] According to Calvin, "In short, from the time when he took on the form of a servant, he began to pay the price of liberation in order to redeem us."[51] This brings us to Christ's public ministry and passion.

2.3.3 Ministry: Words, Works, and Passion

One way to encompass the manifold works and words of Christ in the Gospel accounts is to treat them all under the trope of the strong man's defeat (Matt 12:29; Mark 3:27; Luke 11:21–22). In parabolic form, Jesus speaks of himself (Messiah) binding the strong man (Satan), in order to gain power over him and his possessions (the earth). Jesus defeats Satan through his obedient ministry (tying Satan up). This was a major theme in the work of Irenaeus, who famously saw Christ's life as a recapitulation of Adam's: Jesus "fought and conquered … and through obedience [did] away with disobedience completely: for he bound the strong man and set free the weak."[52] As Crowe states, "the presupposition for this is the coming of the Holy Spirit upon Jesus Christ, which enabled him to renew humanity."[53] The binding of Satan should be seen as something Jesus does both at a point in time (the victory in the temptation narratives; Matt 4:1–17; Mark 1:12–13; Luke 4:1–14) and throughout his ministry.[54] "Jesus's temptations

---

[50] Habets, *The Anointed Son*, 141.
[51] John Calvin, *Institutes of the Christian Religion* (1559), 2.16.5 Library of Christian Classics XX (ed. John T. McNeill, trans. Ford L. Battles; Philadelphia: Westminster Press, 1960), 507.
[52] Irenaeus, *Haer.* 3.18.6 (*ANF* 1:447–448), cited in Crowe, *The Last Adam*, 20.
[53] Crowe, *The Last Adam*, 20.
[54] Walter W. Wessel, "Mark," in *Expositor's Bible Commentary*, vol. 8 (ed. Frank E. Gaebelein; Grand Rapids, MI: Zondervan, 1984), 623, who argues that it is widely accepted that the whole of Mark relates to Jesus' temptation narrative as his entire ministry was one of continuous encounter with Satan.

are therefore presented to the reader within this messianic framework as he begins his ministry of word and deed in the power of the messianic Holy Spirit."[55]

The Spirit is the power of Christ throughout his earthly sojourn. In the Synoptic Gospels, the power of Christ to overcome the strong man is attributed to his reception and use of the Holy Spirit working through him (Matt 12:28, 32; Mark 3:29; Luke 11:20).[56] This accounts for his power over nature, over demons, over sin, and over death itself. As Colin Gunton remarked, "The distinctive work of the Spirit is, through Christ, to perfect the creation. The function of the Spirit in relation to Jesus is, accordingly, as the perfecter of his humanity. Just as the *enhypostasia* reminds us of the origin of our salvation in the eternal love and action of God, so attention to the Holy Spirit reminds us of the way in which the saving action of Jesus is accomplished humanly in time."[57]

A vast number of episodes in the Gospels could be appealed to in order to make the case that Jesus lives and acts as the Spirit-inspired Messiah and that his relationship with the Spirit is the key to his identity and mission.[58] Throughout the life of Christ, we see his vicarious ministry of filial obedience as Jesus remains faithful to his mission. As Crowe noted, "the initial testing of Jesus's messianic sonship catapults Jesus into his ministry of obedient sonship, in which he overcomes all spiritual opposition to his task, even to the point of obediently facing the unjust death on the cross. By his obedience and full possession of the Spirit, Jesus possesses unrivalled spiritual authority on earth."[59]

This unrivaled spiritual authority is exercised over nature (Luke 8:24–25; Matt 14:25; Mark 11:21); over sin (Matt 9:2, 6; Mark 2:5; Luke 5:18–26); over evil (Mark 1:21–28; 5:1–20), and over people (Matt 8:16; Luke 4:40; Mark 3:10; Luke 6:18). In each instance, Jesus is not simply healing and exercising power indiscriminately; rather, he is fulfilling all prophesy and acting out a parable of the Kingdom. As the Gospel of John phrases it, Jesus' vicarious ministry involves actions that function as "signs" (*sēmion*) that point to his

---

[55]Crowe, *The Last Adam*, 31.
[56]Crowe, *The Last Adam*, 73.
[57]Colin E. Gunton, *Christ and Creation* (Grand Rapids, MI: Eerdmans, 1992), 50. Raniero Cantalamessa, *The Holy Spirit in the Life of Jesus* (Collegeville: Liturgical Press, 1994), 11, reminds us that "beginning with the baptism and temptations in the wilderness, there is something new in salvation history: the free and human consent of a God! Human but of God; a yes of fully human quality, but of divine power."
[58]See Habets, "Spirit Christology and the Power of Jesus."
[59]Crowe, *The Last Adam*, 79.

identity as the Messiah and the coming Kingdom. This is confirmed by Jesus when he stood in the synagogue and told the audience that his ministry was the fulfilment of Isaiah 61: "The Spirit of the Lord is upon me, because he anointed me to preach the Gospel to the poor. He has sent me to proclaim release to the captives, and recovery of sight to the blind, to set free those who are oppressed, to proclaim the favourable year of the Lord." After which he said, "Today this Scripture has been fulfilled in your hearing" (Luke 4:18–19, 21).[60]

The vicarious ministry of Jesus results in his passion. The role of the Spirit in the passion of Christ has been grossly neglected in Christian thought; but that is a mistake. Jesus' ministry comes to a climax of sorts at the cross, and here no less than throughout his public ministry, the Spirit is active and essential. How could Jesus remain obedient at the cross? In the face of evil and rejection he forgave his enemies, comforted the penitent on the cross, cared for his mother, and looked out for his disciples. These are superhuman feats and are only explicable in spiritual terms. As John O'Donnell wrote, "In the death of Jesus, the Son surrenders himself totally to the Spirit, entrusting it to the Spirit to rescue his mission after his death."[61] Earlier, in the Garden of Gethsemane, Jesus sought and received the power to endure the cross from the Spirit sent from the Father.

The prayer that ends with the Son's embracing of the Father's will, "not my will but yours" (Mark 14:36), begins with the words, which the early church identified as the witness of the Holy Spirit, that one is a child of God; "Abba" (cf., Mark 14:36; Rom 8:15; Gal 4:6). In light of the fact that this practice was widespread in the early church, why is it only here, in Gethsemane, that Mark records Jesus addressing his Father by the Spirit-inspired words "Abba"? Moltmann rightly concludes that this means Mark is giving a pneumatological interpretation to Jesus' passion. What began with his conception and baptism through the Spirit now ends in his passion through the Spirit. The Spirit that led Jesus into the wilderness is still beside him now in this time of trial and temptation.[62]

The Father earlier called Jesus his "Beloved Son," here Jesus responds with his own words of affection, calling God his "Abba Father." The next day, on the cross, as Christ bears the weight of the sin of the world and stands in our

---

[60] See Habets, *The Anointed Son*, 146–51.
[61] John J. O'Donnell, "In Him and Over Him: The Holy Spirit in the Life of Jesus," *Gregorianum* 70 (1989): 35.
[62] See Habets, *The Anointed Son*, 163, citing Jürgen Moltmann, *The Spirit of Life: A Universal Affirmation* (trans. Margaret Kohl; Minneapolis, MN: Fortress Press, 1992), 64.

place, he can only cry out our words of dereliction, "My God, my God, why have you forsaken me?" (Mark 15:34); and he does so through the power and presence of the Holy Spirit (Heb 9:14). But he knows, by the Spirit, that this is not the end. The stronger man has conquered sin and death, and by the Spirit he will rise again to give new life to all.

2.3.4 Current Session: Resurrection, Ascension, and Session

Having made the case that the accounts of Christ's life and ministry are framed by the presence of the Holy Spirit working within and through him, we need only point to some examples of how the vicarious Spirit-filled ministry of Jesus endures after the passion, into the resurrection, the ascension, and the current session of Christ. Once more, there is too much material to cover in a brief survey and so only a few examples will have to suffice.

As the one who perfects the Father's word in creation, the Spirit is the agent of the eschatological act of resurrection in the midst of time. If the resurrection is designed to do, as well as to show, something (as Scripture maintains), then we must view it as the beginning of an eschatological redemption (see Rom 4:25). Through the resurrection, Jesus' particular humanity becomes the basis of universal redemption. So, what of the Holy Spirit? Christ offered himself up through the eternal Spirit (Heb 9:14) and he lives in the 'life-giving Spirit' (1 Cor 15:45). He endured the sufferings and death through the power of the Spirit and was born again to eternal life by the Spirit (Rom 8:11; 14:9; 1 Cor 15:45; 2 Cor 13:4); hence, the pneumatological-Trinitarian paradigm. The Spirit gives birth to Christ once more, this time to eternal life, through and beyond his death. In Christ's rebirth it is the Spirit who is active, as in Christ's conception.[63]

Following the resurrection, the ascension of Christ is an important Messianic *kairoi* as it is the first stage of the giving of the Holy Spirit to Christ's followers. Enthroned at God's right hand (Mark 16:19), Christ triumphs over his enemies (1 Pet 3:22; Pss 8) and is Lord over all (1 Cor 12:3; Eph 1:22). The ascension acts as an antecedent to Pentecost, as the first part of a two-stage coronation and exaltation.

---

[63] Habets, *The Anointed Son*, 171.

For Paul, "the last Adam became a life-giving spirit" (1 Cor 15:45). Here "Spirit" is best identified as Holy Spirit. Christ on his ascension came into such complete possession of the Spirit, who had so associated himself with Jesus through the incarnation, that an economic equivalence of sorts resulted. The resurrected Christ and the Spirit are now experientially one (although not undifferentiated). From the ascension and then Pentecost, the Spirit is now the *alter Christus* to us, and ministerially he is the *allos paraclētos* (see John 14–16).[64]

From the ascension onwards, the Holy Spirit will have a Messianic shape and everything it touches will be affected by Christ. Pentecost is thus the grand coronation ceremony of Christ, as he takes his throne and rules over all and inaugurates his Kingdom with the giving of the Holy Spirit (Acts 2:33). With Craig Keener we affirm, "As Jesus's announcement of his Spirit-anointing in Luke 4:18–19 … is programmatic for Luke, Acts 1:8 and 2:16–21 … are programmatic for Acts."[65] As Peter proclaimed, Joel 2:28–32 was fulfilled on the day of Pentecost as the Spirit was poured out on all flesh on the basis of the finished work of Christ (Acts 2).

The current session of Christ is an extension of his Lordship made possible by the Spirit, as Christ works through the church in the world ushering in the coming Kingdom. Here Heribert Mühlen's definition of the church is instructive when he writes of the church as "the continuation in history of the anointing of Christ with the Holy Spirit." Cantalamessa comments further, "the church, he says, is not, except in the broad sense, a prolongation of Christ's human body, that is to say of the incarnation, but it is, in the strict sense, a prolongation of the Spirit of Christ, of his anointing and of his grace."[66] This theme is echoed by others including Clark Pinnock, who spoke of the church as "a continuation of the Spirit-anointed event that was Jesus Christ."[67] Developing (improving) on this idea, Liston argues the church is not the "continuation" but in fact the "sequel" to the incarnation.[68]

The current session of Christ brings into consideration the means of grace, which put at our disposal the Christoform and cruciform work of the

---

[64] Habets, *The Anointed Son*, 180.
[65] Craig S. Keener, *The Spirit in the Gospels and Acts: Divine Purity and Power* (Peabody, MA: Hendrickson, 1997), 190.
[66] Raniero Cantalamessa, *The Holy Spirit in the Life of Jesus* (Collegeville, PA: Liturgical Press, 1994), 16. (He does not provide the reference to Mühlen's work.)
[67] Pinnock, *Flame of Love*, 113.
[68] Liston, *The Anointed Church*, 88.

Spirit and the various works of the church by which the body of Christ on earth does the will of the Father in Heaven. Here the baptism in the Spirit, followed by the fruit of the Spirit, are all important as the character of Christ is recreated in his disciples and ministry and mission are conducted in participation with Christ and his ongoing vicarious work. As Cantalamessa puts it, "it is now for the Church, speaking in the first person, to repeat those solemn words pronounced in the synagogue at Nazareth: 'the Spirit of the Lord is upon me ... He has anointed me to bring glad tidings to the poor!' "[69]

The reciprocity of Christ and Spirit evidenced throughout Scripture and within recent theology argues strongly that there can be no conception of Christ that does not encompass an understanding of the Christ event as thoroughly pneumatological in itself. There can be no study of the identity or mission of Christ in abstraction from the mission and identity of the Holy Spirit. In the economy, the Spirit is prior to the Son, hence the rationale for starting with the Spirit; but the Son is always preeminent. Where the Spirit is today, there is also knowledge of the Son; where the Son is, there the power of the Spirit is present also.[70]

2.4 Conclusion

In his survey of Spirit Christology, Sánchez helpfully notes that the three main questions in the field relate to: (1) Christology and Soteriology and how we describe the activity of the Holy Spirit in the life and mission of Jesus; (2) Trinitarian Theology and how we describe the proper mission of the Holy Spirit in God's economy of salvation; and (3) Life in the Spirit and how Jesus' life in the Spirit is different from and similar to his disciples life in the Spirit.[71] We have dealt with the first two issues already, and we will address the final issue more directly in Chapter 5. To briefly anticipate the applied nature of TAT, we could point to issues dealt with in practical theology, including but not limited to anointing, resisting sin, evangelism, praying, and good works. We could also name the ecumenical potential of TAT as a way of doing theology that transcends a traditional or denominational

---

[69]Cantalamessa, *The Holy Spirit in the Life of Jesus*, 41.
[70]Habets, *The Anointed Son*, 227.
[71]Sánchez, *Receiver, Bearer, and Giver of God's Spirit*, xi–xii.

dogmatic approach to theology (without necessarily contradicting any of that dogma).

Chapter 3 details the more precise methodological commitments TAT entails, explaining each in detail, and showing how they can and have been applied to the illustrative example of Spirit Christology explored in this chapter.

3

The Methodology of Third Article Theology

3.1 Introduction

The phrase *Third Article Theology* (TAT) is used in two senses. First, as a specific theological approach that starts with the Spirit, and second, as the theological understanding that emerges when this approach is adopted. In outlining some of the core features of a Spirit Christology, Chapter 2 provided a helpful example of its use in the latter sense—as a theological understanding that arises from intentionally starting with the Spirit. This chapter initially aims to provide a more comprehensive (but still introductory) outline of the phrase's use in the former sense—as an explicit theological methodology. What are the characteristics that describe TAT and distinguish it from other approaches within systematic theology? Building on the work of Dabney and others, Habets has developed a set of ten methodological criteria to describe and distinguish a TAT approach. The next section of this chapter (3.2) works through these criteria, explaining each in detail, and at times using the description of Spirit Christology outlined in the previous chapter as a methodological exemplar. Following this, the latter section (3.3) addresses the question of practical method: how theologians actually go about determining the insights of TAT, and in particular how TAT insights can be extended to doctrines beyond Spirit Christology.

3.2 The Methodology of TAT

The following ten methodological criteria describe the theological approach of TAT and differentiate it from other approaches within systematic theology.

The final and most definitive form of these criteria was articulated by Habets in the edited volume *Third Article Theology: A Pneumatological Dogmatics*, although earlier articles noted the criteria (without explanation).[1] Liston has also offered his own detailed account of these methodological criteria.[2] Some of the criteria (1, 6, 7, 10) clearly build on the work of Lyle Dabney,[3] and others (3, 8) have been independently suggested by Andrew Grosso.[4] The following discussion utilizes all of the above sources, together with other commentary from leading TAT scholars, to provide an overarching and introductory description and explanation of these methodological criteria. Further, as appropriate, it illustrates each of the criteria, using the example of Spirit Christology introduced in Chapter 2.

1. TAT starts with the Holy Spirit. Pneumatological considerations are not left to a postscript or conclusion but are, rather, incorporated into theological discourse right from the beginning.

In contrast to First Article Theology, which (in Dabney's characterization) starts with human capacity, or Second Article Theology, which starts with human incapacity, TAT begins not with universals but with a particular claim, that through the ages particular communities have been and are still being moved toward a redemptive relationship with God *by his Spirit*. From this theological baseline, a TAT views every aspect of God's action in the world intentionally through the lens of his Spirit, from creation to incarnation to eschatology. So, as Chapter 2 illustrated, a TAT approach to Christology means exploring Christ's mission as an aspect of the Spirit's. As Pinnock comments, "Let us see what results from viewing Christ as an aspect of the Spirit's mission, instead of (as is more usual) viewing Spirit as a function of Christ's."[5] The underlying assumption behind this approach is that the Word of God is not, in and of itself, the most basic reality humans can access, but exists only in and through an equally fundamental reality: the Spirit of God. As Pinnock writes, "far from being an incidental or isolated topic in theology, Spirit is a major theme, supplying a standpoint, in fact,

---

[1] Habets, ed., *Third Article Theology*, 14–19. For the earlier listings, see, for example, Habets, "The Surprising Third Article Theology of Jonathan Edwards," 195–7.
[2] Liston, *The Anointed Church*, 23–33.
[3] Dabney, "Starting with the Spirit," 24–7.
[4] Andrew Grosso, "Spirit Christology and the Shape of the Theological Enterprise," in *A Man of the Church: Honoring the Theology, Life, and Witness of Ralph Del Colle* (ed. Michel René Barnes; Eugene, OR: Pickwick Publications, 2012), 206–22.
[5] Pinnock, *Flame of Love*, 80.

for surveying the whole vista of Christian truth."⁶ Mühlen writes similarly that in an approach like TAT, questions of the Spirit will no longer act as an "edifying appendage to the doctrine of God."⁷

2. TAT looks through the Spirit rather than looking at the Spirit, thus it is a "Third Article Theology" and not a "theology of the Third Article" (which would simply be pneumatology).

Although closely related to it, TAT is not pneumatology. The doctrine of the Holy Spirit (characterized in this criterion as "a theology of the Third Article") is sometimes reductively divided into the study of the person and the work of the Spirit, and while connected, is often examined separately from other theological *loci*. TAT, in contrast, examines the full range of theological *loci*, and in these examinations always utilizes the Spirit as a lens. The Spirit thus becomes a means rather than an end to the theological task; it is looked through rather than merely being looked at. Pertinent here is the Spirit's role in connecting theological doctrines. Examined through the lens of the Spirit, it is virtually impossible to treat theological topics in isolation. So, for example, it is the Spirit that forms the members of the church into the body of Christ (1 Cor 12:13), connecting ecclesiology and Christology. TAT thus focuses on the connection between and not just the content of specific theological subjects. As Bobrinskoy writes, "Pneumatology is not so much one specific chapter of Christian theology as an essential dimension of every theological view of the church and of its spirituality and liturgical and sacramental life."⁸ Note the fact that the Spirit is being looked through rather than at does not mean that the Spirit remains faceless or nameless. Indeed, quite the opposite. Naming the Spirit (whose person and work are fully parsed in a Trinitarian context) becomes one of the key means through which the Spirit can be most clearly utilized as a means through which to examine other doctrines.⁹

3. TAT should precede First and Second Article Theology as the most consistent way of coordinating the *ordo salutis*, from which we derive the *ordo cognoscendi*, and come to know the *ordo essendi*—from the

---

⁶Pinnock, *Flame of Love*, 10.
⁷Heribert Mühlen, "The Person of the Holy Spirit," in *The Holy Spirit and Power* (ed. Kilian McDonnell; Garden City, NY: Doubleday, 1975), 12.
⁸Bobrinskoy, "Holy Spirit," 470.
⁹See, for example, Lyle Dabney, "Naming the Spirit: Towards a Pneumatology of the Cross," in *Starting with the Spirit* (ed. Stephen Pickard and Gordon Preece; Hindmarsh: Australian Theological Forum, 2001), 28–58.

Father, through the Son, to the Holy Spirit, and back by the Holy Spirit, through the Son, to the Father.

There are two reasons why Habets claims that TAT should precede First or Second Article Theology. The first is temporal and argues that this methodology should have priority at this moment in history. Reasons for this include historical context (in which both First and Second Article theologies have been rigorously mined as methodologies, leaving TAT as the methodology with the greatest untapped potential), theological context (in which the influence of Schleiermacher is increasingly distant allowing for sufficient distinguishing between the human spirit and God's Spirit),[10] and cultural context (in which the TAT themes of particularity and relationality overlap with postmodern emphases and hence have potential to be more easily heard).[11] But Habets goes further and argues that TAT should be prior in an atemporal sense as well. The logic he uses relates our ontology with our epistemology. It is the Spirit who is our immediate (as opposed to our mediated) point of connection with God. We know of God, and we know God first and foremost through the Spirit. Consequently, according to this criterion, our scholarly understanding of God should also always start with an examination through the Spirit.

While virtually all scholars utilizing TAT acknowledge and agree on the contextual imperatives for the priority of TAT, not all agree with Habets's atemporal point. Liston, for example, argues that to prioritize a TAT atemporally unnecessarily confuses and equates epistemology and ontology.[12] The way we come to know of something does not necessarily correspond with the reality that is. Although an imperfect illustration, the situation can be compared to an understanding of scientific method. A theory can be sourced from anywhere, and in many ways the source is secondary and unimportant. All that matters is the extent to which the predictions of the theory match experimental evidence, something that is decided *after* the theory has been tested and not before. In a similar way, all methodologies of determining knowledge about God and the world are

---

[10] As noted by Barth and discussed in Section 1.1.
[11] See Section 1.2.
[12] Coffey makes similar points to Liston in the following discussion, arguing that "no single method will be ideal for the whole of theology, but it is entirely proper that Third Article method as defined above be allowed its day, particularly as it has been neglected hitherto. But if the proof of the pudding is in the eating, the ultimate test of method will be the quality of its results." David Coffey, "The Method of Third Article Theology," in *Third Article Theology: A Pneumatological Dogmatics* (ed. Myk Habets; Minneapolis, MN: Fortress Press, 2016), 22.

permissible, and in many ways the methodology chosen is secondary and unimportant. What matters is the extent to which the theological outcomes of that methodology match God's revelation.[13]

Habets, unsurprisingly, pushes back on this critique. Pointing to an impressive range of scholars who argue for pneumatological priority,[14] he notes that because TAT aligns our epistemological approach with our existential reality, it will be more likely to result in an understanding closely aligned with God's revelation. Liston's response is that whether this is the case ought to be evaluated *after* the methodology has been outworked, and not before. Just as it is unwise to have an *a priori* prejudice toward one scientific theory over another, it is unwise to advance one theological method as being fundamental and constitutive of others. It is perhaps not inappropriate that in an emerging methodology such as TAT, minor points of disagreement between its proponents occur. The substantial agreement between all scholars about the initial contextual point, however, means that this difference in principled understanding has minimal consequence in the outworking of TAT in practice.

4. TAT complements and thus does not compete with First and Second Article theologies. It is thus a contribution toward a fully Trinitarian theology.

As a theology that self-consciously starts with the Spirit, TAT is not intended as a methodological replacement for First and Second Article theologies, but rather complements these other approaches and in some cases corrects their extremes. The most developed outworking of this is again in Christology, where, as noted in Chapter 2, Spirit Christology is seen as a complement and not a replacement for Logos Christology. If TAT intentionally "competed" with Second Article Theology, then it would argue Jesus' divinity could be *entirely* explained through the Spirit, in contrast to the more common but equally flawed argument that Jesus' divinity is entirely explained through the *Logos*. As noted in Chapter 2, there are some theologians who do argue for such a replacement,[15] but a more nuanced understanding sees

---

[13]See, for example, John Polkinghorne, *The Faith of a Physicist* (Minneapolis, MN: Fortress Press, 1996), 5–7.

[14]Habets points to Dabney, "Starting with the Spirit," 24–6. Also Grosso, "Spirit Christology and the Shape of the Theological Enterprise," 217–18. And even T. F. Torrance, *Theology in Reconstruction* (Grand Rapids, MI: Eerdmans, 1965), 116.

[15]For example, Roger Haight, "The Case for Spirit Christology," *Theological Studies* 53 (1992): 257. Also the discussion in Section 2.2.1.

both Christological approaches as complementary. This complementary approach recognizes that Jesus is *fully and uniquely the person of the Son and fully and uniquely anointed by the Spirit.*[16] TAT, as outlined in this book, argues that if either of these aspects is neglected or downplayed, then neither Jesus' divinity nor his humanity can be adequately understood or explained.

   5. TAT recognizes that the Spirit continues to speak today to the church in a retroactive movement of Triune discourse.

While recognizing human limitations, TAT maintains that the Spirit is at work in the observer as well as in the revelation being observed. Habets terms this a "retroactive hermeneutic."[17] "Retro" refers to the role of the Spirit in the lives of biblical authors, enabling them to accurately recall and record Jesus' words and works (John 16:12). "Active" refers to the role of the Spirit in guiding the interpreters to the true message of the text and its correct application to the new situations the community finds itself in (John 14:26). Habets writes, "It is the Spirit of Light who illuminates the significance of the Christ event (*retro*); it is the presence of the Spirit of Life that moves the church on (*active*); and it is the Spirit of Truth who brings the word of God into new situations (*retroactive*)."[18] Two further features of a retroactive hermeneutic are pertinent. First, following Vanhoozer, it is intrinsically communal. Recognizing the problems of individual subjectivity, the church community has a Spirit-derived "charismatic authority,"[19] evidenced for example in the Jerusalem council: "for it seemed good to the Holy Spirit and to us" (Acts 15:28). Second, following Gunton, a retroactive hermeneutic leads to an understanding of doctrinal development as enrichment. Habets writes, "Enrichment ... is a Spirit inspired reading of the past from the vantage point of the future."[20] This is contrasted with an *evolutionary* development, where new understandings are loosely (or simply not) related to those of the past, and could be contrasted with a *static* resistance, where no development beyond the canon is permitted. A retroactive reading of the

---

[16] See Gregory J. Liston, "A 'Chalcedonian' Spirit Christology," *Irish Theological Quarterly* 81 (2016): 74–93.
[17] For more details, see Habets, *The Anointed Son*, 103–17. Also, Myk Habets, "Developing a Retroactive Hermeneutic: Johannine Theology and Doctrinal Development," *American Theological Inquiry* 1 (2008): 77–89. For a similar argument, see Dabney, "Saul's Armour," 134–6.
[18] Habets, *The Anointed Son*, 105–6. This terminology is also used by Philip J. Rosato, "Spirit Christology: Ambiguity and Promise," *Theological Studies* 38 (1977): 444.
[19] As opposed to a canonical authority, to which it is subject. See, for example, Kevin J. Vanhoozer, *Is There a Meaning in This Text?* (Leicester: Apollos, 1998), 411.
[20] Habets, *The Anointed Son*, 114.

Gospels thus opens us to an encounter with Jesus the Messiah—he who was uniquely and completely anointed by the Spirit of God.[21]

6. TAT unfolds the story of the Trinitarian mission of God in the world.

The central concept in this methodological criterion is "transformation," as Dabney explains: "a theology of the third article is a theology of God's mission of a transforming recreation of creation, a theology of continuity in God's presence and purpose in creation and re-creation through the discontinuity of human sin and death. It is thus a theology of neither continuum nor of contradiction, but rather of transformation."[22] Given that looking through the lens of the Spirit encourages seeing connections between different theological doctrines, the methodology of TAT drives the resulting theological understandings toward having a holistic vision of God's working in the world. This vision is fundamentally dynamic and narrative based. In other words, it is intrinsically transformational, and therefore essentially missional.

But a true TAT methodology leads to participation in, and not just observation of, that overarching mission. As Dabney writes, "a theology of the third article seeks to unfold the story of the trinitarian mission of God in the world, indeed, it seeks to facilitate that mission. It seeks therefore to be a theology for a global Christianity, helping Christianity to 'act its age' in the time and place it now finds itself."[23] As noted more explicitly in the criteria below, in an academic context increasingly characterized by reductionism and noncommittal independence, TAT provides a helpful and welcome contrast in insisting (through its intrinsically pneumatological nature) on an overarching viewpoint that both invites and demands personal commitment.

7. TAT finds its focus in the center of that story—in the life, death, and resurrection of Jesus Christ.

Precisely because of its pneumatological emphasis, TAT is just as Christocentric and crucicentric as the Gospel. This methodological approach may look through the lens of the Spirit, but given such a lens, at the crosshairs in the center of that vision, Christ is always present. Consequently, Dabney

---

[21] A detailed examination and development of a Third Article Hermeneutics is a valuable task that still lies ahead of TAT. However, see the interesting and prototypical TAT of the Scriptures contained in the early chapters of Andrew T. B. McGowan, *The Divine Spiration of Scripture: Challenging Evangelical Perspectives* (Nottingham: Apollos, 2007).
[22] Dabney, "Starting with the Spirit," 25.
[23] Dabney, "Starting with the Spirit," 25.

asserts that TAT "finds its focus—that is, defines what it means by Spirit—in the centre of the story of God's mission: in the life, death, and resurrection of Jesus Christ."[24] It is this episode that illuminates the Spirit's work with particular clarity. It is for this reason that TAT has focused in its early stages of development primarily on the articulation of a Spirit Christology, and even now, most examinations of other doctrines go through Spirit Christology as a first point of access.

As a particularly pertinent example, consider how a Spirit Christology can and has been used to inform our understanding of the immanent Trinity. Rather than philosophically starting with God's unity and "solving" his diversity, or starting with God's diversity and "solving" his unity, TAT focuses on that aspect of revelation where the unity and diversity of the Godhead are most clearly and simultaneously evident: Spirit Christology. It is from here that implications about the immanent Trinity are drawn, and it is for this reason that it is often claimed that Spirit Christology provides a more secure route to understanding the immanent Trinity than other economic launching points.[25]

8. TAT highlights the eschatological nature of God's Trinitarian mission in the world and proleptically incorporates such eschatology throughout its pneumatological dogmatics, whereby the mission of God in Christ remains the center of the divine drama.

In a wide-ranging discussion of Spirit Christology, Grosso concludes with this important and overarching insight: "it comes as no surprise that each of the various dimensions of the theological enterprise thus far identified … manifest in different ways and to varying degrees an eschatological character. The manifestation of the Word and Spirit in the world is an eschatological event … so it is entirely natural that each and every dimension of the theological enterprise … should likewise exhibit an eschatological tenor."[26] This is a methodological insight that is true not just for Spirit Christology, but for all dimensions and *loci* within a TAT. Given that is fundamentally grounded in the person of the Spirit, who is the perfecting perfector, it is an immediate and inescapable consequence that TAT recognizes and requires

---

[24]Dabney, "Starting with the Spirit," 25.
[25]See the collection of essays in Bradford E. Hinze and D. Lyle Dabney, eds., *Advents of the Spirit: An Introduction to the Current Study of Pneumatology* (Milwaukee, WI: Marquette University Press, 2001), 302–46. This point will be explored more fully in Chapter 6.
[26]Grosso, "Spirit Christology and the Shape of the Theological Enterprise," 220–1.

constant movement. As the early church father Basil wrote in *De Spiritu Sanctu*,

> On our hearing, then, of a Spirit, it is impossible to form the idea of a nature circumscribed, subject to change and variation, or at all like the creature. We are compelled to advance in our conceptions to the highest, and to think of an intelligent essence, … to whom turn all things needing sanctification, after whom reach all things that live in virtue, as being watered by its inspiration and helped on toward their natural and proper end; perfecting all other things, but Itself in nothing lacking.[27]

The result of this understanding is that the pneumatologically driven journey of sanctification we participate in is not purposeless or endless. It has a finishing point and a goal. TAT adopts a methodological approach that is constantly mindful that the Spirit's work in the world has as its goal the presentation of the church fully and finally to Christ. "The Spirit is about proclaiming and bringing in the kingdom of God, of which Christ is the King."[28] It is in this *telos* that the present transformation of the church, and our entire theological enterprise, finds its context and character.

9. TAT emphasizes the sanctifying work of the Spirit, who moves believers into further holiness or christification—thus it is existentially viable and apologetically effective in today's postmodern milieu.

In discussing the advantages and approach of an intrinsically pneumatological theology, Kärkkäinen writes that "hardly any other theological topic has such a potential for integrating spirituality and discursive theologizing. … The hegemony of one-sided Western theologizing, notwithstanding its massive accomplishments, must give way to a more comprehensive, intercultural theologizing where the whole life, not just intellectualism, comes to bear on our living and thinking."[29] By recognizing this as a methodological criterion, and deliberately making it a starting reference point, TAT establishes itself as much more than merely an intellectual or theorizing activity, examining God's workings in the world from afar. The Spirit is the relational bond enabling humanity to apprehend and appreciate God's revelation in the world. Consequently, TAT deliberately and consciously aligns our scholarship with

---

[27]Basil, *De Spiritu Sanctu*, chapter 9, section 22, https://www.newadvent.org/fathers/3203.htm.
[28]Habets, "Prolegomenon: On Starting with the Spirit," 18.
[29]Kärkkäinen, *Toward a Pneumatological Theology*, 78.

the Spirit's work so that in our theologizing, as in other areas of our life, we may be drawn together by the Spirit into the life of God.

If a TAT approach to Christology is adopted, for example, then the resulting Spirit Christology cannot merely note interesting insights about the Spirit's role in Christ's life. It must look through these insights to determine the sanctifying work of the Spirit in our own lives, transforming us as individuals and communities to become more and more like Christ. The Lutheran scholar, Leopoldo A. Sánchez M., provides a perfect example of this particular methodological aspect of TAT in his ground-breaking work *Sculptor Spirit*.[30] In this volume, Sánchez directly builds from Spirit Christology and outlines five models of transformation that naturally emerge, noting how each of them can lead to our ongoing personal sanctification.

10. TAT is a thoroughly ecumenical theology. Ecumenical is used here in two senses; first it indicates a commitment to the ecumenical creeds and confessions of Christendom; and second, it indicates the potential for doctrinal unity among the currently divided traditions of Christianity.

In an article that is rightly referred to as the first explicit and detailed articulation of a TAT, Lyle Dabney concludes his clarion call to develop a TAT with the important methodological insight that such a theology "intends to be a thoroughly ecumenical theology. The time for polemics and party-spirit in Christian theology is over: ours is an age that demands of us a thoroughly ecumenical theology."[31] He elaborates that "theologically, we must act our age. This does not mean conforming the faith to the age, it means proclaiming that faith in a manner that is appropriate to the age, in a way that is both faithful to God and authentic to God's world today."[32]

TAT's ecumenical potential is easy to see. As a relatively unexamined theological subject, it allows Christian groups a meeting place without too many preconceived opinions or agendas. The fact that it starts from particularity allows the contextual distinctives of each position and community to be acknowledged up front. And the reality that the Spirit has always been understood as a binding factor, not just within the Trinity but within the church, suggests that starting with the Spirit may develop an emerging commonality not just in our thinking but in our practice. But

---

[30]Sánchez M., *Sculptor Spirit: Models of Sanctification from Spirit Christology*.
[31]Dabney, "Starting with the Spirit," 25.
[32]Dabney, "Starting with the Spirit," 26.

Dabney and Habets, in listing ecumenism as a methodological characteristic of TAT, are making a bolder claim than this. Not only does TAT have ecumenical potential, this criterion affirms that it *must* be developed in a way that draws disparate believers together rather than driving them apart. Of course, our very understanding of what it means to be united may well be affected by this journey, as Dabney also noted in his original article: "Ecumenical theology … would thus be best understood not simply as the task of resolving our 'internal' disputes concerning faith and practice, but rather as the common task of living and thinking as disciples of Christ in the new 'external' situation in which we now find ourselves."[33]

In bringing this description of the methodological criteria to a close, two final summative comments are in order. First, these criteria are not offered and should not be adopted as a methodological straitjacket to which anyone attempting to undertake a TAT must conform, but rather as a general locus of intent. They are presented with an acknowledgment and desire for spaciousness appropriate to any emerging discipline. While there may be some dissent about some of the criteria or their specific wording, the claim is nevertheless that many and perhaps most of those working in the field of TAT concur with the list above to some degree. Second, it will also be noticed that the criteria, very roughly, can be divided into three categories. Criteria 1 to 4 specifically and deliberately *distinguish* TAT from other methodologies within systematic theology. Their primary goal is to explain how TAT is different from the way theology has been conducted in the past. Criteria 5 to 8 *describe* the way in which TAT should be done, and it could be argued that to some degree these methodological criteria are reflective of all good theology. Their inclusion in the list, however, illustrates how adopting a pneumatological priority leads naturally toward the production of a theology of quality. Criteria 9 and 10 are *aspirational* and *restrictive*, providing intentional guides for the direction that a TAT approach can and should profitably face.

3.3 The Method of TAT

As noted in the description of Criterion 7, the majority of work in TAT to date has been in the area of Spirit Christology, and while they don't necessarily have to, even now, current examinations of other doctrines utilizing a TAT

---

[33]Dabney, "Starting with the Spirit," 26.

approach usually go through Spirit Christology as a first point of access. This section explores how a TAT approach can provide insights beyond Spirit Christology. It argues that the dialogical insights described by Nicholas Wolterstorff in his profound and concise masterpiece *Reason within the Bounds of Religion* provide an eminently suitable approach and language for analyzing and describing this method.[34]

Over a decade ago, Habets maintained that (broadly conceived) there were at least fifty theologians pursuing Spirit Christological research.[35] While the number of theologians explicitly extending TAT beyond Christology at that time would have been less than this by nearly an order of magnitude, the assemblage of those pursuing this kind of theological research has significantly increased over the last decade. Clark Pinnock and Lyle Dabney can justifiably lay claim to being the progenitors and pioneers of this extension. In 1996, Pinnock published a monograph that examined all the main theological doctrines through a pneumatological lens.[36] While it was a birds-eye view, it indicated some profitable anticipatory directions for the coming TAT movement. Three years later, Dabney called for the development of a detailed systematic theology that intentionally starts with the Spirit.[37]

Since the work of these early pioneers, and particularly within the last decade, the group of theologians who have begun to explicitly explore TAT beyond Christology has grown not just in number but in breadth. Those involved in the movement include Roman Catholics (e.g., Ralph Del Colle, David Coffey), Pentecostals (e.g., Amos Yong, Veli-Matti Kärkkäinen, Stephen Studebaker), and Protestants (e.g., Leo Sánchez, Myk Habets, Greg Liston), among many others. It is a testament to the intrinsically ecumenical nature of TAT that the theologians engaged in it are so broadly arrayed. Perhaps the variegated nature of the movement is best illustrated by looking through the expansive author list that contributed to Habets's massive, edited work: *Third Article Theology*.[38]

While very few of these theologians explicitly refer to Wolterstorff's dialogical epistemology as they extend Spirit Christology into a TAT examination of other doctrines, their approaches bear similarities that, when

---

[34]Nicholas Wolterstorff, *Reason within the Bounds of Religion* (Grand Rapids, MI: Eerdmans, 1976).
[35]Habets, *The Anointed Son*, 200.
[36]Pinnock, *Flame of Love*.
[37]Dabney, "Starting with the Spirit," 26–7.
[38]Habets, ed., *Third Article Theology*.

abstracted, can be helpfully explained through utilizing his terminology and concepts. So, while the previous section with its methodological criteria attempted to be spacious and inclusive, this section will attempt rather to outline a single specific method that is reasonably precise and defined. Of course, all work done from every TAT theologian will not fit exactly within the framework of the method outlined, but the specific descriptions given helpfully illustrate the method often adopted in the TAT research being undertaken by many of these leading scholars.

3.3.1 Method Design

The first two methodological criteria mentioned in Section 3.1 were that a TAT starts with pneumatology, and that it looks through, rather than at, the Spirit. As noted, when discussing those criteria, looking through the Spirit makes it abundantly clear that doctrines cannot be examined in isolation. For it is primarily through the Spirit that individual doctrines are connected. A framework and approach for developing TAT beyond Spirit Christology emerges directly from this recognition. Rather than looking directly at the doctrine through the Spirit, the constituent features of a TAT doctrine are illuminated by looking *at* the doctrine *through* the lens of the Spirit *from the vantage point* of other theological *loci*.[39]

To illustrate, consider the view of *ecclesiology* seen from the vantage point of Christology. First, the link between the two subjects is primarily pneumatological. The church is connected historically, metaphorically, and organically with Christ, and each of these connections is pneumatologically enabled.[40] For example, just as the Spirit birthed and empowered Jesus during the incarnation, so the Spirit births and empowers the church. Second, the link between the two *loci* is analogical. The church's identity is related to but not identical with Jesus' identity. The continuities are real, but not exact, and determining the limits to which the analogy can be taken and how the analogy can best be utilized is pivotal in obtaining an accurate ecclesiological understanding. Third, the vantage point utilized illuminates some but not all ecclesiological features. So, the link from Christology to

---

[39]As also noted above, given the significant work already done to date on Spirit Christology, the vantage point most commonly used by TAT scholars at the moment is Spirit Christology, but there is no reason this currently favored perspective should be the exclusive case going forward.

[40]The church was founded by Christ (historical); the church is like Christ (metaphorical); and the church is in Christ (organic). For further discussion of this, see Liston, *The Anointed Church*, 121–4.

ecclesiology illuminates the ontology of the church, but (because of Jesus' individuality) sheds little light on internal ecclesial relationships. It appears that other vantage points also need to be utilized to clearly comprehend all aspects of ecclesiology in a comprehensive manner.[41]

Recognizing these features of the Spirit-enabled connection between theological doctrines suggests how a systematic method for exploring doctrines within TAT can be developed. Working backwards, the third insight above (that each vantage point sheds light on only particular features) means that a variety of perspectives will be needed to move toward a truly comprehensive understanding of the doctrine. It is not sufficient to view ecclesiology only from the vantage point of Christology, for example. Other doctrinal vantage points will be required. The pneumatological perspectives from other theological *loci*—the Trinity, eschatology, and others—also need to be included. Section 3.3.2 outlines this multiple vantage point approach utilizing some seminal concepts from Nicholas Wolterstorff. Wolterstorff outlines a rigorous, postcritical, and dialogical epistemological approach that is particularly suited to the integrated nature of TAT. The first and second insights above (the pneumatological enabled, and analogical connection between doctrines) provides insight into how TAT research can actually go about utilizing one doctrine as a vantage point from which to inform another. Section 3.3.3 will examine how these correspondences can be helpfully applied within a TAT approach.

3.3.2 Multiple Vantage Points

In his seminal work, *Reason within the Bounds of Religion*, Wolterstorff argues (*together* with much postmodern thinking) that there is no indubitable, foundational knowledge.[42] He also asserts (*against* much postmodern understanding) that humans can nevertheless approach a true understanding of an objective and independent reality. This can occur through the analysis and interchange of background beliefs, data beliefs, and control beliefs.

---

[41] It is recognized here that a pneumatologically informed TAT understanding of these doctrines may need to be developed. So, for example, we would need to explore what understanding of the Trinity is fully compatible with a Spirit Christology before that Trinitarian vantage point can be used to view ecclesiology.

[42] See Wolterstorff, *Reason within the Bounds of Religion*.

To take an illustrative example to which Wolterstorff regularly refers, consider the way an astronomer measures a star's position. Put simply, the optical features of a telescope are utilized to determine the star's coordinates. Indeed, astronomers usually integrate several measurements to obtain the most accurate results possible. Applying Wolterstorff's framework to this example, the star's position is the data belief—the reality the astronomer is determining. The telescope's optical features are the control beliefs—the basis on which the astronomer determines the star's position. Everything else, such as Newton's laws of motion, is simply assumed. These are background beliefs. Wolterstorff claims that scientists regularly swap the positions of the data beliefs, control beliefs, and background beliefs. So, for another experiment, the astronomer will simply assume how the telescope works (background belief) and measure a star's position (control belief) in order to test Newton's laws of motion. The star's position in the sky, which was originally a data belief, becomes a new control belief.

In order to illustrate a Wolterstorffian epistemological approach's applicability to contemporary theology, consider the prominent issue of the relationship between the economic and the immanent Trinity. A simple and direct application of Rahner's *Grundaxiom* implies an approach where we examine God's biblical revelation of himself and deduce from this the nature of God's immanent Being.[43] The direction of consideration is thus always vertically upwards, from the economy to God's immanent reality. Using Wolterstorff's terminology, in this approach the biblical, economic Trinitarian accounts are the control belief, the immanent Trinity is the data belief, and everything else is in the background. Using Rahner's approach, each of these beliefs permanently stays in its initially assigned positions. The biblical Trinitarian accounts are always the control; the immanent Trinity is always the data.

Coffey suggests an extension of this approach, where initially the biblical accounts are utilized to gain an understanding of the Trinity, from which the immanent reality of the Godhead is deduced. Then, as a second step, this understanding of the Trinity is applied to other doctrines such as soteriology and ecclesiology.[44] Describing this approach in Wolterstorff's

---

[43] Rahner's *grundaxiom* is, "the economic Trinity is the immanent Trinity and the immanent Trinity is the economic Trinity." Karl Rahner, *The Trinity* (trans. Joseph Donceel; Tunbridge Wells: Burns & Oates, 1997), 22.

[44] Coffey outlines this approach in several of his theological papers. Most clearly in David Coffey, *Deus Trinitas: The Doctrine of the Triune God* (New York: Oxford University Press, 1999), 9–32. For

terminology, the first stage matches the simple and direct application of Rahner's *Grundaxiom* above. But in Coffey's second stage, the doctrines that are control, data, and background beliefs get swapped, so the immanent Trinity becomes the control belief, other theological *loci* such as soteriology and ecclesiology become the data belief, and the biblical Trinitarian data become the background belief.

While this is a positive step forward, a Wolterstorffian approach would go even further. It would apply the *new* control belief of the immanent Trinity not just to other *loci*, but also to the *original* control belief of the biblical accounts of the Trinity. In other words, a Wolterstorffian approach would say that our newly derived immanent Trinitarian understanding should inform even our reading of the text: what is currently termed a theological interpretation of Scripture.[45] Further, it would also use the revised understandings of soteriology and ecclesiology as control beliefs. Indeed, every area of knowledge is used as a vantage point to examine every other area, and the revised understanding gained from this examination immediately becomes a new vantage point from which to observe all others. This is the crux of the Wolterstorffian approach to theology. All aspects of our understanding—our biblical interpretation, our apprehension of the immanent Trinity, our understanding of the Trinity's actions in the church, all other theological *loci*, and even beyond this to other areas of human knowledge—each of these is to be utilized as both control and data beliefs, so that our entire system of knowledge is consistent, coherent, and always developing.

So, the application of Wolterstorff's epistemological approach to theological methodology does not assign a definitive starting point—a single indubitable foundation from which all other understandings are derived. The *subjective source* of an understanding is of secondary importance in Wolterstorff's framework; of primary importance is the consistency and coherence of the understanding developed—the extent to which it matches the breadth of experimental evidence (from a scientific perspective), or the breadth of revelation (from a theological perspective).[46]

---

a comparison of the methodological approach of Rahner and Coffey, see Declan O'Byrne, *Spirit Christology and Trinity in the Theology of David Coffey* (Bern: Peter Lang, 2010), 155–84.
[45]See, for example, Daniel J. Treier, *Introducing Theological Interpretation of Scripture: Recovering a Christian Practice* (Grand Rapids, MI: Baker Academic, 2008).
[46]See Polkinghorne, *The Faith of a Physicist*, 5–7.

Having described a Wolterstorffian approach, consider the natural fit that exists between it and a TAT, which, looking through the lens of the Spirit, intrinsically emphasizes the links between theological *loci*. For many TAT research projects, there are background beliefs—Holy Scripture and the Creeds, or other doctrines—which are crucial reference points, but not the initial focus of a particular TAT project. Then, there are several control beliefs—Third Article doctrines such as Spirit Christology, Trinity, or eschatology—that form the basis or vantage points from which the examination occurs. And finally, there is the data belief—another doctrine such as ecclesiology, or the Trinity—that is the specific area being examined. Each of the views of this doctrine gained from the different perspectives through the lens of the Spirit is integrated to determine as complete and coherent a view of the doctrine as possible. In this sense, a TAT approach might be likened to a surveyor traveling around a vast and beautiful mountain and setting up a telescope at different locations to examine the view of the mountain from a number of vantage points. The mountain examined is the doctrine in question, or the data belief. The different vantage points are various theological doctrines being used as control beliefs. And the telescope being looked through is the Spirit.

This dialogical or Worlterstorffian approach of developing a TAT understanding naturally follows from the way that the Spirit connects doctrines together. Perhaps in this sense, Catholic theologian Heribert Mühlen is correct in asserting that "the doctrine and person of the Holy Spirit is not one doctrine among others, but a fundamental doctrine and reality in the church."[47] While such a combined understanding represents the initial TAT project, it does not form the end of the TAT program, though. Because the new understanding gained can then be utilized as a control belief—a vantage point from which other TAT doctrines can be examined.[48]

3.3.3 Analogical Connections

Using Wolterstorff's terminology, then, a TAT method initially chooses one doctrine as a control belief, and then looks from this vantage point

---

[47] Mühlen, *Una Mystica Persona*, 5. As quoted and translated by Vondey, *Heribert Mühlen*, xv.
[48] Grosso develops a similar understanding of how a comprehensive TAT could be developed but utilizes the epistemological framework of Polanyi rather than Wolterstorff. See Grosso, "Spirit Christology and the Shape of the Theological Enterprise," 215–22.

through the lens of the Spirit at another doctrine that forms the data belief. The immediate question that arises from this method is exactly how a truth or insight in one particular doctrine can inform our understanding of the reality in another doctrine. For example, by what criteria can we determine whether a Trinitarian "truth" can be applied to ecclesiology? Given the former are truth claims about God, and the latter are truth claims about humanity, it is wise to be extremely cautious in too closely identifying the two. Indeed, it could justifiably be questioned whether anything concrete can be determined by regarding humanity as analogous to deity, or vice versa. A TAT method extensively utilizes the insight that a valid correspondence between doctrines exists, and that it is pneumatologically enabled, intrinsically analogical because of it being Christologically informed.

First, consider the analogical correspondence that exists between doctrines. (The intrinsically pneumatological nature of these correspondences will be explored later.) This "analogous" pathway of determining theological insight has been traveled by former theological giants, on whose shoulders TAT researchers stand. For example, Barth's examination of reconciliation in *Church Dogmatics* IV extensively utilized the notion of analogy (or correspondence as he often termed it) to explore the church from the vantage point of Christology. Barth argued that the correspondence between ecclesiology and Christology, for example, and indeed the relationship between all human and divine interactions, parallel the correspondence between the human and divine natures of Christ.[49]

Kimlyn Bender's analysis of Barth's work notes three repeated elements of this parallel.[50] The first element is the "Chalcedonian pattern."[51] Between the divine and human nature of Christ—and consequently, according to Barth, between all divine and human relationships—there is unity, differentiation, and asymmetry: unity in that the two need to be considered together—"without division or separation"; differentiation in that they cannot be so mingled that either loses their own integrity—"without confusion or change"; and asymmetry in that the relationship is ordered so the first is independent and superior, the second dependent

---

[49]See, for example, Karl Barth, *Church Dogmatics* (trans. G. W. Bromiley and T. F. Torrance; Peabody, MA: Hendrickson, 2010), IV.3.2 532-3. See also Kimlyn J. Bender, *Karl Barth's Christological Ecclesiology* (Aldershot: Ashgate, 2005), 5–7.

[50]For a more detailed discussion, see Bender, *Karl Barth's Christological Ecclesiology*, 3–8. In developing these three elements, Bender is building upon the work of Hunsinger, Holloway, Torrance, and Gollwitzer, among others.

[51]George Hunsinger, *How to Read Karl Barth: The Shape of His Theology* (New York: Oxford University Press, 1991), 185.

and subordinate. According to Hunsinger, "there is virtually no discussion of divine and human agency in the *Church Dogmatics* which does not conform to this scheme."[52] The second element expands on the asymmetry of the Chalcedonian pattern. Within Christology, it is expressed as the *anhypostasia/enhypostasia* formula, which establishes (negatively) that the human nature of Jesus has no existence without the Word (*anhypostasia*), and (positively) that the human nature has a true, genuine existence in the Word (*enhypostasia*). Barth analogically affirms similar truths about all divine/human relations, noting that the human side depends on the divine in a manner akin to the *anhypostasia/enhypostasia* formula. The third and final element expands on the *enhypostasia* and its analogical extension into all divine/human relationships. This element is termed "correspondence" by Barth (and Bender) and refers to human actions reflecting the divine in a manner appropriate to the creature. Using these insights, the analogical correspondence between a variety of doctrines can be explored. For example, these insights enable theologians to explore the relationship between Christ and the church, such as Barth does in volume IV of *Church Dogmatics*, or between the economic and the immanent Trinity, as suggested in the first half of Rahner's famous *grundaxiom*.

Turning to the second aspect noted earlier—the intrinsically pneumatological nature of these correspondences—a TAT approach enables a valuable extension and a necessary correction to this commonly trodden analogical approach, however. For, as has been repeatedly noted in this chapter, all doctrines are connected through the Spirit. Consequently, TAT provides not just a new vantage point from which to examine doctrines (e.g., starting from a Spirit Christology and not just a Logos Christology), but the fact that Spirit Christology has enabled a more nuanced view of the hypostatic union, providing new insights into the relationship between Christ's divine and human natures, means that the very nature of analogical relationship between various doctrines can be viewed in a new way, as the very nature of the analogous relationship between the doctrines is intrinsically pneumatologically enabled and Christologically conditioned.

At this early point, two examples will suffice to illustrate the outworking of this extension and correction.[53] First, consider the relationship

---

[52]Hunsinger, *How to Read Karl Barth*, 187.
[53]Note that Part II of this volume provides many more examples of this approach. See particularly Chapters 6, 7, 8, 9, 10, and 11.

between Christology and ecclesiology. Moving beyond the analogical correspondences developed by Barth and others between Logos Christology and the (resultingly rather static) ecclesiology, a TAT approach can look at the correspondences between a Spirit Christology and the church. Moreover, it can explore the intrinsic pneumatological enabling of that relationship. So, in terms of continuities, just as Christ's divine and human natures are one, and this unity is pneumatologically enabled, so Christ and his church are one, and the two entities are joined together through the Spirit. In terms of discontinuities, just as Christ's divine and human natures must be differentiated and not confused, so Christ and the church must be differentiated and not confused, for the role and relationship of the Spirit within each is distinct and not identical. And finally, in terms of asymmetries, just as there is an asymmetry between Christ's divine and human natures with the Spirit enabling the relationship, so there is an asymmetry between Christ and the church, with Christ always the source and life of the church, which is again enabled through the Spirit. A detailed TAT approach to exploring ecclesiology could outline the parallels between a Spirit Christology and a pneumato-ecclesiology in much more detail, exploring in each case the continuities, discontinuities, and asymmetries, resulting in significant insight into the workings of Christ and the Spirit within the church.[54]

As a second (and more briefly considered) example, consider the relationship between the doctrines of Christology and the Trinity. While a Logos Christology provides some insight into the immanent Trinity, a Spirit Christology, and particularly exploring the active relationship that Christ enjoyed through the Spirit with the Father during the incarnation, provides an excellent insight into the working of the immanent Trinity. As the Franciscan Friar Thomas Weinandy says, for example, "The Father begetting his Son in the womb of Mary by the Holy Spirit becomes, I believe, a temporal icon of his eternally begetting the Son by the Holy Spirit."[55] Exploring the continuities, discontinuities, and asymmetries that exist between those relationships has resulted in some of the most compelling and insightful accounts of the Trinity to be developed in recent years.[56]

---

[54]See Chapter 7 for further detail on this.
[55]Weinandy, *The Father's Spirit of Sonship*, 42.
[56]See Chapter 6 for further details on this.

3.4 Conclusion

Building on the example of Spirit Christology as a first exemplar of TAT, this chapter has outlined more generally the approach adopted by scholars pursuing a TAT. It first (in Section 3.1) listed and explained a series of methodological criteria that together distinguish, describe, and provide an aspirational *telos* for a TAT approach. Then (in Section 3.2) it proposed a specific method through which TAT investigations into theological doctrines can be accomplished. Both this methodology and method have been presented without justification. In this chapter, it has simply been assumed that TAT is a valid and acceptable theological approach. Of course, if the proof of the pudding is in the eating, then much of this justification for TAT will come in the second half of this volume where the specific outcomes of applying TAT to various doctrines will be considered. But before moving on to this application, the question of TAT's viability and acceptability as an overall theological approach needs to be explicitly addressed. What specific reasons exist for adopting such a TAT approach, and can this approach be defended against actual or potential critique? This exploration of TAT's justification is the subject of Chapter 4.

4

Critiques and Questions

4.1 How Has TAT Been Received?

This chapter examines what critiques and questions have been leveled against TAT and offers responses. As TAT is a relatively new way of doing theology, it has not yet occasioned much in the way of formal, published critiques or questions. Spirit Christology has been around for much longer, and so there are several critiques leveled at this that can be addressed in this chapter. No theological system or approach will be foolproof or problem-free, given that architectonic structures and approaches to theology act as provisional theories that are always open to revision and refinement. That being said, TAT is a robust and coherent way of doing theology, and it can adequately address the questions leveled at it, and its weaknesses do not negate its strengths. Specifically, this chapter will first address the critiques leveled against Spirit Christology before addressing the critiques leveled against TAT. With regard to Spirit Christology, charges of adoptionism will be addressed, as leveled by Donald Bloesch, Gregg Allison, Andreas Köstenberger, and Steve Wellum. Allison, Köstenberger, and Wellum are relying on each other's scholarship and arguments and so a genealogy of argument is provided below. Ultimately, Wellum is reliant upon certain critiques of Oliver Crisp over agency, and so Crisp is interacted with as well. Finally, an objection raised by Steven Studebaker is replied to, namely, that our account does not go far enough. With regard to critiques of TAT, Gregg Allison and Andreas Köstenberger's criticisms are addressed first, namely that starting with the Spirit necessarily corrupts the divine *taxis*. This view is traced back to the critique of Christopher Holmes and addressed clearly. Steven Wellum extends his critique of Spirit Christology into TAT more generally, critiquing an idiosyncratic theology from below and associating TAT with that. Finally, the criticisms of Andréa Snavely are addressed, namely that we should come to Jesus with no presuppositions!

4.2 Addressing the Main Critiques of Spirit Christology

Given the proximity between Spirit Christology and TAT, several persistent critiques of Spirit Christology will be treated first. As mentioned in an earlier chapter, many theologians working today wrongly assume that Spirit Christology is a sophisticated form of an Adoptionist heresy. As Cornelis van der Kooi and Gijsbert van den Brink have written,

> Nowadays many try to follow the alternative route of Spirit-Christology … Quite often this Spirit-Christology has been dismissed because it was thought to make the distinction between Jesus and ordinary people purely quantitative, as if Jesus simply had a little extra of what we possess in more limited measure. This impression is indeed created in the proposals for a Spirit-Christology by H. Berkhof, P. Schoonenberg, R. Haight, and others. … It replaces [orthodox accounts] with an adoption approach.[1]

Van der Kooi and van den Brink quickly point out, "Such a conclusion is not inevitable, however."[2] Van der Kooi develops an orthodox Spirit Christology in line with our account.[3]

We find evidence of scholars too quickly identifying Spirit Christology with adoptionism in many systematic theologies; the following are merely a representative sample. When influential evangelical scholar, Donald Bloesch, released the fifth of his seven-volume systematic theology, *Christian Foundations*, he turned to a treatment of the Holy Spirit and briefly addressed

---

[1] Cornelis van der Kooi and Gijsbert van den Brink, *Christian Dogmatics: An Introduction* (Grand Rapids, MI: Eerdmans, 2017), 410.
[2] Van der Kooi and van den Brink, *Christian Dogmatics*, 410. The work of Habets is then appealed to as a representative example of how to construct an orthodox Spirit Christology (page 411).
[3] Van der Kooi has gone on to argue for an orthodox account of Spirit Christology in both his essay "On the Identity of Jesus Christ: Spirit Christology and Logos Christology in Converse," in *Third Article Theology: A Pneumatological Dogmatics* (ed. Myk Habets; Minneapolis, MN: Fortress Press, 2016), 193–206, and in his work *This Incredibly Benevolent Force: The Holy Spirit in Reformed Theology and Spirituality* (Grand Rapids, MI: Eerdmans, 2018).

the topic of Spirit Christology.[4] Bloesch laid out the theological landscape of the time and noted the polarity created by advocates of a Logos Christology versus those of a Spirit Christology. He rightly argued for their complementarity but wrongly identified Spirit Christology as a form of mysticism or spiritualism. Later in the work, Bloesch identifies Spirit Christology with the post-Trinitarian work of Michael Welker and the process-theology-like theology of Philip Rosato.[5] Bloesch then levels his critique at a Spirit Christology, which he believes advocates Adoptionism whereby Jesus is a "man totally possessed by the Spirit."[6] Bloesch's critique is clearly only leveled at what we have earlier termed "post-Trinitarian" proposals; he does not identify or address the orthodox account of Spirit Christology offered here.

Other systematic theologies followed suit in misidentifying Spirit Christology and rejecting it on that basis. A good recent example of this mistake is found in the work of Gregg Allison and Andreas Köstenberger. Allison and Köstenberger have the mistaken idea that Spirit Christology necessarily posits the Holy Spirit as the sole acting agent in the incarnation.[7] They acknowledge that the Spirit empowers the incarnate Son, and this relationship of the Son's dependence upon the Spirit is new at the incarnation. Still, they do not think this equates to a Spirit Christology, which, according to them, necessitates the Spirit as the sole divine cause of Jesus' actions. This critique is also made by Oliver Crisp and Steve Wellum and will be addressed further below.

Allison and Köstenberger primarily base their definitions of Spirit Christology on the work of Gerald Hawthorne, Garrett DeWeese, and Klaus Issler, primarily as mediated by the work of Stephen Wellum.[8] As Allison and Köstenberger illustrate, DeWeese and Issler posit a weak type of kenotic Christology whereby the Son's attributes or their use lies dormant

---

[4]Donald G. Bloesch, *The Holy Spirit*, Christian Foundations (Downers Grove, IL: Intervarsity Press, 2000), 222–3.
[5]Bloesch, *The Holy Spirit*, 261, 262.
[6]Bloesch, *The Holy Spirit*, 265. In private correspondence with Bloesch, I (Myk) had the opportunity to share what I meant by Spirit Christology, and Bloesch kindly wrote back saying he thought on this matter we were "kindred spirits." Unfortunately, he was not able do a second edition of his work on the Spirit to update his comments on Spirit Christology.
[7]Gregg R. Allison and Andreas J. Köstenberger, *The Holy Spirit* (Nashville, TN: B&H Academic, 2020), 353.
[8]Gerald F. Hawthorne, *The Presence and the Power: The Significance of the Holy Spirit in the Life and Ministry of Jesus* (Eugene, OR: Wipf and Stock, 2003); Garrett J. DeWeese, "One Person, Two Natures: Two Metaphysical Models of the Incarnation," in *Jesus in Trinitarian Perspective: An Introductory Christology* (ed. Fred Sanders and Klaus D. Issler; Nashville, TN: B&H Academic, 2007), 114–53; Klaus Issler, "Jesus' Example: Prototype of the Dependent, Spirit-Filled Life," in *Jesus in Trinitarian Perspective*, 189–225; and Klaus Issler, *Living into the Life of Jesus: The Formation of*

in the incarnation, so Christ relies upon the Holy Spirit for all his divine prerogatives and power.⁹ The only exception is that some proponents of this view claim that in exceptional circumstances (the transfiguration, for example), Christ reverts to using his divine nature directly.[10] Allison and Köstenberger rightly argue that this is an "improper approach to the incarnation."[11] We agree, but more to the point, this is not the way that the most robust or comprehensive Spirit Christologies argue. It certainly does not represent the Spirit Christology represented in this book.

Allison and Köstenberger rightly argue that the Spirit Christology of Issler and others "is an improper approach to the Christ-Spirit relationship. It suffers from misunderstandings of the divine nature, trinitarian relations, inseparable operations, and divine agency."[12] Allison and Köstenberger then recognize that the Spirit Christology we propose (they focus on the work of Habets) is of a very different kind and is thoroughly orthodox.[13] No discussion of our orthodox account of Spirit Christology is offered, leaving readers again with the false impression that Spirit Christology itself is wrong.[14]

The work of Stephen Wellum is the basis for Allison and Köstenberger's critique of Spirit Christology. Turning to Wellum directly, he believes that Spirit Christologies occupy a theological position between classical Christology and "Ontological Kenotic Christology" (OKC) and labels them a form of "Functional Kenotic Christology" (FKC).[15] Included in the list of FKC are Hawthorne, Issler, and DeWeese (and Bruce Ware, but in more muted terms) and those not espousing Spirit Christology, such as William Craig, J. P. Mooreland, and Millard Erickson. Wellum establishes four criteria for FKC: first, in line with classical Christology, there is no "essential-accidental" distinction regarding the divine nature such that the Son does

---

Christian Character (Downers Grove, IL: InterVarsity, 2012). See Stephen J. Wellum, *God the Son Incarnate: The Doctrine of Christ* (Wheaton, IL: Crossway, 2016), 382–8.

[9] Allison and Köstenberger, *The Holy Spirit*, 362. They cite Hawthorne, *The Presence and the Power*, 208. Wellum, *God the Son*, 383 calls these representatives of "Functional Kenotic Christology."
[10] Allison and Köstenberger, *The Holy Spirit*, 363. They cite Klaus Issler as an example where he names examples of Jesus using his divine nature directly: forgiveness of sin, the transfiguration, the miracle of turning water into wine, and his use of the phrase "I am."
[11] Allison and Köstenberger, *The Holy Spirit*, 364.
[12] Allison and Köstenberger, *The Holy Spirit*, 364.
[13] Allison and Köstenberger, *The Holy Spirit*, 366.
[14] I (Myk) am grateful to Allison and Köstenberger for at least noting that my own contribution to Spirit Christology is orthodox, as a result of my brief comments on the prepublication proofs of their book. I take this to be an act of two gracious Christian scholars.
[15] Wellum, *God the Son*, 380.

not give up any of the divine attributes in the incarnation. This distinguishes FKC from OKC. Second, in line with OKC, a will attaches to a person, not a nature; hence there is an affirmation of Monothelitism. Related to this, there is an identification of "person" with "soul" such that the soul of the Son becomes the soul of Jesus Christ (this would be Apollinarianism, but Allison and Köstenberger do not make that connection).[16] Third, apparently, FKC argues that "the Incarnate Son" never (or seldom) uses his divine attributes directly.[17] Wellum seems to think that what he calls FKC and, within that, what is termed Spirit Christology, necessarily denies a *Logos asarkos* or at least denies the Son transcends the human nature even during the incarnation (the *extra Calvinisticum*).[18] Fourth, FKC "is often associated with the term 'Spirit-Christology.'"[19] Here the guilt-by-association argument is overt! Wellum appeals to the conclusions made by Hawthorne at the end of his critical study to the effect that the incarnate Son renounces all use of divine attributes in the incarnation. Wellum offers two examples of FKC; the first is the Spirit Christology of DeWeese and Issler. It won't pay to rehearse the arguments against Issler and DeWeese again; suffice it to say that we agree with Wellum's critique that theirs is a form of FKC. What is important to point out is that Wellum fails to address the form of Spirit Christology represented in this work or other significant works by Del Colle, Sánchez, van der Kooi, Claunch, and others. In short, Wellum only interacts with various forms of unorthodox Spirit Christology.

In addressing Wellum's critique, it is best to recapitulate his four points. First, the Spirit Christology developed in this work, and by others such as Del Colle and Sánchez, agrees the "essential-accidental" distinction is illegitimate. The eternal Son cannot give up divine attributes because God is a simple being, not composed of parts that can be given up. Second, our Spirit Christology is classically conceived, so it agrees with the church councils on affirming Dyothelitism. The incarnate Son has two wills: one divine and one human. The conciliar tradition has not specified how the two wills of Christ relate to one another. So, the supposition of our Spirit

---

[16]Wellum, *God the Son*, 381, n. 39 appeals to Crisp's definitions at this point and appears to be relying on his argument.
[17]Wellum, *God the Son*, 380.
[18]Wellum, *God the Son*, 382. For a reply to Wellum on this point, see Kyle Claunch, "The Son and the Spirit: The Promise of Spirit Christology in Traditional Trinitarian and Christological Perspective." (PhD diss., The Southern Baptist Theological Seminary, 2017), 208–13. Claunch is defending his own interpretation of an Owenite Trinitarian Spirit Christology, but the critique shares much in common with our own approach.
[19]Wellum, *God the Son*, 382.

Christology, based upon the consistent biblical evidence that the Holy Spirit is intimately involved in mediating the divine presence and will to the human will and mind of Christ, falls within orthodoxy. Third, any pro-Chalcedonian Christology, such as our Spirit Christology, affirms the *extra Calvinisticum* and, in fact, takes this more seriously, perhaps, than advocates of classical theism such as Wellum (or Allison and Köstenberger). To explain, to make sense of the eternal Son's consistent use of the divine attributes (we prefer to speak of divine perfections rather than attributes, given there is no generic "divine nature" that consists of "divine attributes" the Trinity must conform to) and the concomitant commitment that Jesus is *homoousios to patri*, the *extra Calvinisticum* has to be deployed to the effect that the eternal Son exists everywhere[20]—to simply take the perfection of omnipresence—*and* at the same time he exists somewhere as the incarnate Son, Jesus the Christ. As Calvin (echoing Athanasius) declared, "The Son of God descended from heaven in such a way that, *without leaving heaven*, he willed to be borne in the virgin's womb, to go about the earth, and to hang upon the cross; yet he continuously filled the world even as he had done from the beginning!"[21] In Wellum's account, this is not clearly affirmed or presented. Finally, identifying *all* Spirit Christology with that of Issler, DeWeese, or Hawthorne is the most egregious form of guilt-by-association argument.[22]

It is notable that Wellum's work has a brief appeal to the Spirit Christology of Habets.[23] In referring to the work of Habets, Wellum mistakenly thinks he teaches that the incarnate Son only occasionally uses his divine nature directly; at all other times, the divine nature is not in use.[24] No evidence is provided that this is what Habets is affirming, and the very pages Wellum cites contain no supporting argument for this unusual view. What is argued by Habets in the pages Wellum cites is the Athanasian Christological

---

[20] Or "nowhere," if we were to speak in strictly metaphysical terms.
[21] John Calvin, *Institutes of the Christian Religion*, vol. 1, 481 (emphasis added). Athanasius wrote: "For he was not enclosed in the body, nor was he in the body but not elsewhere. Nor while he moved that [body] was the universe left void of his activity and providence. ... And the most wonderful thing was that he both sojourned as a human being, and as the Word begot life in everything, and as Son was with the Father," *On the Incarnation*, section 17, trans. John Behr (Yonkers, NY: St Vladimir's Seminary Press, 2011), 87.
[22] Sánchez, M., *T&T Clark Introduction to Spirit Christology*, offers his defense of Spirit Christology against its critics and advocates of alternate Christology: James Dunn (36–42), Gerald Hawthorne (42–8), Jürgen Moltmann (94–104), David Coffey (104–11), Jenkins (141–9), Sammy Alfaro (153–7), and Lucy Peppiatt (157–64).
[23] Wellum, *God the Son*, 382, n. 42, 45; 407, n. 43.
[24] Wellum, *God the Son*, 382. He appeals to Habets, *The Anointed Son*, 118–87, 260–7.

argument that the Son does not live *in* a man but *as* a man, Jesus of Nazareth, and hence he has a true human nature and lives out of that.[25] Wellum has wrongly associated the Spirit Christology offered by Habets with that of Issler, DeWeese, Ware, and Hawthorne without providing an argument, illustration, or evidence that he subscribes to anything like their faulty Christology.

On occasion, Wellum refers to the work of Bruce Ware, noting a few areas where his Christology is faulty, despite the fact that Ware espouses a radically unorthodox form of Spirit Christology, very similar to that of Issler and DeWeese.[26] Wellum notes that Ware does not equate "person" with "soul," and hence he does not espouse FKC,[27] and yet Wellum fails to see that our Spirit Christology does not espouse this either and yet he still views our understanding as a species of FKC.[28] There is a radical inconsistency in Wellum's critique of Spirit Christology, and none of his critiques interacts with the substance of the Spirit Christology offered in this work.

The more serious objection to Spirit Christology leveled above comes from Oliver Crisp, and it concerns who exactly is the divine agent in the life of Christ.[29] Others have raised this objection as well. John Owen is thought to be the genesis of the view that the Son has no direct agency in the incarnation as that is given over to the Holy Spirit. Although this reading of Owen is challenged in recent Owen studies, it still needs to be addressed as it concerns our understanding of Spirit Christology.[30] Crisp and others are under the impression that a Spirit Christology *necessarily* argues that at the moment the Son assumes human nature, he ceases to have any direct agency in the incarnation, as that is handed over to the Holy Spirit. In providing an interpretation of Owen's Christology, Crisp writes:

> The principal cause for concern is that Owen's doctrine seems to generate a distinction between the [sic] God the Son and his agency "in" or "through" his human nature at all moments after the first moment of the assumption of human nature in the very act of becoming incarnate. Thereafter, his divine

---

[25]Habets, *The Anointed Son*, 265–6.
[26]Wellum, *God the Son*, 383, n. 49; 383, n. 77; 407, n. 43. See Bruce A. Ware, *The Man Christ Jesus: Theological Reflections on the Humanity of Christ* (Wheaton, MA: Crossway, 2013). For a critique of Ware's Christology, see Claunch, "The Son and the Spirit," 69–80.
[27]Wellum, *God the Son*, 381, n. 38.
[28]For further critique, see Claunch, "The Son and the Spirit," 91–112.
[29]See Oliver D. Crisp, *Revisioning Christology: Theology in the Reformed Tradition* (Farnham: Ashgate, 2011), 91–109.
[30]See Ty Kieser, "The Holy Spirit and the Humanity of Christ in John Owen: A Re-examination," *International Journal of Systematic Theology* 25 (2023): 93–113.

nature does not act directly upon his human nature, but only mediately, via the agency of the Holy Spirit. But this seems theologically dubious.[31]

In short, Crisp believes that Spirit Christology (at least of the sort Owen provides) "introduces a theologically damaging cleavage between God the Son and his human nature."[32]

The problem is that this view is nowhere argued in our account of Spirit Christology or a TAT. In fact, Crisp hints at this when, in a footnote, he writes, "In conversation, Lucy Peppiatt pointed out to me that the *krypsis* Christology outline given above is consistent with a species of Spirit Christology."[33] Peppiatt's Spirit Christology is a species of the Spirit Christology Habets and Liston advocate, so it appears that Crisp has no objection to our version of Spirit Christology.[34]

This criticism (as outlined here by Crisp) has also been responded to already by Habets.[35] The essence of the response revolves around seeing dual agency at work in the incarnation. The Son is the subject of the incarnation, but, a Spirit Christology adds, not without the agency of the Holy Spirit. In an earlier work, Habets argued:

> In the economy, the missions of God are coordinated with the eternal processions such that we might be led to think that while the Son is the subject of the incarnation, this is not without the Father and the Spirit. Thus personal agency in God is more complex than it is with human creatures, and especially so when the actual human being we are considering—Jesus Christ—is unique in having two natures "unconfusedly, unchangeably, indivisibly, and inseparably" (as per Chalcedon). Add to this the actual scriptural accounts of Jesus' life lived in dependence on the Spirit—his conception, baptism, vocation, passion, exaltation—and a more complex picture emerges than that of simply a Logos Christology. In fact, Christ's mission is specifically situated within the prior mission of the Spirit and can only adequately be understood in that light.[36]

Keith Johnson's critique of Issler, Hawthorne, and Ware is helpful when he appeals to the doctrine of inseparable operations and argues:

---

[31] Crisp, *Revisioning Christology*, 100.
[32] Crisp, *Revisioning Christology*, 93.
[33] Crisp, *Revisioning Christology*, 108, n. 27.
[34] See Lucy Peppiatt's doctoral thesis, "Spirit Christology and Mission" (PhD diss., Otago University, 2011); and "New Directions in Spirit Christology: A Foundation for a Charismatic Theology," *Theology* 117 (2014): 3–10.
[35] Habets, "Spirit Christology: The Future of Christology?" in *Third Article Theology*, 207–32.
[36] Habets, "Spirit Christology: The Future of Christology?" in *Third Article Theology*, 225.

We are now in position to see more clearly the trinitarian problems besetting the proposals of Hawthorne, Ware and Issler. All three wrongly assume that only one person of the Trinity can function as divine agent when Jesus performs miraculous actions like healing. In the case of Hawthorne, that divine agent is exclusively the Holy Spirit. In the case of Issler and Ware, that agent is predominantly the Spirit. According to Issler and Ware, on rare occasions Jesus performed some miracles by his own divine power. The point is that in any situation, only one trinitarian person can be the source of divine power in the ministry of Jesus Christ. In this model of divine action, no consideration is given to the possibility that all three divine persons might be involved. This is rejected *a priori*.[37]

We agree, but we also appeal to that same argument to respond to criticisms such as Crisp's. With Ian McFarland, we agree, "the confession that the Word is the subject of Jesus' thoughts and actions … must be distinguished from the claim that the Word is the cause of Jesus' human operations. … On biblical no less than Chalcedonian terms, however, it is much more profitable to ascribe this divine activity to the Holy Spirit."[38]

Another critique of Spirit Christology, and TAT by implication, comes from Pentecostal scholar Steven Studebaker.[39] Studebaker is sympathetic to TAT, being one of the original contributors to *Third Article Theology*, but he does not think Habets's Spirit Christology goes far enough.[40] Specifically, he posits *separate* missions for the Son and the Spirit. Studebaker thinks Habets keeps the missions of the Son and Spirit too close after Pentecost, whereas they should be separated.[41] In making his argument, Studebaker overextends the argument of Habets and, in the process, offers a skewed presentation of the Spirit Christology being argued for here. Liston has critiqued Studebaker and rightly argues for the simultaneous economic activity of the Son and

---

[37]Keith E. Johnson, "The Work of the Holy Spirit in the Ministry of Jesus Christ: A Trinitarian Perspective" (paper presented at the annual meeting of the Evangelical Theological Society, San Diego, CA, November 20, 2014), 11, cited in Claunch, "The Son and the Spirit," 75.

[38]Ian A. McFarland, "Spirit and Incarnation: Toward a Pneumatic Chalcedonianism," *International Journal of Systematic Theology* 16 (2014): 153.

[39]Steven M. Studebaker, *From Pentecost to the Triune God: A Pentecostal Trinitarian Theology* (Grand Rapids, MI: Eerdmans, 2012), 174–85.

[40]Studebaker objects to the fact that in the work of Habets, there is a "traditional Christocentrism." Studebaker, *From Pentecost to the Triune God*, 176. Habets considers this a compliment more than a critique.

[41]This claim is made on the basis that Studebaker argues for "The Son and the Spirit's identities are mutually constituted, but they both—and the Father as well—retain unique identities and work that flow from their identities." Studebaker, *From Pentecost to the Triune God*, 181. I take "unique" work to constitute separate missions.

the Spirit post-Pentecost.[42] Studebaker's account of a Spirit Christology is compelling, but it is not the account we are offering.

4.3 Addressing the Main Critiques of TAT

When we turn our attention specifically to TAT, there is much less to go on due to the relative newness of this approach to theology. In his survey, the *SCM Study Guide to Theology in the Contemporary World*, Ben Pugh considers TAT to be one of the more valuable developments in contemporary theology.[43] He rightly notes that TAT accepts the insights of Chalcedon but seeks to complement them with a robust pneumatology. Pugh thinks the dogmatic precursor for a TAT goes as far back as the Puritan John Owen but that the real genesis for TAT goes "back to the way the first Christians themselves theologized: they began with their experience of the Spirit. … Third Article Theology attempts to retrieve this, to start doing theology at exactly the place where our discipleship is supposed to start: life in the Spirit."[44]

Earlier in their work Allison and Köstenberger clarify that they will not be following the suggestion of the recent TAT approach to start with the Spirit, labeling it an "extreme" approach to theology to be avoided.[45] Instead, "out of respect to the traditional taxis" that gives priority to the Father, then Son, then Spirit, Allison and Köstenberger reject a TAT approach.[46] No argument for this preference is given other than that it is a traditional commitment from the time of Thomas Aquinas.

In reply to Allison and Köstenberger, it should be pointed out that a TAT seeks to comprehensively represent the traditional exposition of the trinitarian *taxis* but to do so in a more thoroughly biblical way. This means that while the katabatic movement of the triune missions is normally (but not exclusively) from the Father, through the Son, and by the Spirit, the anabatic

---

[42] Liston, *The Anointed Church*, 229, n. 134.
[43] Ben Pugh, *SCM Study Guide to Theology in the Contemporary World* (London: SCM Press, 2017), 33, 46–52. Pugh names the following as the key people working in TAT: Myk Habets, Greg Liston, Kirsteen Kim, Amos Yong, Veli-Matti Kärkkäinen, and Clark Pinnock.
[44] Pugh, *SCM Study Guide to Theology*, 52.
[45] Specifically, Allison and Köstenberger are not following the suggestions of D. Lyle Dabney, Myk Habets, or Sarah Coakley. Allison and Köstenberger, *The Holy Spirit*, 226.
[46] Allison and Köstenberger, *The Holy Spirit*, 226.

return is clearly stated in Scripture as by the Spirit, through the Son, to the Father.[47] TAT thus respects the traditional trinitarian *taxis* of the Trinity but recognizes the diversity of the biblical presentation and thus the legitimacy of starting with the Spirit in constructing a Christian dogmatics following a TAT. It is not the case, as TAT advocates have made clear, that one *must* start with the Spirit as if starting with the Father is wrong; it is, instead, that starting with the Spirit fits a theology that starts from below and follows the biblical model of the anabatic return to the Father.[48]

Allison and Köstenberger appeal to the work of Christopher Holmes as their supporting evidence for the illegitimacy of TAT.[49] Given this appeal to Holmes, it is only fitting that we turn attention to his critique of Spirit Christology and, by implication, a critique of TAT.[50] Holmes has argued against starting with the Spirit in theology generally (TAT) or Spirit Christology particularly. The essence of Holme's critique centers on two issues: first, a commitment to the idea that the *taxis* evident in the divine processions must be matched *in every way* in the divine missions, and a commitment to a Thomistic theology that will not allow the Spirit to occupy any active role in the processions or the missions. This type of theology refuses to focus on the Spirit for too long, believing that the Spirit is always "self-effacing," and as such, it is wrong to start with the Spirit. Second, Holmes believes that starting with the Spirit "is a confusion of the order of knowing and teaching in relation to the order of being."[51]

It is difficult to address Holmes's critique clearly and simply as it is loaded with implicit Thomistic assumptions that are not shared by the TAT we are constructing. For Holmes, the theological assumptions made about the divine procession of the Spirit revolve around the Spirit as Gift and Love

---

[47]Rodrick K. Durst, *Reordering the Trinity: Six Movements of God in the New Testament* (Grand Rapids, MI: Kregel Academic, 2015), clearly shows there are many exceptions to the Father–Son–Spirit taxis in Scripture and provides a statistical analysis that shows the F-S-Sp pattern makes up 24 percent of the New Testament presentation, S-Sp-F makes up 20 percent, S-F-Sp makes up 19 percent, F-Sp-S makes up 15 percent, Sp-F-S makes up 12 percent, and Sp-S-F makes up 10 percent. According to Durst, "Research indicates that there are seventy-five Trinitarian references in the New Testament. Just eighteen instances (twenty-four percent) do follow the expected order of Father, Son, and Spirit," 73.
[48]See the discussion by Liston and the interaction with suggestions made by David Coffey (200–10), Jürgen Moltmann (210–17), Weinandy and Habets (217–26), and Kathryn Tanner (226–32), *The Anointed Church*. A key part of Liston's discussion concerns the divine *taxis* where he offers the insightful view that the Son and Spirit are simultaneously equal in the economic *taxis*.
[49]Allison and Köstenberger, *The Holy Spirit*, 226, citing Christopher R. J. Holmes, *The Holy Spirit* (Grand Rapids, MI: Zondervan, 2015), 123–30.
[50]Claunch, "The Son and the Spirit," 205–8, offers his own critique of Holmes.
[51]Holmes, *The Holy Spirit*, 128.

of the prior relationship of the Father and Son: "In terms of the Trinity in itself, the Spirit proceeds from the Father and Son as gift, which is the key to the Spirit's identity," writes Holmes.[52] That is Thomism writ large and with it, a large proportion of Latin trinitarianism.[53] But, and this is the important point, that is not pro-Nicene or pro-Chalcedonian theology *simpliciter*, and so to reject parts of Thomism and hence parts of the Latin tradition is not to be wrong (unorthodox); to simply believe Holy Scripture points us in a different direction.[54]

Holmes correctly associates the trinitarian theology of Habets with that of Thomas Weinandy.[55] Habets builds upon the work of Weinandy in making his case for the immanent Trinity and for starting with the Spirit in theological discourse. In the work of Habets, there is no confusion over the *ordo essendi* and the *ordo cognoscendi*, as Holmes suggests there is.[56] In the economy, we come to know the Father only through the work of the Spirit, who unites us with the incarnate Son. The divine *taxis in se* of Father–Son–Spirit is inverted in the incarnation as the Spirit creates, convicts, converts, and recreates. There is nothing new in this suggestion as theologians have routinely said God reveals himself by the Father, through the Son, and in the Holy Spirit, and we return and respond to this loving revelation by the Spirit, in the Son, to the Father. This does not decenter Christ or bring the Father low; rather it merely expresses the biblical narrative of how the triune God works in the world.[57] TAT follows this biblical pattern by following the economic *taxis* of Spirit–Son–Father.

Wellum, for his part, makes some brief but unusual comments on theological methodology in general that relate to the methodology of

---

[52] Holmes, *The Holy Spirit*, 128.
[53] See Myk Habets, "Review Essay, Matthew Levering, *Engaging the Doctrine of the Holy Spirit: Love and Gift in the Trinity and the Church* (Grand Rapids: Baker Academic, 2016)," *Modern Theology* 34 (2017): 677–9.
[54] At the very least, Thomism can be seen to have different interpretations. For comments on the Creed in support of TAT, see Raniero Cantalamessa, "The Incarnation and the Mystery of the Anointing: Christology and Pneumatology in the Early Centuries of the Church," in *Third Article Theology: A Pneumatological Dogmatics* (ed. Myk Habets; Minneapolis, MN: Fortress Press, 2016), 175–92.
[55] See Weinandy, *The Father's Spirit of Sonship*.
[56] See Habets's articulation of this point in his "Prolegomenon: On Starting with the Spirit," in *Third Article Theology*, 15.
[57] More could be said about the immanent Trinity, but that would take us well beyond the scope of this chapter. Holmes would be right, as a Thomist, to have disagreements with Weinandy's reconceived Trinity and my (Myk's) own attempts to go even beyond Weinandy. But these trinitarian models are not necessary to TAT and so we won't pursue the discussion here. See Myk Habets, "Getting beyond the *Filioque* with Third Article Theology," in *Ecumenical Perspectives on the Filioque for the Twenty-First Century* (ed. Myk Habets; London: Bloomsbury T&T Clark, 2014), 211–30.

TAT. Wellum provides a brief discussion on the "necessity of Christology 'from above'" as opposed to a theology from below.[58] Wellum makes the extraordinary move to define Christology from above and Christology from below in a novel and idiosyncratic way, that is, in a way not found in the literature, and then with this redefinition, to label anything that espouses a theology from below as illegitimate. For Wellum, a Christology from below is necessarily committed to "historical-critical research, independent of a commitment to the full authority of Scripture." A Christology from above, however, "refers to starting with Scripture as God's own accurate and authoritative word written in texts, so that we do Christology from the point of view of those texts."[59] That is an extremely unusual way to define these terms and is at odds with how they are normally used.[60] While Wellum does not address TAT in this part of his book, clearly he would conclude that a TAT that starts from below would be ruled out as unorthodox on the premises of his definition offered above.

The problem, of course, is that advocates of a theology from below, such as those espousing a TAT, do *not* adopt Wellum's odd definitions, and hence his critique of this method is incorrect. Habets has extensively dealt with the issues involved in methodologies from above and below.[61] According to Habets, it is better to follow Rahner's terminology at this point and speak of a *descending* Christology (a Christology from above) and an *ascending* Christology (a Christology from below) to retain the continuity of the person of Jesus Christ and not drive a wedge between his divinity and humanity.[62] Habets concludes his discussion with the following:

> In the awkward language of theological precision the model of Spirit Christology presented here is an inspirational-incarnational Christology, a Christology that proceeds from below to above. Not in a sequential linear movement as Pannenberg advocates, for this concedes too much to reason. Nor in a double movement which lays great stress on a transcendent

---

[58] Wellum, *God the Son*, 86–91.
[59] Wellum, *God the Son*, 86.
[60] See Wolfhart Pannenberg, *Jesus—God and Man* (trans. L. L. Wilkins and D. A. Priebe; London: SCM, 1968), 33; Gunton, *Yesterday and Today*, 33–43; Karl Rahner, *Theological Investigations*, vol. 13, *Theology, Anthropology, Christology* (trans. D. Bourke; London: Darton, Longman & Todd, 1974), 218; Millard J. Erickson, "Christology from Above and Christology from Below: A Study of Contrasting Methodologies," in *Perspectives on Evangelical Theology* (ed. Kenneth S. Kantzer and Stanley N. Gundry; Grand Rapids, MI: Baker Books, 1979), 47.
[61] Habets, *The Anointed Son*, 29–52.
[62] See Habets, *The Anointed Son*, 30 and Rahner, *Theology, Anthropology, Christology*, 213–23.

anthropology as Rahner proposes, for this tends towards an adoptionistic conclusion. By contrast, I propose a Christological methodology that seeks to bridge the gulf between Jesus's humanity and divinity (the two nature Achilles heel of classical Christology) by means of the Holy Spirit. This movement lays equal stress on faith and understanding, on Spirit and reason, and on transcendence and immanence. Spirit Christology is a method that holds out the great promise of returning Christian discipleship to its roots; the simple faith and practice of seeking to be like Jesus. At the same time, a Spirit Christology when applied to theology proper, is able to lead us up from Christology (and anthropology), into Trinitarian theology, from the economic Trinity to the ontological Trinity, and from the economy to God's eternity.[63]

The above conclusion from Habets is a far cry from the inventive Christology from below that Wellum has created. Once again, what appears to be a critique of the methodology of TAT is nothing more than a case of mistaken identity.

A final critique of Spirit Christology will be examined here, that of Pentecostal scholar Andréa Snavely.[64] This is the oddest of the critiques examined to date, as Snavely's work is mired in ambiguity and contradiction. Snavely wants to build a Spirit Christology that starts with Jesus himself and applies insights gleaned from Christ directly to the lives of believers.[65] There is nothing odd about this *prima facie* until Snavely clarifies that we must come to Jesus with no presuppositions and the posture of knowing nothing of Christ before reading about him in the Gospels. Snavely divides Spirit Christologies into three camps and critiques each before offering his account. First, there are those Spirit Christologies of religious experience that eclipse Jesus' life and death.[66] Pentecostals wrongly, he argues, start with the experience of the Spirit and read that back into the Christ event.[67] In such a Christology, "Jesus' life is relegated to the 'best' moral example."[68] To rectify this error, we must go back to Jesus' life and passion as the starting point for the Spirit's work in believers' lives.

---

[63]Habets, *The Anointed Son*, 52.
[64]Andréa Snavely, *Life in the Spirit: A Post-Constantinian and Trinitarian Account of the Christian Life* (Eugene, OR: Pickwick Publications, 2015), 53–9.
[65]Snavely, *Life in the Spirit*, 29.
[66]Snavely, *Life in the Spirit*, 30–6.
[67]Snavely, *Life in the Spirit*, 30.
[68]Snavely, *Life in the Spirit*, 31.

Snavely misidentifies this type of theology as a form of TAT. This would be inaccurate, however, as Snavely merely seems to mean pneumatology.[69] Next, there are Spirit Christologies of divine presence that deny Jesus' life as transformative.[70] In such accounts, there is no discontinuity between Jesus and believers, and Jesus is reduced to a moral example. Geoffrey Lampe and James Dunn's work fits into Snavely's account (what we earlier termed "post-trinitarian Spirit Christology"). The third kind of Spirit Christology eclipses Jesus' life and death as defining life in the Spirit.[71] Habets's account of Spirit Christology is included in this group, along with the work of Sammy Alfaro, Ralph Del Colle, and David Coffey.

Snavely says that the work of Habets "uses immanent Trinitarianism as a framework to describe Jesus' death." As a result, it is "inadequate to explain the Christian life as life in the Spirit due to … [its] eclipsing of *how* Jesus lived his life as constitutive for defining the Spirit's presence in the body of Christ."[72] This appears to be a blatant *non-sequitur*. Snavely takes exception to Habets's commitment to reconciling Spirit Christology with Logos Christology, which appears to mean that he disagrees with any Christology that assumes Jesus' divinity. Snavely writes, Habets's "account eclipses Jesus' death on a cross, the result of the kind of life he lived as the Son of God, for what it meant for Jesus to live in the Spirit."[73] The problem is that it is simply not evident why this should be the case. How can one *not* know that Jesus rose again when reading the Gospels as Christian Scripture? Snavely offers no argument to support his conjecture that Habets's Christology "short-circuits a view of Jesus' life as he lived in the Spirit which, as a result, obscures the cross Jesus died on as a result of *how he lived* in the Spirit."[74] Snavely believes it is possible to read the Gospels without a post-Pentecostal knowledge of Jesus' divine identity. He argues that knowing that Jesus is resurrected and is the Divine Son means we cannot explain Jesus' life, death, and resurrection as necessary for believers. "Why not begin with Jesus' life as he was living it without importing a prior epistemological understanding of his divine nature from a post-Pentecost theological foundation back into his

---

[69]Snavely's exemplars are the work of Amos Yong and Veli-Matti Karkkainen, who he believes start from general religious experience and read that back into the life of Christ. Snavely, *Life in the Spirit*, 32.
[70]Snavely, *Life in the Spirit*, 36–44.
[71]Snavely, *Life in the Spirit*, 44–59.
[72]Snavely, *Life in the Spirit*, 44.
[73]Snavely, *Life in the Spirit*, 54.
[74]Snavely, *Life in the Spirit*, 56.

life and death?"⁷⁵ This is an astounding claim, given that the Gospel writers were each writing *post-Pentecost*!⁷⁶ Snavely is critical of Habets's stereoscopic approach to the biblical narrative; in its place, he wants to claim theological amnesia regarding Christ each time the Gospels are read. This radical act of anti-Christ scriptural reading is hardly a critique of the Spirit Christology or the TAT proffered in this work.

Finally, Snavely writes, "Habets's most telling weakness resides in his account not allowing for Jesus' life and death to *bring death* to the sinner and *resurrection* in the Spirit within one's own life *solely* on account of Jesus' life and death."⁷⁷ It is hard to know what this criticism even means, let alone refute it. Perhaps it is enough to say that we can't correctly know the interpretation of Christ's life, death, and resurrection without the risen Lord's help and the Spirit's illumination; hence we do read back into the life of Christ later revelation. This is what the Gospel writers do and invite fellow disciples to do. Snavely defends Sánchez's Spirit Christology, despite the fact that Sánchez, Habets, and Liston share the same species of Spirit Christology. What Snavely praises in Sánchez is found first in the work of Habets and then of Liston. This is evident in that Snavely follows Sánchez who is following Habets in his theological method⁷⁸ and in narrating the Messianic disclosure episodes, but under another name.⁷⁹

4.4 Conclusion

Kyle Claunch expresses a view we share: "Unfortunately, the variegated character and broad spectrum of ideological commitments of Spirit Christology are not always given sufficient weight when critiques of various proposals are put forward."⁸⁰ We have seen evidence of this throughout this chapter. Claunch also notes that most critiques of Spirit Christology (and we could add, TAT) are made based on "a small representative sample."⁸¹ In many cases, such sampling did not include the work being described and put forward in this volume. When theologians have interacted with such

---

⁷⁵Snavely, *Life in the Spirit*, 57.
⁷⁶Snavely acknowledges this point but fails to see the inconsistency of his argument. Snavely, *Life in the Spirit*, 77.
⁷⁷Snavely, *Life in the Spirit*, 57–8 (emphasis in original).
⁷⁸Snavely, *Life in the Spirit*, 65.
⁷⁹Snavely, *Life in the Spirit*, 79–93.
⁸⁰Claunch, "The Son and the Spirit," 205.
⁸¹Claunch, "The Son and the Spirit," 205.

proposals, we have seen a consistent inattentiveness to the details of the argument, and thus an often inadequate and unjustified critique is offered.

TAT and the Spirit Christology it encompasses is a biblical, orthodox, and contemporary way to do theology that respects and works within the conciliar tradition and is a genuine contribution to contemporary constructive theology. It is hoped that the responses to various critiques of TAT in this chapter bear this out. What remains in Part I is to offer an account of the implications, applications, and benefits TAT offers to the contemporary church.

5

Third Article Theology Applied

5.1 Introduction

Theology is often criticized for its impractical, disembodied, and rational nature. While such claims are an exaggeration, TAT offers a way of doing theology that can address these concerns. In light of the claims that TAT is both a grounded theology from below and that it has existential viability, this chapter sketches the practical applicability of TAT, one that recognizes and incorporates faith and experience, grace and nature, and how it is compatible with a range of methodologies from the humanities, especially critically realist approaches and qualitative methodologies. Dogmatics and practical theology are brought together in this theological-applied synthesis. This chapter only offers a series of highlights as it concludes Part I of this work, and as we move into Part II, many of the themes introduced here are developed in detail.

5.2 Conciliar and Ecumenical Theology

TAT has an ecumenical goal or interest.[1] This point has been made before, and in the literature, this is borne out by the wide acceptance of TAT across traditional and denominational lines and how it is being developed across

---

[1] This is also highlighted in Habets, "Prolegomenon," 18.

the church.² TAT is not a Pentecostal, Catholic, Protestant, or Orthodox theology if that means it is uniquely and solely at home on Pentecostal, Catholic, Protestant, or Orthodox soil. Many Pentecostal, Catholic, Protestant, and Orthodox theologians are adopting TAT into their theology and are finding it a valuable resource to articulate the central features of their theological tradition. TAT is a Christian theology, and because it is orthodox and conforms to the conciliar tradition, most notably Nicaea and Chalcedon, it is ecumenical.

5.2.1 Conciliar

An essential ingredient in the kind of TAT we are constructing is the criterion that it must conform to the ecumenical Creeds, and as such, it must be conciliar. The Nicene Creed (381) and the Chalcedonian Definition (451) are the most important. The consensus of the church holds to the doctrine of the Trinity and the two natures of Jesus Christ (among other doctrines, but these two are foundational). TAT seeks to uphold these commitments and work within the tradition, not to challenge or dispute it. One advantage of theology in an orthodox key is that it forces one to go narrow and deep, not broad and shallow. This has always been a feature of the conciliar tradition.

What the Creeds and Definitions provide, however, is, at best, a dogmatic sketch of what Christ and Scripture teach, being clear to chart boundaries and clarify the center of the faith.³ The creedal tradition provides a stable, if not unchanging, base upon which to construct a theology that is faithful to Holy Scripture and attentive to context.⁴ The Creeds, because they are partial and contextual, are authoritative and reliable guides, but they are just that— guide books, not instruction manuals. We have many creeds and confessions because we have many church communities, each seeking to express the faith in their unique contexts. TAT is a contextual theology seeking to build upon the conciliar tradition to bring new insights and perspectives to contemporary issues and contexts. As Georges Florovsky once remarked,

---

²Sánchez examines ways in which Spirit Christology is applied across traditional lines in *T&T Clark Introduction to Spirit Christology*, 153–72, paying specific attention to Latino theology.
³Whether or not the conciliar tradition offers a centered set or bounded set is not the focus of this chapter.
⁴On the feature of continuity and change within the creeds, see Jaroslav Pelikan, *Creedo: Historical and Theological Guide to Creeds and Confessions of Faith in the Christian Tradition* (New Haven, CT: Yale University Press, 2003), 7–34.

"the spiritual experience of the Church is also a form of revelation."[5] This means that TAT will express theological ideas in new idioms, it will often begin from different starting points, and it will bring new insights to old issues, and at times this may challenge some old "orthodoxies." Working within the Creeds offers the ability to, in the words of the Barth commentator Gabriel Vahanian, be "both in strict conformity with orthodoxy and—we must admit—wholly unorthodox."[6] This will be apparent in the relational ontology at the heart of TAT, in the emphasis upon a Spirit Christology, the eschatological or Christological theological anthropology it advocates, and the form of proleptic eschatology it espouses (among other commitments).[7]

5.2.2 Ecumenical

If TAT is conciliar, then it is also ecumenical.[8] Being intentionally ecumenical is important for a TAT, given that the work of the Spirit is so tied to unity and communion. Ecumenism is also a profoundly Christian orientation. On one level, being ecumenical means not being sectarian or parochial. Being ecumenical means privileging what C. S. Lewis (via Richard Hooker and Richard Baxter) famously called "mere Christianity": that set of beliefs and convictions all Christians everywhere hold in common.[9] This is not to deny the legitimate and important theological distinctions within the many theological traditions (both authors of this book are Baptist and hold that identity dearly). Still, it is to make the affirmation so often overlooked today that Christians have more in common than they disagree over. Across traditional and denominational lines, the central contours of the Christian faith remain the same, anchored in the teachings of Holy Scripture, the recitation of the creeds, and the ongoing communion of the Holy Spirit.

---

[5] Georges V. Florovsky, *Collected Works*, 14 vols (Belmont, MA: Nordland, 1972–89), vol. 7, 156, cited in Pelikan, *Creeds*, 28.
[6] Gabriel Vahanian, "Introduction," in Karl Barth, *The Faith of the Church: A Commentary on the Apostle's Creed* (London: Fontana, 1960), 10.
[7] At times, the conclusions of TAT will be misunderstood, as is the case with Joseph A. Bracken's response to Myk Habets's *The Anointed Son*. See Joseph Bracken, "Trinitarian Spirit Christology: In Need of a New Metaphysics?" *Theological Studies* 72 (2011): 750–67, and the response by Habets, "Getting beyond the *Filioque* with Third Article Theology," 211–30 (see especially 230, n. 80).
[8] Kirsten L. Guidero offers two significant works on receptive ecumenism from a TAT perspective, the first lays a foundation, "'In the Unity of the Spirit': A Third Article Theology of Receptive Ecumenism," in *Third Article Theology* (ed. Myk Habets), 463–78; and the second provides a working example, "Filled with 'The Fullness of the Gifts of God': Towards a Pneumatic Theosis" (PhD diss., Marquette University, Wisconsin, 2020).
[9] Clive S. Lewis, *Mere Christianity* (London: Collins, 2012), viii–ix.

With the apostle Paul, we affirm there is one body, one Spirit, one hope, one Lord, one faith, one baptism, and one God and Father of all "but to each one of us grace was given according to the measure of Christ's gift" (Eph 4:4-7).

Receptive ecumenism is a specific commitment of TAT and includes the reception of Christians and Christian traditions other than our own in the spirit of listening and learning, seeking first to understand and only then to be understood.[10] This form of ecumenism is conducive to TAT and its commitments because it is not the old-style ecumenism that devolves into an agreement on the lowest common denominator with the result that real learning, growth, and communion are hampered from the beginning. Instead, receptive ecumenism allows diverse communities and thinkers to come together, agreed on the core of the faith (the conciliar tradition), and then learn from the other in the spirit of humility. TAT can start from below in specific contexts of Christian faith and community and then work from function to ontology, faith to knowledge, and communion to intercommunion. It is the Spirit that creates and sustains real communities of faith (Matt 18:20; Eph 4:3), so a theology that starts with the Spirit will naturally work toward a receptive ecumenism.

5.3 Systematic Theology

Commenting on the Spirit Christology of John Owen, Oliver Crisp notes several benefits of this approach, benefits that are equally applicable to TAT as a whole. The benefits Crisp mentions include "a means by which to marry the two-natures doctrine of catholic Christology with the biblical narrative."[11] Crisp reminds readers that one unforeseen drawback of the Catholic creeds is that "all they yield is a metaphysical description of certain aspects of the relation between God the Son and his human nature. ... For one of the things that immediately strikes readers of the canonical Gospels is the way in which Christ is sustained by the Holy Spirit at key moments [messianic *kairoi*] of his ministry."[12] This leads to a second benefit Crisp notes that can apply to TAT as well as to Spirit Christology, namely the "pastoral,

---

[10] Among the vast literature, see the useful and practical summary by Graham Buxton, *Dancing in the Dark: The Privilege of Participating in God's Ministry in the World*, rev. ed. (Eugene, OR: Cascade Books, 2016), 265–9.
[11] Oliver Crisp, *Revisioning Christology: Theology in the Reformed Tradition* (Farnham: Ashgate, 2011), 93.
[12] Crisp, *Revisioning Christology*, 93, 94.

as well as dogmatic advantage over traditional, orthodox views that do not take with sufficient seriousness this pneumatological dimension to the life and work of Christ."[13] In the words of Leo Sánchez, "the relative continuity between the Spirit's activity in Christ and his disciples is axiomatic in the field."[14] Two theological *loci* are worth considering at this point as examples of the usefulness and practicality of TAT in dogmatics, namely Christology and theological anthropology. Both of these *loci* are discussed at length in other parts of the work, but in what follows, the practicality of approaching them by means of a TAT is emphasized and illustrated.

5.3.1 Christology

TAT provides a way to understand the hypostatic union and the ontological dynamics of the incarnation in ways guided by Holy Scripture and compatible with the tradition. A traditional and dominant Logos Christology posits two metaphysically determined natures in the one person of Christ and sets up theological investigation on that level. The result has been centuries of debate over the two natures of Christ and the well-known divides between Lutheran-Reformed, Protestant-Catholic, and other rival Christological constructions. These debates are not without merit, but a TAT approach believes they are not the only way to think about the Son's incarnation. Instead, starting with the person of the incarnate Son, the Messiah sent by the Father in the power of the Spirit, we can work from his economy and humanity up, as it were, to consider his divinity.

The eternal Son assumes an (*anhypostatic*) human nature and, in that act, takes humanity to himself in an act of incarnation such that his human nature is now personal (*enhypostatic*). Jesus of Nazareth is that person: born of the Spirit and born of a woman, Mary. Chalcedon affirms that both natures remain fully intact and operative at all times. The practical issue is how we understand the operations of the incarnate Son, given the constraints of the flesh. The Son lives as Christ and lives through a (fallen)[15] human nature. Jesus thinks, feels, and acts as a human being because he is a human being, in every way like us, yet without sin (and a dual nature). But if Christology

---

[13]Crisp, *Revisioning Christology*, 94. Crisp does not personally own these views, he is merely representing those that do.
[14]Sánchez, *T&T Clark Introduction to Spirit Christology*, 151.
[15]The assumption of fallen human nature is contingent for this argument, hence the brackets. See Myk Habets, "The Fallen Humanity of Christ. A Pneumatological Clarification of the Theology of Thomas F. Torrance," *Participatio* 5 (2015): 18–44.

remains at the level of the *what*—how natures work—then it misses the all-important *who*—the identity of the one doing the action. TAT starts with the *who* to ascertain the *what*.

With the doctrines of the *communio idiomatum* and the *extra Calvinisticum/catholicum* at work in the background, we can say that the eternal Son thinks, feels, and acts in the incarnation through the human nature of Jesus (not apart from it) and that Jesus is the human thinking, feeling, and functioning of the eternal Son. If the Son overwhelms and bypasses the human nature in any way, then it is not incarnation that we are talking about but alien possession or some such. If the Son thinks, feels, and acts through Jesus *simpliciter*, his human nature is merely instrumental and unnecessary (even contradicted). But redemptive history tells us that the Son had to become human for us and our salvation. Conversely, if the Son gives up his identity, will, and power and all that is left is a human somehow empowered by God, then Jesus is just another prophet, priest, or holy man, and again, disqualified from being the Savior. TAT posits a third way that focuses not on the what/nature but on the who/person and moves from function to ontology.

According to TAT, the Son and the Spirit work in the incarnation (in different ways) to bring about our salvation. The Gospels tell us as much—the Father sends the Son, and the Holy Spirit anoints Jesus (his body at conception and his ministry at baptism). On a mission from the Father and born of the Spirit, Jesus is the incarnate Son, and as such, he is the eternal radiance of his Father, the Word of God, light from light, the radiance of the Father's glory, the image of God *in human form* (Col 1:15–20). At the same time, he is veiled, concealed, clothed in the flesh of (fallen) humanity, occupying a real mind, will, and emotions (Phil 2:6–8). Like all other humans, he, too, needs the Holy Spirit to vivify, gift, equip, lead, guide, comfort, convict, and communicate with God. Relating to God the Father, in the Son, by the Holy Spirit is simply the human thing to do. And the incarnate Son of God does this impeccably. The one who eternally loves God now also loves God with the flesh of a Jewish man. The one who eternally knows God now knows God through the process of human maturation as he grows in wisdom and stature and in favour with God and humans (Luke 2:52). The eternal Wisdom of God, there at his side fashioning all that is (Prov 8:22–31), now learns obedience from what he suffers in the flesh (Heb 5:8). And how, we ask, can a human do this? How can Jesus do this? TAT says that he can do this by the power of the indwelling Holy Spirit. The Holy Spirit mediates knowledge of God and his ways to the incarnate

Son such that the human nature of Christ receives insight, faith, wisdom, love, hope, power, and knowledge from God through the Spirit. This is one way the axiom *opera trinitatis ad extra indivisa sunt* ("all external works of the Trinity are one and undivided") is upheld and understood. In the first instance, TAT has practical benefits to how we understand the incarnation and how Christ perfectly embodies the divine and human natures.

5.3.2 Theological Anthropology

A direct implication of the incarnation is how others are recreated and conformed to Christ (theological anthropology). Raniero Cantalamessa reminds us that the Spirit anoints Jesus as the Messiah and anoints us as Christians, the Spirit urges Jesus and the church to struggle against Satan, the Spirit urges Jesus and the church to evangelize, and the Spirit urges Jesus and the church to pray.[16] We could add that the Spirit urges Jesus and the church on to good works. At this stage, TAT's principle is that what is true of Christ is made true of those united to Christ. In Christ, full of the Spirit, the Christian too has their mind, will, and emotions affected by the Holy Spirit of Jesus Christ, who baptizes and fills us to become like Christ. As Christ turned his (fallen) flesh back to the Father with every act of obedience and love, so too the Spirit of Christ recreates fallen creatures (regeneration), makes them right with God (justification), enables faith and repentance (conversion), and equips them for a life of good works (sanctification/Christification). As it was with Christ, it is with us as we are united to Christ.

The difference between Christ and us is not the what—we each have the same (fallen) human nature—it is the who—only Christ is divine, the eternal Son of God. My sinful inclinations, personal sins, and relentless disobedience are taken hold of by the Spirit, and I am united to Christ, who, in his perfection, perfects me through that same Spirit. Jesus Christ really is our faithful, sympathetic High Priest (Heb 4:14–15). He has gone before us and perfected our humanity so that united to him, the Spirit may do in and for us what he did in and for the incarnate Son. That is the basis of our Christlikeness and conformity to Christ. We never become Christ or replace Christ, but we do become like him from glory to glory. A TAT can bring these practical aspects of the Christian life to the fore.

---

[16]Cantalamessa, *The Holy Spirit in the Life of Jesus*.

5.4 Practical Theology

Another applied aspect of TAT is that it is more than compatible with various approaches of practical theology, especially qualitative projects. James Fowler explains the aims and scope of practical theology as follows:

> Practical theology aims at a kind of knowing that guides being and doing. While concerned with theory, it is not *theoria*; while concerned with techniques, it is not *poesis*. Its knowledge is a *practical knowing*—a knowing in which skill and understanding cooperate; a knowing in which experience and critical reflection work in concert; a knowing in which disciplined improvisation against a backdrop of reflective wisdom, marks the virtuosity of the competent practitioner.[17]

Added to this definition, John Swinton and Harriet Mowat describe the intent of practical theology as

> Critical, theological reflection on the practices of the church as they interact with the practices of the world, with a view to ensuring and enabling faithful participation in God's redemptive practices in, to and for the world.[18]

To achieve these ends, practical theology often adopts a qualitative methodology.[19] Given the focus on ecclesial practices, faith, embodied existence, and the work of God in the world, practical theology and some forms of qualitative methodology are suitable vehicles for TAT. But what type of qualitative study? Qualitative studies are often phenomenological or ethnographic (as but two examples) and struggle to make a case for any sense of generalizability. As a form of theology, TAT has a commitment to a realist epistemology, and as such, critical realism immediately suggests itself as a viable methodology for TAT study.[20]

Central to a Christian worldview is that the truth can be known and apprehended, and this knowledge represents a genuine disclosure of what is

---

[17]James Fowler, "Practical Theology and the Shaping of Christian Lives," in *Practical Theology* (ed. Don S. Browning; Philadelphia: Harper and Row, 1983), 154–5.
[18]John Swinton and Harriet Mowat, *Practical Theology and Qualitative Research* (London: SCM, 2006), 6.
[19]This is the focus of Swinton and Mowat, *Practical Theology*.
[20]On the use of critical realism in the humanities, see Berth Danermark, Mats Ekström, Liselotte Jakobsen, and Jan Ch. Karlsson, *Explaining Society: Critical Realism in the Social Sciences* (London: Routledge, 2002). On Christian realism in theological science, see Thomas F. Torrance, *Reality and Scientific Theology* (Edinburgh: Scottish Academic Press, 1985); and Alister E. McGrath, *Reality: A Scientific Theology*, vol. 2 (Grand Rapids, MI: Eerdmans, 2002).

real. Christian theology and natural science operate with an understanding of knowledge that has its ontological foundations in objective reality. When critical realism is used in theology (perhaps it should be called "theological realism"?), it proposes that Scripture is an authoritative guide to truth and reality. Yet, it comes from God in various linguistic forms and expressions that a fallible reader must interpret. Critical realism identifies three ontological levels or domains: Empirical, Actual, and Real. The Empirical domain refers to what can be observed and experienced. This involves experiences. The Actual domain refers to what is known but cannot always be seen. This involves experiences and the events within which they occur. The Real domain refers to the hidden but necessary precondition for the actual and the empirical. The level of the Real contains causal mechanisms that explain the Actual conditions and are experienced in the Empirical domain.[21] A mechanism can affect an outcome or event in the world.[22] When used as a research paradigm or epistemology, a recognition of a realist worldview is being made, and this becomes a justification for the generalizability of the research. The stratification of truth or reality into the three fields of the Empirical, Actual, and Real allows the researcher to provide explanatory reasons for events and experiences that are derived from causal mechanisms in the real.

The same process of moving from the Empirical through the Actual, to the Real is followed by TAT, when it starts from below and takes seriously the embodied, contextual, and realistic nature of faith in the world. Even when the reverse is happening in forms of formal theology, our knowledge of God still comes from the economy and is mediated by the epistemic structures of creation—the mind, the church, Holy Scripture, experience, and so forth. TAT and critical realist methodology make for good bedfellows and create the conditions for fruitful practical theology.[23]

5.5 Conclusion

There are many other practical outcomes and benefits of TAT, many of which will be touched on in the chapters that follow. What has been offered here is merely an entrée to the field.

---

[21] Roy Bhaskar, *A Realist Theory of Science*, 2nd ed. (London: Routledge, 2008), 2.
[22] Danermark et al., *Explaining Society*.
[23] Both authors have supervised numerous graduate and postgraduate students in TAT and critical realism and TAT and qualitative research.

This brings Part I of this work to a close. In many ways, Part I forms a coherent unit in its own right. Some readers may find this sufficient for their purposes as a self-contained overview of TAT—its definition, scope, method, justification, and practicability. For others, a more technical and substantial interrogation of theological topics is required, and that is what follows in Part II as we focus on the Trinity, ecclesiology, soteriology, anthropology, missiology, and eschatology. Part II is intended to provide an overview of the kind of theology possible for TAT and a stimulus for others to follow.

Part II

The Content and Consequence of Third Article Theology

6

Trinity: Viewing God through a Pneumatological Lens

6.1 Introduction

It is not uncommon to hear from those in churches sentiments such as, "I know a lot about God, but I don't know much about the Trinity." In formal academic guise this sentiment is camouflaged by the more technical sounding commitment to speak of a doctrine of God before one speaks of God's triunity.[1] This is not the way of Christian theology. Instead, we speak of the one God who is triune or the triune God who is one. Following the lead of Thomas F. Torrance, we affirm that "we apprehend the self-revelation of God to us in his indivisible wholeness as *one Being, three Persons, three Persons, one Being*."[2] Torrance was following a long line of thinkers from the early church through to today. The claim being made here is that we don't start with one (Being or *ousia*) or three (Persons or *hypostases*) but instead with both at the same time: three Persons one Being, one Being three Persons. Gregory Nazianzen famously stated in AD 381 that

> No sooner do I conceive of the One than I am illumined by the Splendour of the Three; no sooner do I distinguish Them than I am carried back to the One. When I think of any One of the Three I think of Him as the Whole, and my eyes are filled, and the greater part of what I am thinking of escapes me. I cannot grasp the greatness of That One so as to attribute a greater greatness

---

[1] This is not simply an appeal against separating *De Deo Uno* from *De Deo Trino*, nor is it simply a trenchant argument against starting with *De Deo Uno* over and against *De Deo Trino*, although those arguments are compatible with the doctrine of the Trinity outlined here.

[2] Thomas F. Torrance, *The Christian Doctrine of God: One Being Three Persons*, Cornerstones ed. (London: Bloomsbury T&T Clark, 2016), 113 (emphasis in original).

to the Rest. When I contemplate the Three together, I see but one torch, and cannot divide or measure out the Undivided Light.[3]

Boris Bobrinskoy registers his uneasiness at any theology (he levels his criticisms at Western scholastic theology) that would separate the one God from the three persons: "the mystery of living God is a mystery of *Tri-unity*. This concept … unites the Three and the One in a single expression."[4] Both Bobrinskoy and Torrance, to use two giants of East and West, are adamant that a doctrine of God simply is a doctrine of the Trinity. That is the first point to be clearly made at the start of this chapter.

A second point to make early on is methodological and epistemological: we move from the economy of redemption to a constructive and theo-logical account of God before moving back to the economy.[5] Torrance is again a reliable guide when he clarifies what this kind of scientific theology involves, namely:

> A stratified structure of several coordinated levels of understanding in which the conceptual content and structure of basic knowledge becomes progressively disclosed to inquiry. We moved from the ground level of evangelical or biblical knowledge of God as he is revealed to us in the saving activity of his incarnate Son, to a distinctly theological level in an attempt to grasp and give intelligible expression to the unbroken relation in Being and Act between Christ and the Holy Spirit to God the Father, which belongs to the very heart of the Gospel message of God's redeeming love.[6]

We follow the same procedure here in a TAT: beginning with the biblical account of the Spirit, we are drawn to Christ, and through Christ to the Father,

---

[3] Gregory Nazianzen, "Oration on Holy Baptism," *Oration 40.41*, in *NPNF²*, 7:375.

[4] Boris Bobrinskoy, *The Mystery of the Trinity: Trinitarian Experience and Vision in the Biblical and Patristic Tradition* (Crestwood, NY: St Vladimir's Seminary Press, 1999), 1. Both Bobrinskoy and Torrance cite as patristic support Gregory Nazianzen's famous quip about not being able to think of one without three and three without one from *Orations* 40:41, in *NPNF²*, 7:375.

[5] Each of these moves is imperative but in a single essay such as this, a more organic approach has had to be taken due to the limitation of space. Adonis Vidu provides a concise summary of this methodology: "While it is natural that one starts with the divine economy and proceeds to an understanding of the immanent Trinity, the knowledge of the divine economy should be regarded as provisional, as a sort of first naïveté. Having 'known' the immanent Trinity by way of the economic operations, one must return, in a second naïveté, to the economic works. Thus, our principle does not yield a simplistic and unidirectional application but rather a creative tension, whereby the immanent pole is ascribed a principled priority, with full awareness that the two poles cannot be divorced and are unavailable apart from one another," Vidu, *The Same God Who Works All Things*, 92–3.

[6] Torrance, *Christian Doctrine of God*, 113. For the same movement in different words, see Bobrinskoy, *The Mystery of the Trinity*, 2–3.

only then can we develop a doctrine of the immanent Trinity and allow a theo-logic to enable a constructive theology applicable to all times, peoples, and places. What TAT highlights in this very standard theological method is the mission and procession of the Spirit as a starting point in understanding God's economic work and how this informs our doctrine of the immanent Trinity. TAT allows the relational character of God to be clearly perceived and enriches the received tradition by removing obstacles to ecumenism and retrieving a dynamic trinitarianism eclipsed at times throughout church history. Each of these points is established by the Holy Spirit and his spiration and mission. The specific claim of TAT is that by focusing on the person and work of the Spirit we can (more?) clearly establish the fundamental tenets of orthodox trinitarianism while also gaining new insights into the Being and Act of the triune Lord. This methodological approach is consistent with that discussed earlier in Chapter 3, where it was shown how Spirit Christology and the doctrine of the Trinity are properly basic beliefs and as such, Spirit Christology offers one of (the?) best entry points into a doctrine of the Trinity.

For the sake of clarity and space, in Section 6.2 we consider the basis for the inseparable operations of the three persons of God in the economy in order to highlight the triunity of God. Then, in Section 6.3, we reflect upon the triune reciprocal relations and a dynamic trinitarianism or a relational ontology. Finally, a theological reflection is offered on the way Jesus taught his disciples to pray to "our Father" in Section 6.4.

6.2 Inseparable Operations

Athanasius was adamant that "it is more pious and more accurate to signify God from the Son and call Him Father, than to name Him from His works only and call Him Unoriginate."[7] We call God "Father" because that is how he has been revealed to us by the eternal Son, and we come to know the Son through the revelatory work of the Holy Spirit.[8] Knowledge of God is thus triune in content and trinitarian in the manner in which we come to know God. In the face of Jesus, we see the Father, made possible by the presence

---

[7] Athanasius, "Four Discourses against the Arians," 1.34, in *NPNF*², 4:326.
[8] In like fashion to Athanasius, Larry Hurtado reminds us that "the NT does not present 'God' as 'Father' to believers through creation or in some universalizing sentimental sense. Instead, for Christians to address 'God' as 'Father' is to affirm that they know this God effectually through Jesus and affirm Jesus' relationship to this God as his 'Father,'" Larry W. Hurtado, *God in New Testament Theology*, Library of Biblical Theology (Nashville, TN: Abingdon, 2010), 41.

of the Holy Spirit. Knowledge of the triune God is possible only because of the revelatory work of the triune God: only God can reveal God. As the Scriptures say, "no one has seen God at any time, the only-begotten Son who is in the bosom of the Father he has declared him" (John 1:18), and "no one knows the Son but the Father, neither does anyone know the Father but the Son, and he to whom it shall please the Son to reveal him" (Matt 11:27). Also, "The Spirit searches all things, even the deep things of God" (1 Cor 2:10), and "the Spirit will receive from me what he will make known to you" (John 16:15). "Hence only the divine persons themselves, who dwell in the inaccessible light of the Godhead, can know themselves in their distinction from one another and also in their mutual relations."[9] Matthias Scheeben even goes so far as to say, "In the entire created universe there is nothing that could bring one to the thought of a Trinity of persons in God."[10] It is, Scheeben rightly reminds us, a revealed mystery of the faith and a mystery revealed by all three persons of the Godhead. When we start with the Spirit, as TAT does, then we are aware of the work of the Spirit revealing the Son and through the Son, the Father. TAT cannot be unitarian nor can it first talk of an abstract deity or "god" and only then seek to articulate a doctrine of the Trinity: it is trinitarian from the start. And it is trinitarian from the start because in Scripture we see the dogmatic rule that theologians would later term *opera trinitatis ad extra sunt indivisa* ("all external operations of the Trinity are one and undivided"), namely, the doctrine of inseparable operations.[11]

As with the Father, so too with the Spirit, Athanasius was equally clear that we do not know the Spirit from the manifestations of spirit (human or ethereal) or even the operations of the Holy Spirit in creaturely existence, but rather, we know the Spirit from his inner relation to the Son and the Father.[12] The Spirit is the Spirit of the Father and the Son and only as such can we know him in his external works.[13] Once again, when TAT starts with the Spirit in the doctrine of God, it is trinitarian from start to finish because the

---

[9] Matthias J. Scheeben, *The Mysteries of Christianity* (trans. Cyril Vollert from the 1941 original; New York: Herder and Herder, 2006), 27–8.
[10] Scheeben, *The Mysteries of Christianity*, 28.
[11] For one of the few full-scale works on the dogmatic rule, see Vidu, *The Same God Who Works All Things*.
[12] Athanasius, *Adversus Serapion*, 1.30; 3.1, 16.
[13] Hurtado agrees with this sentiment when he states that "in the NT writings the Spirit is linked specifically with Jesus in remarkable and unparalleled closeness," such that "the NT already reflects a certain 'triadic' shape to the early Christian experience of 'God' and to discourse about this God," Hurtado, *God in New Testament Theology*, 45.

Spirit reveals the Son and through the Son the Father, and the Spirit is sent by the Father with the Son to do this revealing work, hence the Spirit does not reveal a God-idea nor does he enlighten creatures with a metaphysical interest; rather, the Spirit reveals the Son of the Father and in that revelation, he reveals God as the Trinity.

The contention of Spirit Christology, as argued for earlier, is that the biblical writers present Jesus to us as the *Messiah*, the Spirit anointed and incarnated Son of God the Father. Throughout the Gospels, we have various moments or Messianic *kairoi* that present Jesus to us as the eternal Son of the Father made known by the Spirit. Knowledge of the Son is only made possible by the Holy Spirit just as knowledge of the Father is only made possible by the Son (and the Spirit). The Holy Spirit is God, *homoousios* with the Son and the Father,[14] and essentially one with them, hence the economic activity of God is undivided and triune, thus the doctrine of what is called inseparable operations. As Torrance reminds us, "the Spirit is not outside the Being of the Word or Son but inherent in him as he is inherent in God the Father, and as the Father is in him, and so through the Son the Spirit is inherent in the Father."[15] Torrance then cites Athanasius in support: "The Holy and Blessed Trinity is indivisible and one in himself. When mention is made of the Father, there is included also his Word and the Spirit who is in the Son. If the Son is named, the Father is in the Son, and the Spirit is not outside the Word. For there is … one divine nature and one God."[16]

TAT establishes the doctrine of the Trinity in the economy of God's divine self-revelation, starting with the Spirit, before then offering a constructive account of the reciprocal relations. This does not mean we are reliant upon diachronic or synchronic readings of Scripture (helpful as they are) and are left to decide whether or not to give priority to Father, Son, or Spirit in the divine revelation. Rather, "the doctrine of the Holy Spirit is derived, therefore, not merely from biblical statements, nor from doxological formulae alone, but from the supreme truth that God reveals himself through himself, and therefore that *God himself* is the content of his revelation through the Son

---

[14] Athanasius, Didymus, Gregory Nazianzen, and Epiphanius had no hesitation in speaking of the Holy Spirit as *homoousios* with the Son and the Father in the same sense that Nicaea speaks of the Son as *homoousios* with the Father. See Thomas F. Torrance, *The Trinitarian Faith: The Evangelical Theology of the Ancient Catholic Church*, Cornerstones Series (London: Bloomsbury T&T Clark, 2016), 202–5.
[15] Torrance, *The Trinitarian Faith*, 201.
[16] Torrance, *The Trinitarian Faith*, 201–2 citing Athanasius, *Adversus Serapion* 1.14.

and in the Spirit."[17] Revelation of God is centered in the incarnate Son who is both *homoousios* with the Father and with us and as such, he is able to reveal God to us. But this is not without the Spirit whose mission is to make known to us the Son of the Father. "He comes to us as the Spirit of the Father and of the Son, revealing the Father in the Son and the Son in the Father, and thus as himself God through whom God reveals himself."[18] And so to start with the Spirit, we are led to the Son and through the Son to the Father.

Textbook accounts of the Trinity in Scripture take their cues from the theology articulated above and present the progressive unveiling of the three persons of the Godhead.[19] The earlier chapter on Spirit Christology illustrated how this work of biblical theology can be done in ways that bring out the inseparable operations of the Trinity in the economy. This chapter is not concerned to work through this inseparable work, but rather it provides the basis for it; and in the next section on reciprocal relations, it begins to develop a constructive theological account of the one triune God.[20]

---

[17]Torrance, *The Trinitarian Faith*, 202 (emphasis in original). Torrance goes on to cite a number of church fathers in support including Athanasius, Didymus, Gregory Nazianzen, and Epiphanius.
[18]Torrance, *The Trinitarian Faith*, 203.
[19]See, for example, Habets, *The Progressive Mystery*.
[20]There are many works that examine the extent to which the Old and New Testaments themselves are trinitarian or triadic or implicitly trinitarian. Arthur W. Wainwright, *The Trinity in the New Testament* (London: SPCK, 1962, 1969), speaks of a triadic or threefold pattern; Gordon Fee, *Pauline Christology* (Peabody, MA: Hendrickson, 2007), speaks of a divine triad in the Pauline corpus. Richard Bauckham, *God Crucified: Monotheism and Christology in the New Testament* (Carlisle: Paternoster, 1998), speaks of Jesus sharing the divine identity. Hurtado, *God in New Testament Theology*, speaks of the triadic shape of God discourse in the New Testament. Both Fee and Hurtado also speak of the "proto-trinitarian" nature of the New Testament and even of the need to see the Trinity as presuppositional to many New Testament texts. Newer works have established a more robust and comprehensive basis for arguing for a trinitarian reading of both Old and New Testaments. Here, Christopher R. Seitz's work, *The Elder Testament: Canon, Theology, Trinity* (Waco, TX: Baylor University Press, 2018), is important as he argues that the Old Testament contains within it the clear and compelling foundations of what becomes the doctrine of the Trinity. In a similar vein but focusing on the Pauline corpus is Wesley Hill, *Paul and the Trinity: Persons, Relations, and the Pauline Letters* (Grand Rapids, MI: Eerdmans, 2015), who provides exegetical arguments for the conceptual continuity of Paul's God-language and what later theologians would call the relations that obtain between the trinitarian persons. These are only a small selection of works, of course, but they do show the growing consensus in biblical theology for the continuity between the Christian Scriptures and later theological construction on the Trinity. Francis Watson, for example, states that "traditional Jewish God-language is relocated within a framework in which the word 'God' is misunderstood and misused if it is not always and everywhere accompanied by reference to Jesus and his Spirit," Francis Watson, "The Triune Divine Identity: Reflections on Pauline God-Language, in Disagreement with J. D. G. Dunn," *JSNT* 80 (2000): 105. Also worth consulting on how to read Scripture theologically is R. B. Jamieson and Tyler R. Wittman, *Biblical Reasoning: Christological and Trinitarian Rules for Exegesis* (Grand Rapids, MI: Baker, 2022).

6.3 Reciprocal Relations

At the heart of the Christian confession is belief in one God, three persons. The unity of God and the triunity of God are not in any tension with each other, but, rather, are mutually defining. In this section, we provide a dogmatic sketch of the reciprocal triune relations of the Godhead and highlight ways in which a TAT articulates a doctrine of the Trinity. As indicated earlier, the doctrine of the Trinity is often underappreciated, even among those who should know better. As Scheeben reminds us, "God would appear as a dead Monad, as a rigid motionless unity, if we did not think of Him in the Trinity of persons."[21] TAT sees in the biblical portrayal of God a deeply relational and dynamic Trinity, a doctrine fecund with applications and importance.

Thomistic scholar Gilles Emory once noted, "if 'Father' and 'Son' are indeed mutually related names, then whenever there was a Father, there must have been a Son."[22] Emory could have, perhaps he should have, completed the sentiment with something like, "and whenever there was a Father and Son, there must have been a Spirit." The divine persons are constitutive of the one Godhead and as such, something of a dynamic trinitarianism has to be articulated. This is the way of TAT because it is embedded in the tradition as a way of further describing what is revealed in Holy Scripture.

For his part, another Thomistic scholar, Matthias Scheeben,[23] correctly asserted that, "the persons are not absolute, but relative persons; that is, the characteristic of the personality of each consists in the fact that each possesses the nature only in relation to the others, and consequently in common with them."[24] Scheeben clarifies what he means by this when he

---

[21]Scheeben, *The Mysteries of Christianity*, 30. Later he writes, "The Father in knowing Himself confronts Himself with the Son, as the expression of this self-knowledge and the image of its object; and inasmuch as the Father and the Son love each other reciprocally, this love seeks its bond and its expression in the Holy ghost. But this productivity in the process of the divine self-consciousness can be inferred neither from the nature of self-consciousness in general, nor from the nature of the divine self-consciousness in particular, as far as our reason can know it," Scheeben, *The Mysteries of Christianity*, 36.
[22]Gilles Emery, *The Trinitarian Theology of St. Thomas Aquinas* (trans. Francesca A. Murphy; Oxford: Oxford University Press, 2007), 80.
[23]By working with theologians such as Emery and Scheeben (and later, Weinandy), Thomistic scholars in the scholastic tradition, I am highlighting the continuity of a TAT with the received tradition of the church. TAT is not a theological novelty. Khaled Anatolios calls Scheeben "the most lucid and rigorous modern exponent of the classic Augustinian-Thomistic trajectory of that tradition …," *Deification through the Cross: An Eastern Christian Theology of Salvation* (Grand Rapids, MI: Eerdmans, 2020), 241–2.
[24]Scheeben, *The Mysteries of Christianity*, 51.

says, "This is evident in the case of the two persons who are produced [Son and Spirit], since they have the nature from the First Person [Father], and accordingly are what they are only in relation to Him."[25] This is affirmed by all branches of orthodox Christianity. But Scheeben continues, "But the same is no less clear with regard to the First Person [Father], too; for He possesses the nature only so far as He possesses it in a characteristic manner, as a special person, to give it to the other two persons."[26] It is this reciprocity between the divine persons, *including the reciprocity of the Father*, that makes them persons and as such, that makes God-God. Scheeben then turns this into a theological maxim, namely: "the three persons cannot really be three divine persons, cannot possess the nature as their common good, unless they stand in essential relationship to one another, in a relationship which is the reason both for community of possession and for distinction in possession."[27] This is well said but needs to be clarified. In what ways is the Father personal in "a characteristic manner," and what is the "essential relationship" the Father has from the Son and the Spirit that makes him Father? Relations of opposition is the standard answer to these questions, and indeed, that is part of the answer Scheeben gives himself, albeit with some suggestive modifications.[28] One of the key modifications Scheeben offers has to do with the Holy Spirit, and that is where his theology is of interest for our TAT account of the Trinity. It is the Person of the Spirit that illuminates the dynamic of the Triune life. While Scheeben was not doing TAT per se, many of his insights are helpful for just that.

The Christian tradition teaches that the Father is an unproduced person, the one who is not derived from others. The Father's personal distinction is his being unbegotten and the begetter of the Son and spirator of the Spirit. The Son proceeds from the Father as the perfect expression or Word of his wisdom. The Spirit's spiration is different, he is the mutual love or sigh or sweet kiss[29] between the Father and the Son and as such "he possesses

---

[25]Scheeben, *The Mysteries of Christianity*, 51.
[26]Scheeben, *The Mysteries of Christianity*, 51.
[27]Scheeben, *The Mysteries of Christianity*, 51.
[28]"We shall take pains to enrich St. Thomas' train of ideas by the addition of other elements, and where necessary to paint his thought more sharply and develop it further, or, as the case may require, to modify it," Scheeben, *The Mysteries of Christianity*, 55.
[29]Scheeben is taken with the idea that the Holy Spirit is the love, sigh, kiss, or breath of the Godhead which he borrows from various Fathers. It is, however, Bernard whom Scheeben turns to for the language of the Spirit as the "sweet kiss of Father and Son," Scheeben, *The Mysteries of Christianity*, 65, 100 etc. According to Scheeben, the most common expression of the Fathers for the Spirit is that of the *osculum* or kiss; "the kiss is the caress of love in the most exquisite sense," Scheeben, *The Mysteries of Christianity*, 65.

the divine nature as truly and perfectly as does He to whom it originally belongs."³⁰ In Scheeben's words, "the bliss which these two enjoy in the possession of the same nature can achieve a real expression in no other way than by taking a third person into this communion, by sharing with a third the entire and indivisible good which they possess, without losing it."³¹

Here it can sound like a form of modalism is at work whereby the Father, the real God, produces a second, the Son, and then together they produce a third, the Spirit. This is not, of course, what the tradition means by this language. These are hypostatic productions in which the fullness of deity is possessed by each Person not because the divine nature is produced (as in a reproduction) but because the divine nature is communicated, in its entirety, to each person and in that communication (or procession) the Godhead is triune.

This again raises the question of the status of the Father as a person. If, as the tradition is clear, he is not the Father without the Son and the Spirit, and if, as the tradition is equally clear, the processions in part define God, then the Father is relationally dependent upon the Persons produced by the processions (Son and Spirit) as much as the Persons produced by the processions are relationally dependent upon the Father. Scheeben is aware of this when he affirms the three persons as "personal in a way that is quite special; for the producing principle, which constitutes the persons, *is also manifested as a person in them*."³² Later he elaborates, "the First person, too, is relative to the others in His possession, because He owes His possession of the nature to the communication of it just as much as they do. And the First person is for His part essentially bound up with this communication, because He possesses the nature only to communicate it. And thus the divine persons are perceived to be such only in and through the relations in which they stand to one another."³³ Scheeben turns this too into another helpful and correct theological maxim, "the divine persons are relative proprietors of the divine nature … they are proprietors of the divine nature in and through their relationship to other proprietors of the same nature."³⁴

---

[30] Scheeben, *The Mysteries of Christianity*, 75.
[31] Scheeben, *The Mysteries of Christianity*, 76.
[32] Scheeben, *The Mysteries of Christianity*, 79 (emphasis added).
[33] Scheeben, *The Mysteries of Christianity*, 81.
[34] Scheeben, *The Mysteries of Christianity*, 81. Later he explains, "the dissimilarity between divine and created hypostases lies in this, that in God distinct possession is based not on a multiplication of the object possessed, but on the communication of the same object," Scheeben, *The Mysteries of Christianity*, 83.

We read, "The term 'Son' designates the first product in God as a suppositum, and likewise as a personal suppositum, as a person. And since the First Person is perceived to be subsistent only when He appears as the generative principle of the Son, the name Father is just as fitting and significant for Him as the name Son is for the Second person."[35] Once again, it is important not to miss the essential detail found in this affirmation, namely that the Father is personed by the Son in the very act of the Father begetting the Son (and spirating the Spirit). Scheeben is overt about this: "The Father cannot be God and possess the divine nature without the Son, nor can the Father and the Son without the Holy Spirit. Each possesses the nature in Himself and for Himself, but only in so far as He possesses it also from another or for another: from another, from whom He receives it; for another, to whom He gives it. Thus distinction in possession not only does not exclude common possession, but essentially requires it."[36]

There is no Father without Son and Spirit, and no Son without Father and Spirit, and no Spirit without Father and Son. Speaking of the consubstantiality of the three persons, Scheeben writes, "But they [Son and Spirit] can well be equal to the producing person if the latter has an essential ordination to the production and possesses His own subsistence only in His productivity of them."[37] Hence, no processions no Father and no Father or processions, no God. God is essentially triune or he is nothing.

Knowing what implications a genuine commitment to God's triunity has, Scheeben adds, "This union and communion among the persons appear in higher relief when we reflect that not only are any two of the persons immediately related and united to each other, but that *each of the three persons is in His own way a center and focus to which the other two are related and in which they are united to each other*."[38] It is this very principle that a TAT begins with (despite taking necessary time to come to). We can start with the Father and see how he unites the other two persons with himself through the begetting of the Son and with (through) the Son, spirating the Spirit. Here the Father is the *fons divinitatis* of the Godhead and we have the common Western articulation of the relations of opposition in the West or the common Eastern articulation of the monarchy of the Father. Or we could start with the Son as the one begotten of the Father and together with

---

[35] Scheeben, *The Mysteries of Christianity*, 95.
[36] Scheeben, *The Mysteries of Christianity*, 115.
[37] Scheeben, *The Mysteries of Christianity*, 121.
[38] Scheeben, *The Mysteries of Christianity*, 115–16 (emphasis added).

the Father as spirator of the Spirit. Here the Son "occupies a central position, and is thus a link which joins the other persons in Himself to form a golden chain."[39] Or, Scheeben argues, we could start with the Spirit who "unites the Father and the Son with and in Himself, not as their principle, but as their common and immediate product; and more accurately, as the product of their mutual love, in which they manifest their unity and show themselves to be one Spirit."[40] Starting with the Spirit is, of course, the central motif for a TAT.

We see this most clearly when we focus on the spiration of the Holy Spirit. The Holy Spirit is love and he is the love of the Father and the Son, hence, in some real sense, the Holy Spirit is the love of the Father that begets the Son, and the Spirit is the love of the Son in being begotten. Begetting and being begotten are dependent upon love and as such on the Spirit, and so the begetting of the Father, and the being begotten of the Son, are commensurate with the spiration of the Spirit. No contemporary theologian has articulated this as well or as comprehensively as Thomas Weinandy. Weinandy is important for TAT as the Holy Spirit is the key to his understanding of the Trinity.

Thomas Weinandy's work on the Trinity offers an orthodox and constructive account of the reciprocal relations by suggesting that in the Western theological tradition, the Holy Spirit does not seem to be very personal given he is not an active person, and alongside this concern a certain "sequentialism" whereby it is hard to see how the Spirit is a real "who" or person at all.[41] Weinandy also takes issue with the Eastern theological tradition and its adoption of the Platonic principle of emanation whereby the whole Godhead resides in the Father alone and only in the Son and Spirit as they emanate out of him.[42] Weinandy's constructive solution is as follows:

> The Father begets the Son in or by the Holy Spirit. The Son is begotten from the Father in the Spirit and thus the Spirit simultaneously proceeds from the Father as the one in whom the Son is begotten. The Son, being begotten in the Spirit, simultaneously loves the Father in the same Spirit by which he himself is begotten (is Loved).[43]

---

[39]Scheeben, *The Mysteries of Christianity*, 116.
[40]Scheeben, *The Mysteries of Christianity*, 116.
[41]I have appropriated Weinandy's work on the Trinity in my constructive accounts of TAT elsewhere, including Habets, "Getting beyond the Filioque with Third Article Theology," 211–30.
[42]For the full argument, see Thomas G. Weinandy, *The Father's Spirit of Sonship: Reconceiving the Trinity* (Edinburgh: T&T Clark, 1995).
[43]Weinandy, *The Father's Spirit of Sonship*, 17.

More recently, Weinandy has slightly corrected his thesis and updated the argument.[44] Working on the agreed theology of East and West, and with particular attention to the doctrine of the Trinity put forward by Thomas Aquinas, Weinandy states that "what distinguishes the divine persons is the actual relations that they possess among themselves, for their divine identities are constituted by their inter-relations. Since these inter-relations are ontologically constitutive of the Trinity, they constitute the very nature of God, his essence."[45] After detailing the relations of opposition, Weinandy then concludes, "Thus, there is a perichoretic union, an intertwining ontological communion among the Father, the Son and the Holy Spirit, in and through which they subsist as who they distinctively are in relation to one another."[46] So far, this is classical Trinitarianism. Weinandy then proceeds to use these theological agreements to question parts of the received tradition in the attempt to construct a *more orthodox* account of the Trinity (hence "reconceived") that takes into full consideration the person of the Spirit.

Central to Weinandy's corrective of the tradition is the person of the Spirit. We cannot recount his entire argument here but "If the Spirit did not proceed from them [Father and Son] as Love fully-in-act, the Father would not be paternity fully-in-act nor would the Son be filiation perfectly in act."[47] Weinandy's specific complaint is recounted here:

> Though the Holy Spirit proceeds from the Father and the Son, there is no passivity within the Holy Spirit himself. As the Son is begotten of the Father as sonship-fully-in-act, since there is no passivity in the Son in his being begotten of Father, so the Holy Spirit proceeds from the Father and the Son as Love-fully-in-act: there is no passivity in the Spirit in his being spirated by the Father and the Son. All processions within the Trinity, whether as begotten as Son or as spirated as the Holy Spirit, are fully-in-act, for they originate from, and so partake of, the Father's fatherhood fully in act. ... For Aquinas, although we speak of the Son and Holy Spirit coming forth from the Father, and thus of their "passivity," yet that "passivity" does not imply their inactivity, for in accordance with the Father being fatherhood-fully-in-act, they come forth from the Father as fully-in-act. Thus, the Son comes

---

[44]Weinandy, "The Trinity and the Father's Spirit of Sonship: Further Considerations on Reconceiving the Trinity," in *Engaging Catholic Doctrine: Essays in Honor of Matthew Levering* (ed. Robert Brown, Scott W. Hahn, and James R. A. Merrick; Steubenville, OH: Emmaus Academic, 2023), 455–78. Weinandy is responding to critiques of his earlier work, especially those coming from fellow Thomistic scholars such as Levering.
[45]Weinandy, "The Trinity and the Father's Spirit of Sonship," 463.
[46]Weinandy, "The Trinity and the Father's Spirit of Sonship," 466.
[47]Weinandy, "The Trinity and the Father's Spirit of Sonship," 468.

forth from the Father as sonship-fully-in-act and the Holy Spirit proceeds from the Father and the Son as Love-fully-in-act. The Holy Spirit is "Love proceeding" (*ST* I, q. 37, a. 2). The Spirit's "proceeding" is the fully enacted Love that the Spirit is. Thus, the Father, the Son, and the Holy Spirit possesses no passive potency that requires further actualization.

What can never be lost sight of is that the persons of the Trinity are verbs; that is, they are subsistent relations fully-in-act and what distinguishes them is the singular defining act that each enacts in relation to the others. Ultimately, the good news is that Aquinas agrees with the thesis being proposed here, at least on this point—that the Spirit is identical to his own act of proceeding, and so is an active person in relation to them. What remains absent is his failure to grasp that the Spirit's procession from the Father and Son as their mutual Love is simultaneous with the Father's begetting of his Son in the Love that is the Spirit, whereby the Son is empowered to love the Father in the same Love wherein he himself is begotten.[48]

In his critique, Weinandy is surely correct. The tradition, East and West in their own ways, has eclipsed the role of the Holy Spirit within the Godhead and as such has threatened a fully personal understanding of the Spirit.[49] The Spirit is the impetus to love, if we can put it that way, and not simply the result of a prior love of the Father and the Son. The sequentialism of the West and the *monarchia* of the East is here corrected. There is no begetting that is not also involved with the spirating, and no spirating that is not also involved with the begetting, and no being begotten that is not also involved with spiration and begetting and so forth. The reciprocal relations of the Trinity are just that, fully reciprocal and constitutive of the Godhead and they are seen most clearly when we start with the Holy Spirit as the gift, love, donum, sigh, kiss, and spiration of the Father with the Son. This principle can be summarized with Weinandy's affirmation that "the fully enacted

---

[48]Weinandy, "The Trinity and the Father's Spirit of Sonship," 469–70. For a more concise critique, he writes in Weinandy, *The Father's Spirit of Sonship*, 77: "East and West ... never quite saw that the Father breathes forth the Word by the breath of the Spirit. The East never perceived this because their conception of the Trinity is neo-Platonic, and thus the Spirit ranked third in the hierarchy and so proceeded through the Son. ... Likewise, the West, in patterning its conception of the Trinity after Aristotelian epistemology, maintained that the Spirit proceeded from the will of the Father as his life for the Son only 'after' the Son was begotten and thus known. So, again, the Spirit here could not be perceived as the breath of the Father in whom the Word was spoken."

[49]Kathryn Tanner, "Beyond the East/West Divide," in *Ecumenical Perspectives on the Filioque for the Twenty-First Century* (ed. Myk Habets; London: Bloomsbury/T&T Clark, 2014), 205–6, agrees: "Neither side [East nor West], I contend, pays full attention to the gospel narration of Trinitarian relations."

fatherhood of the Father and the fully enacted sonship of the Son demands the simultaneous enacted Love that is the Holy Spirit, for in the Trinity *to be* and *to understand and love* are one and the same."[50] Without the Spirit, there is no begetting or being begotten. Tanner is equally insistent: "The Spirit is the love or power of the Father that helps bring the Word about as an animated and efficacious expression of the Father."[51] What Weinandy has articulated is a consistent application of the doctrine of *perichoresis*.[52]

Considering the above, Weinandy has clarified his earlier thesis on the Trinity by replacing the word "by" with the word "in" as follows:

> The Holy Spirit proceeds from the Father as the Father's fully enacted Love in whom he begets his Son, and proceeds from the Son as the Son's fully enacted Love in whom he loves his begetting Father, and thus the Father and the Son love each other *in* Love proceeding, the Love that simultaneously proceeds from the Father and the Son within the Father's begetting his Son.[53]

By replacing the word "by" with "in," Weinandy removes any objection that the Spirit is a causal agent or another principle in the begetting of the Son in addition to the Father.

Weinandy further argues for the coherence of his thesis based on mutually reciprocal triune relations as follows:

> As the fount of the perfect plentitude of love, the Father, in begetting his Son, wills simultaneously to spirate the Holy Spirit, for his paternal Love wells up within Him, and so proceeds from him, as he lovingly begets his Son. In begetting his Son in the Love that is the Spirit, the Father gives to his Son the gift of Love, that is, the Holy Spirit himself. Being begotten by the Father in the Father's paternal Love for him, the Son therefore loves his Father in the same Spirit of Love, the Father's gift of Love, in whom he is begotten. Thus, the Spirit finds his full expression as Love in proceeding from both the Father and the Son as their premier gift of mutual Love for one another.[54]

---

[50]Weinandy, "The Trinity and the Father's Spirit of Sonship," 471–2 (emphasis in original).
[51]Tanner, "Beyond the East/West Divide," 209.
[52]Eastern Orthodox and patristic Scholar, Khaled Anatolios, writes similarly: "while each of the divine persons is a distinct 'I,' each 'I' is 'interior' and 'transparent' to the others, so as to constitute 'another self.' We can understand this formulation as a transposition into a psychological framework of the classic pro-Nicene understanding of the coincidence of ontological self-understanding and mutual reference in the trinitarian persons, such as we find in the felicitous description of Gregory of Nazianzus: 'Each of these persons possess unity, not less with that which is united to it than with itself, by reason of the identity of essence and power,'" Anatolios, *Deification through the Cross*, 253.
[53]Weinandy, "The Trinity and the Father's Spirit of Sonship," 473 (emphasis in original).
[54]Weinandy, "The Trinity and the Father's Spirit of Sonship," 475.

The key to understanding this is the person of the Spirit. If the Spirit were not the one in whom the Son is begotten of the Father and the one in whom the Son loves the Father, then the Spirit would not be Love-fully-in-act as he is affirmed to be.

> If the Spirit is not Love-fully-in-act, then the Father would not be fatherhood-fully-in-act nor would the Son's sonship be fully-in-act, for they would then not love one another with the full perfect divine plentitude of Love. Moreover, if the Spirit is not Love-fully-in-act, he would not be as divine as the Father and Son are divine, for he would not partake totally of their fully-in-act divine nature or essence.[55]

Because the Father, Son, and Spirit define one another, the Holy Spirit defines the Father and Son to the same extent as Father and Son define the Holy Spirit. The Father begets the Son and the Son is begotten of the Father but not without the "co-relative defining act of the Spirit as Love-fully-in-act in relation to Father and Son." According to Weinandy, "Proceeding from the Father and the Son within the act of the Father begetting his Son, the Holy Spirit enacts the act wherein the Father loves his begotten Son and the Son loves his begetting Father."[56] Tanner recounts the same thing in different words when she writes, "The Spirit is a kind of 'amen,' a joyful sound, rounding off those loving relations between Father and Son that the Spirit itself bears up or sustains across their course. In sum, the Son and Spirit come forth together from the Father and return together in mutually involving ways that bind one to the other … in each case of coming out or return a single three-person movement in which they both come out or go back together in complex dependence upon what the other has from and gives back to the Father"[57] is in view.

By looking at the Father and the Son through the Spirit, the doctrine of the Trinity takes on a distinctly relational ontology whereby there is an "eternal simultaneous non-sequential symmetrical perichoretic fully-in-act relations of the fully-in-act Father, the fully-in-act Son, and the fully-in-act Holy Spirit."[58] It is just this doctrine of the triunity of God that is classically orthodox and yet, subtly underrepresented in much contemporary theology. TAT has an ecumenical interest, and by looking at the Trinity through the Spirit we may find more common ground between the various Christian

---

[55] Weinandy, "The Trinity and the Father's Spirit of Sonship," 475–6.
[56] Weinandy, "The Trinity and the Father's Spirit of Sonship," 476–7.
[57] Tanner, "Beyond the East/West Divide," 203.
[58] Weinandy, "The Trinity and the Father's Spirit of Sonship," 477.

traditions.[59] This chapter has deliberately drawn upon Orthodox, Scholastic, and other central features of the Great Tradition to show continuity with that tradition and to counter any claims to pure novelty.

6.4 On Learning to Pray "Our Father"

The practical implications of the triunity of God are many. What follows is a brief reflection on learning to pray Our Father of Matthew 6:9–13; Luke 11:1–4, with a special emphasis or awareness of the Spirit-enabled act of praying. The first two words of the Lord's Prayer, "our Father," in many ways encapsulate the doctrine of the Trinity and our response to that. In these two words, we have an entire theology (and lexicon). We also have a fruitful application of TAT to the everyday life of believers.

The disciples had been living with Jesus on and off for several years by this stage of the Gospel story. They had left their homes and jobs and were following Jesus, watching what he did, listening to what he said, and observing the way he held himself. They also saw him pray. He prayed often. He prayed for short periods and long periods. He prayed in public and in private. And when he prayed, he prayed to *Abba*, an Aramaic term for an intimate expression equivalent in English to "Father" or perhaps to the modern sentiment "Dad."[60] Jesus revealed himself to be *the* Son—*the* Son of *the* Father. Jesus taught that he was *the* eternal Son, a unique Son, an only Son. Jesus taught that he had a Father, an only Father, an eternal Father. He and the Father were one, were eternal, were united, were God. And the

---

[59]In this chapter, Western scholastic Thomistic scholars have been primarily utilized in order to highlight the fact that what is presented here is classically Christian, not an aberrant or novel doctrine of God. TAT does not advocate social trinitarianism, for instance. For a selection of other authors whose work on the doctrine of God is sympathetic to the TAT presented here, see: Thomas H. McCall, *Which Trinity? Whose Monotheism? Philosophical and Systematic Theologians on the Metaphysics of Trinitarian Theology* (Grand Rapids, MI: Eerdmans, 2010); Coakley, *God, Sexuality, and the Self*; Kathryn Tanner, *Jesus, Humanity and the Trinity: A Brief Systematic Theology* (Minneapolis, MN: Fortress Press, 2001); Stanley J. Grenz, *The Named God and the Question of Being: A Trinitarian Theo-Ontology* (Louisville, KY: Westminster John Knox Press, 2005); Dumitru Stăniloae, *Orthodox Dogmatic Theology*, vol. 1: *Revelation and Knowledge of the Triune God: The Experience of God* (trans. and ed. Ioana Ionita and Robert Barringer; Brookline, MA: Holy Cross Orthodox Press, 1994), Thomas F. Torrance, *The Christian Doctrine of God*, to name but a few.

[60]See Hurtado, *God in New Testament Theology*, 89–90. But *Abba* does not mean "daddy"! See "Father/Abba," in *The Baker Expository Dictionary of Biblical Words* (ed. Tremper Longman III and Mark L. Strauss; Grand Rapids, MI: Baker Books, 2023), 292.

disciples watched and heard all this. They watched while Jesus was baptized, and his Father called him *his* Son and his Spirit rested on him (Matt 3:17).[61]

For thousands of years, the Jewish people, the covenant people, had been taught how to worship, serve, sacrifice, live, tax, sing, and pray. For thousands of years, a staple prayer of the Jewish people is of course the Shema of Deuteronomy 6:4: "Behold the Lord your God, the Lord is one." They would pray this multiple times a day as their act of devotion and worship to the Lord, to YHWH. This and other prayers formed the spine of their worship of God. If anything, the Jewish people in the Bible are a praying people! The disciples come to Jesus to ask to be taught how to pray, just as John the Baptist taught his disciples. They are clearly not asking about technique, and they are not even really asking the *how to* question at all. They are asking a *who to* question. Who do we pray to?

Now notice, this is *not* how Jesus prays! Jesus never prays "Our Father"; if he did, he would just be another one of us, no different except by degree. When he prayed, it was "My Father," or simply "Father," or "Abba."[62] Soulen sums up the importance of the language nicely when he writes, "'Father, Son, and Spirit' is not a chance grab bag of unrelated terms, but a privileged set of mutually interpreting designations that leads to the heart of the gospel."[63] Jesus is the only one who can fully and truly claim the Father as his own.[64] And that is because Jesus is the only Son of the only Father in the communion of the only Holy Spirit.[65] Jesus is claiming to be one in essence with the Father, he is claiming to be distinct in person from the Father, and

---

[61]R. Kendall Soulen, *The Divine Name(s) and the Holy Trinity: Distinguishing the Voices* (Louisville, KY: Westminster John Knox, 2011), 213, helpfully makes the connection between the Lord's Prayer and the baptism of Jesus when he notes the term "Father" "implies an already existing familiar relationship between God the one who speaks. ... The term finds its divine counterpart in God's words to Jesus when he was baptized in the river Jordan by John."

[62]Noting the fact that the term "Father" for God is used almost exclusively by Jesus, Soulen comments, this "is not the result of chance. It is a subtle but powerful way the Synoptic writers underscore Jesus' identity as the 'Beloved,' the one through whom God's paternal zeal enters at last triumphantly on the scene," Soulen, *The Divine Name(s) and the Holy Trinity*, 221. It is noteworthy, but not germane to this chapter, that in the Gospel of Mark, Jesus once prays simply to "my God," and that is in the cry of dereliction from the cross (Mark 15:34). See the significance of this for Spirit Christology in Habets, *The Anointed Son*, 166–70, 254–6.

[63]Soulen, *The Divine Name(s) and the Holy Trinity*, 214. The citation continues: "Through them, God, Christ, and Spirit make themselves known to us in terms of the relationships of origin, mutual presence, and availability that characterize their eternal life together, relationships that, by the Father's sending of the Son and Spirit, they open up to the world as well." Soulen's work also shows the importance of other terms and names for God that Jesus uses, especially highlighting the use of God's unspoken name, or the Tetragrammaton.

[64]On the Old Testament use of Father-language for God and the prehistory of the idea of fatherhood in Israel, see Soulen, *The Divine Name(s) and the Holy Trinity*, 30–6, 53–7.

[65]See the important study of Marianne Meye Thompson, *The Promise of the Father: Jesus and God in the New Testament* (Louisville, KY: Westminster/John Knox, 2000), who provides an excellent

all this he claims is made possible by the Spirit. Why the Spirit? We know from the works of Paul that the Spirit is the only means by which the Father can be called "Abba" (Gal 4:4–6 and Rom 8:9). This is true for believers because it was first true for Jesus. As Weinandy reminds us, "The word 'Abba' contains within it this trinitarian ontology. ... The Father is 'Abba' in that he begets the Son, and the Son is Son ... by crying out 'Abba!', to the Father. Moreover, this 'Abba,' as pertaining to the Father and to the Son, is suffused with the Holy Spirit. The Spirit makes this mutual and reciprocal 'Abba'-love to be 'Abba'-love." Why? Because "It is the Spirit who conforms the Father as 'Abba' to the Son and conforms the Son to cry 'Abba!' to the Father."[66] And because of that, Jesus says, this is how *you* should pray—"our Father."

In what ways is God our Father if he is exclusively the Father of the Son in the Holy Spirit? For us to pray "Our Father," we would have to take the place of the eternal Son, and that is both impossible and blasphemous. So that is ruled out. Jesus is *not* inviting us to become the eternal Son and to take his place or pretend to be him. Instead, we have the Gospel preached in two words. To call God "our Father" we need to be children of God, and that is just what the Father has done in Christ by the Spirit (Gal 4:7). And this makes all the difference. Julie Canlis has brought out well how this change in identity affects the way we pray. For Canlis, we have here the radical change from a "slave narrative" to a "Son narrative."[67] Canlis writes, "This is about whether or not we pray to a God of legalism or communion."[68] This is how the deeply relational ontology of the Trinity affects all other aspects of theology and the Christian life. Canlis reminds us that "many of us profess our faith in one story, but pray from another. Prayer is where the story that controls our spiritual life is revealed."[69]

Canlis illustrates how a relational ontology works its way into relational communion by means of the Lord's Prayer, saying, "Others of us, despite praying the 'Our Father,' continue to pray deep down from Moses's story of a good, loving God—but who is still impersonal. This God is the sovereign 'I AM' but who cannot be counted on as *Father*."[70] Jesus revealed that the

---

analysis of the theological importance of God-language, especially that of Father, in the New Testament.

[66] Weinandy, *The Father's Spirit of Sonship*, 74–5.
[67] Julie Canlis, "Trinitarian Prayer: Praying from Slave-Narratives to Son-Narratives," in *Essays on the Trinity* (ed. Lincoln Harvey; Eugene, OR: Cascade Books, 2018), 178–91.
[68] Canlis, "Trinitarian Prayer," 185.
[69] Canlis, "Trinitarian Prayer," 186.
[70] Canlis, "Trinitarian Prayer," 187.

Father and the Spirit unites us with the Son so that God is indeed our Father. "In prayer, we enter this Father–Son relationship. Jesus modeled this new way of being for us, when he taught us to pray 'Our Father.' Calling God 'Abba—Father' is not just giving God a friendly nickname. It is entering into the same trusting, intimate, liberating relationship that Jesus had with his Father."[71]

Why then is it so difficult for Christians to move from what Canlis calls "slave narratives" to "Son narratives," or from non-relational prayers, functional prayers, or the cold formality of simply petitioning prayers to a seemingly capricious deity into a new relationship whereby we are beloved children engaging with our gracious and generous Father in conversation and communion? In a word, Sin. We are fallen creatures who think the worst and when it comes to the triune God of grace and glory, we are constantly tempted to think of him as a tyrant, or distant, or distracted, and to think of ourselves as merely chattel, or slaves. That is why "It is the Spirit who actually helps us claim the words as our own, crying for us, '*Abba*'—Jesus's very words. For those of us for whom slave-narratives come as second nature, we need help. … We need the Spirit to lift us up into Christ's prayer life (which is the relational life) to the Father."[72] Adopted by the Spirit, we are united to Christ and made children ("sons") of the Father such that in Christ and in the Spirit, we can cry out "Abba, Father" (Gal 4:6).[73] "For through Christ we both have access to the Father by one Spirit" (Eph 2:18). Could there be a more beautiful picture of the Gospel than that!

6.5 Conclusion

This chapter has defined and discussed the Christian doctrine of God as one Being three Persons and it has shown how, from the vantage point of TAT, we develop a relational ontology of the divine nature and think about the one God who is Father, Son, and Holy Spirit. We concluded by looking briefly at one implication that the doctrine of the Trinity related to, the basis upon which we can pray to God as "our Father." The Spirit, no less than the Son or the Father, is essentially God and in his economic mission he conforms

---

[71]Canlis, "Trinitarian Prayer," 188.
[72]Canlis, "Trinitarian Prayer," 188.
[73]See Hurtado, *God in New Testament Theology*, 90.

believers into the image of God that is the incarnate Son, Jesus Christ. The biblical writers have no qualms about speaking of this transformation in the most elevated of ways, as a form of *theosis* or deification. The church becomes the locus of this salvific and sanctifying activity, discussed in Chapter 7, and salvation itself is addressed in the chapter after that.

7

Ecclesiology: The Church as a Community of the Spirit

7.1 Introduction

The contemporary need for a renewed understanding of ecclesiology is significant and urgent. For the institutional church, at least in the Western world, is crumbling. While in the Global South the church is growing rapidly, its more established counterpart is experiencing an ever-accelerating loss of size, status, and significance. The many responses that simplistically urge the church to "do" better are primarily motivated by an attempt to return to Christendom. Such an approach is shortsighted, shallow, and ultimately unhelpful. Before we even begin to consider what the church should do—many thoughtful commentators reply to such simplistic responses—we need to recover a meaningful understanding of what the church actually is—precisely who God has called us to be.[1] A TAT perspective suggests that insight into this profound and important question of the church's identity can be gained through prioritizing the Spirit. Such a pneumatologically informed approach to ecclesiology is traditionally endorsed.[2] And the call for such a renewed pneumatological emphasis is repeatedly echoed by noted contemporary

---

[1] See, for example, Cheryl M. Peterson, "Who Is the Church?," *Dialog* 51 (2012): 24. Or for more details, Cheryl M. Peterson, *Who Is the Church? An Ecclesiology for the Twenty-First Century* (Minneapolis, MN: Fortress Press, 2013).

[2] For example, the Apostles Creed places the Spirit and church side by side, declaring "I believe in the Holy Spirit, the holy catholic church, the communion of saints." See Pelikan and Hotchkiss, eds., *Creeds and Confessions: Early, Eastern and Medieval*, 669.

theologians.³ From its very inception, proponents have argued that TAT will help "Christianity to 'act its age' in the time and place it now finds itself."⁴ It is particularly in the application of TAT to ecclesiology that this claim is tested and found to be extremely valuable.

How then, can such a pneumatologically informed understanding of ecclesiology be developed? In Section 3.3, it was argued that the constituent features of a TAT doctrine are best illuminated by looking *at* the doctrine *through the lens* of the Spirit *from the vantage point* of other theological *loci*. This chapter follows this approach, in that we take the two theological doctrines that have already been developed—Christology and the Trinity—and use both these doctrines as vantage points from which to explore ecclesiology through the lens of the Spirit. So, in Section 7.2, we start from the vantage point of Spirit Christology, and explore ecclesiology from this perspective through a pneumatological lens. Then, more succinctly in Section 7.3, we start from the vantage point of the Trinity (and in particular a Trinitarian understanding consistent with Spirit Christology, as outlined in Chapter 6) and view the pneumatological parallels it has with ecclesiology. Finally, Section 7.4 explores the practical implications the developed understanding of pneumato-ecclesiology has for the practice of worship.

7.2 The Church as a Sequel to the Incarnation

The aim of this section is to view ecclesiology from the vantage point of Christology, using the mediating lens of pneumatology. Using Wolterstorff's terminology, Spirit Christology is the control belief, ecclesiology is the data belief, and all other doctrines are background beliefs. Following this approach, two core premises inform the development of a Third Article Ecclesiology. The first is that significant insight into the ontology of the church can be gained through comparing it with the ontology of Christ. This analogical understanding was compellingly derived and worked out by Karl Barth with his utilization of the "Chalcedonian pattern."⁵ The second is

---

³For example, Colin Gunton argues that a greater focus on the church's constitution by the Spirit is the "first and crying need" if responses to the collapse of Christendom are not to descend into new authoritarianisms. See Colin Gunton, "The Church on Earth: The Roots of Community," in *On Being the Church* (ed. C. Gunton and D. Hardy; Edinburgh: T&T Clark, 1989), 62–5.
⁴Dabney, "Starting with the Spirit," 25.
⁵See, for example, Hunsinger, *How to Read Karl Barth*, 185.

that this correspondence cannot be adequately examined without giving the Spirit prominence, for it is the Spirit that forms the church as Christ's body. This is a point that Barth often overlooks. As Badcock argues, "The church as the body of Christ cannot be considered apart from [the Spirit's presence], for the ecclesiastical 'body' is something that is mediated by the work of the Spirit, and cannot exist without the Spirit."[6] Pneumatological insights into how the eternal Son became human inform our understanding of how the perfect Christ indwells an imperfect church. As Veli-Matti Kärkkäinen asserts, "the only way to construe a viable pneumato-ecclesiology is to reflect very carefully on the relationship between Christ and the Spirit on the one hand, and on the relation of the Spirit to the church on the other hand, and then try and see these three as mutual entities that inform each other."[7]

Prioritizing the pneumatological connection between Christ and the church reveals an important ecclesiological tension to navigate. Ecclesiologies traditionally aim for an appropriate balance between the divine and the human aspects of the church. Ecclesiologies that do not achieve such balance are labeled as ecclesial Docetism (if they overemphasize the church's divinity at the expense of its humanity) or ecclesial Ebionism (if they do the reverse). Using Spirit Christology as a vantage point from which to explore ecclesiology reveals that it is equally important for the Son and the Spirit's ecclesial involvement to be balanced—both must be logically distinguished without being existentially separated. The Son's ecclesial involvement must not be subsumed into or subordinated below that of the Spirit, and the Spirit's ecclesial involvement must not be subsumed into or subordinated below that of the Son. This insight directly parallels the similar recognition noted in the development of Spirit Christology. Just as Jesus' divinity needs to be understood through the twin categories of Logos and Spirit, and overemphasizing one or the other leads to a deficient Christology, so Christ's indwelling of the church as his body needs to be understood as occurring through the interrelated missions of the Son and the Spirit.

Such ecclesiological balance is best achieved by exploring the pneumatologically inspired parallels that exist between Spirit Christology and Third Article Ecclesiology:

- The Spirit conceives (Christ and the church)
- The Spirit sustains the communion (of Christ and the church)

---

[6] Gary D. Badcock, *The House Where God Lives: Renewing the Doctrine of the Church for Today* (Grand Rapids, MI: Eerdmans, 2009), 85.
[7] Kärkkäinen, *Toward a Pneumatological Theology*, 93.

- The Spirit conforms (Christ and the church)
- The Spirit directs and empowers (Christ and the church)
- The Spirit is displayed and mediated (by Christ and the church)

Examining ecclesiology in such a parallel manner enables the balance, coherence, and consistency gained in Spirit Christology to be equally applied to the church.

On the basis of these parallels, we are justified in characterizing the church as the *sequel* of the incarnation. Like a movie sequel's relationship with its original, the church has a clear continuity with the incarnation. Many of the same characters emerge and similar themes are explored. But (also like a sequel) the church is not simply a continuation or repetition of the incarnation. Just as disaster awaits attempts to make a movie sequel too like its original, so disaster awaits attempts to identify the church too closely with Christ. The church cannot add to or replicate Christ's already completed work—in attempting to do so it becomes not more but less than it should be. Finally, there is a necessary asymmetry. Just as there is no movie sequel without an original, there is no church without Christ. Jesus is God's Son become human independent of what the church is or does. In contrast, the church is Christ's or it is not the church at all.

Exploring in detail the Spirit-inspired parallels arising from the church being the sequel of the incarnation allows some fundamental questions to be asked and answered, such as the following.[8] What is the church? The church is the Spirit-enabled union that exists between the incarnate Christ and the human community of faith. Who is in the church? The church consists of those humans who have been united by the Spirit to Christ. How is a church recognized? A church can be identified by having both a Christ-centered orientation and an overall momentum toward Christlikeness. What does the church do? The church is cruciform in shape, missional in purpose, narrative in character, and relational in identity. The examination of each of these parallels and their accompanying insights provides a rich, full, and—most importantly—balanced view of the church as seen from the vantage point of Christology through a pneumatological lens.

Perhaps most significantly, the Christological perspective utilized illuminates the church's indivisibility: the historical church is one. This ecclesiological insight is derived and follows directly from Christ's

---

[8] For more detail on how these answers emerge from an examination of the parallels between Spirit Christology and a pneumato-ecclesiology, see Liston, *The Anointed Church*, chapter 5.

uniqueness. One Christ means one church. It is insufficient, though, to say that the church is one merely because of Christ. One Christ without the ontologically establishing presence of the Spirit within the present state of fallen humanity leads inexorably to a logically and practically divided church. The reverse is also true. One Spirit without the separate otherness of Christ as a distinct and separate eschatological goal requires a present perfection that simply doesn't exist. The historical church is one because there is one Christ and one Spirit, in and through whom we as one church participate in Christ's one relationship of Sonship with his one Father.

The pneumatologically enabled oneness also leads to the recognition of the church's unique context: having a relationship with Jesus and being a part of the church cannot be distinguished. The argument here is not for precedence but for equivalency. When a person is united to Christ by the Spirit, then that uniquely occurs through the transformation of that person into the church, the body and bride of Christ. As Gunton puts it, "the Spirit works in the church: his is a churchly rather than an individual sphere of activity."[9] The church consists of individuals who are pneumatologically united to Christ. To express this differently, the church is precisely identifiable as the human community of the baptized, those who have been baptized into Christ's body by the Spirit, leading to union both with Christ and with other believers.

The immediate and obvious consequence is that there is, quite simply, no such thing as a lone or anonymous Christian. Friedrich Schleiermacher famously distinguished between the two major denominational streams by noting "Protestantism makes the individual's relation to the church dependent on his relation to Christ" while Catholicism "makes the individual's relation to Christ dependent on his relation to the church."[10] Whether this statement is theologically and historically accurate or not,[11] TAT goes to neither extreme, but logically identifies one's relationship to Christ with one's membership in the church. It is not membership in the church first, or relationship with Christ first, but membership in the church and relationship with Christ are one and the same.

In this understanding, then, the church consists of those individuals who are pneumatologically united with Christ. Or, to utilize more intentionally

---

[9]Colin Gunton, "Baptism: Baptism and the Christian Community," in *Father, Son and Holy Spirit: Toward a Trinitarian Theology* (London: T&T Clark, 2003), 213.
[10]Friedrich Schleiermacher, *The Christian Faith* (London: T&T Clark, 1999), 103.
[11]See Veli-Matti Kärkkäinen, *An Introduction to Ecclesiology: Ecumenical, Historical and Global Perspectives* (Downers Grove, IL: IVP Academic, 2002), 11–12.

biblical language, it consists of those who have been baptized into the body of Christ by the Spirit (Spirit baptism).[12] But this invisible relationship has clear and visible markers, of which water baptism is primary.[13] Spirit baptism and water baptism thus have a complementary relationship, which can be understood according to a pneumatologically conditioned version of Barth's Chalcedonian logic.[14] First (following the Chalcedonian pattern), Spirit baptism cannot be separated from or confused with water baptism. Second (following the *anhypostasia/enhypostasia* formula), water baptism has no meaning beyond being a human rite without an accompanying Spirit baptism, but Spirit baptism imbues water baptism with a genuine reality. Third, water baptism corresponds to and reflects the genuine reality of Spirit baptism. It thus can be said that through baptism (both of water and Spirit) a person genuinely becomes united to Christ in his body the church. Just as all those who are in a marriage relationship have had a wedding, all those who are in the church and participate in his body have been baptized. The church is precisely the community of the baptized: those who are a part of the body of Christ, which is relationally connected to him through the Spirit.

This understanding, of course, requires some alteration of the "conventional" understanding of baptism. As Gunton notes, "It is not first of all the expression of the faith of an individual or some invisible inner cleansing, but it is public and communal: it is the means by which a person is brought into relation with Christ through the medium of his body, the church."[15] The clearest way to demonstrate this understanding of baptism is to recognize the potential errors it seeks to avoid. The initial two errors correspond to the classical christological heresies. An ecclesially Docetic understanding of baptism excessively focuses on Spirit

---

[12]Note that Spirit baptism here, as explained further below, is not seen as a second event but something commensurate with conversion.

[13]In utilizing the term "water baptism," the immediate question that arises is whether it is paedo or credo baptism that is being referred to. A pneumato-ecclesiology does not draw a sharp distinction between the two competing interpretations of water baptism, and both can fit within this framework. The key recognition is the correspondence between Spirit baptism and water baptism, as discussed below. Credo baptism fits perhaps more naturally with the pneumato-ecclesial perspective, as the rite of water baptism chronologically follows the event of Spirit baptism that it corresponds to and from which its significance and meaning are drawn. But paedo baptism, if considered as a proleptic anticipation of Spirit baptism, can also fit within the framework, through a pneumatologically enabled time reversal.

[14]See, for example, George Hunsinger, "Baptism and the Soteriology of Forgiveness," *International Journal of Systematic Theology* 2 (2000): 247–69.

[15]Gunton, "Baptism," 208.

baptism at the expense of water baptism, reducing water baptism to merely a responsive gesture, a "public testimony of one's faith in Jesus Christ."[16] This is a common position espoused in certain baptistic settings, and at the extreme can even treat baptism as a nonessential practice (e.g., the Quakers or the Salvation Army). The opposite error is ecclesial Ebionism, which completely neglects any mystical aspect of water baptism, and views it merely as an initiatory rite into the human community of the church. Examples can be seen in some liberal mainline churches and nominal Roman Catholicism.

But the examination of ecclesiology through a pneumatological lens reveals that there is a balance required not just between the divine and human elements of baptism, but also between the involvement of the Son and the Spirit in the act. Subsuming the Son's involvement into the Spirit leads to *confusing* water baptism and Spirit baptism. Many theologians of the Middle Ages, for example, claimed that baptismal regeneration occurred in and of the act itself (*ex opere operato*).[17] But the act of water baptism, in and of itself, is not regenerative. Union with Christ cannot be brought about through the performance of a physical act in and of itself. Further, as Stanley Grenz notes, "Baptismal regeneration survives in some form in the contemporary expressions of the more sacramental traditions, including the Roman Catholic and Eastern Orthodox churches and also among certain Lutherans."[18] John Zizioulas's overemphasis on the Spirit at the expense of Christ in the life of the church, for example, leads directly to him holding such a position.[19] His overemphasis on the Spirit comes as a direct consequence of lacking an understanding of Christ's person external to his corporate personality in the church. In Zizioulas's work, because an individual's connection to Christ and to Christ's church is literally and not just logically identified, Spirit baptism and water baptism also must be literally identical and not just logically complementary.

The opposite error subsumes the role of the Spirit into that of the Son, with the consequence that water baptism and Spirit baptism are excessively distinguished. This view does not neglect the importance of either form of

---

[16] Erickson, *Christian Theology*, 1023.
[17] Stanley J. Grenz, *Theology for the Community of God* (Grand Rapids, MI: Eerdmans, 1994), 526.
[18] Grenz, *Theology for the Community of God*, 526.
[19] John Zizioulas, *Communion and Otherness: Further Studies in Personhood and the Church* (London: T&T Clark, 2006), 80. See also Jonathan Martin Ciraulo, "Sacraments and Personhood: John Zizioulas' Impasse and a Way Forward," *The Heythrop Journal* 53 (2012): 995-7. For more details, see the discussion in Liston, *The Anointed Church*, chapters 4 and 6.

baptism, but it views them as separate and (more importantly) separable. Some argue that Barth's work trends in this direction. For example, toward the end of his *Church Dogmatics*, on the basis that Jesus Christ is the one and only sacrament of God, Barth maintains the nonsacramental nature of water baptism,[20] a claim that perplexes even his most ardent supporters. George Hunsinger writes that Barth's "argument is peculiar. Although, for Barth, Jesus Christ is the Word of God in the strict and proper sense, that did not prevent God's Word from having a threefold form. ... A similar logic immediately suggests itself for thinking about baptism and the Lord's supper as sacraments."[21] Barth's tendency to overemphasize that the human and the divine within the church are "unconfused" results directly from his tendency to subsume the role of the Spirit in ecclesial life into that of the Son. It is perhaps in his characterization of the sacraments, and baptism in particular, that the problematic implications of Barth's tendency to subsume the Spirit in the work of the Son are seen at their clearest.

So, beyond simply not emphasizing water baptism over Spirit baptism or vice versa, a *christological* Third Article Ecclesiology also balances the tendency to merge Spirit baptism and water baptism (arising from an overemphasis on the Spirit's ecclesial role) and the tendency to excessively separate them (arising from an overemphasis on the Son's ecclesial role). Viewed through the lens of the Spirit, water baptism becomes the sign and analogy of Spirit baptism, the human counterpart of a divine action. While this is only one of many balanced insights attained through this TAT methodology, it reveals the gains obtained from viewing the church, and this action in particular, through the lens of the Spirit. Moreover, it affirms the pneumato-ecclesial understanding of the church as the *unique context* in which a person's relationship with Christ is outworked and enabled. As Gunton rightly asserts, "the Holy Spirit is the agent of our incorporation into Christ through the medium of the community of faith."[22]

---

[20] See Barth, *Church Dogmatics*, IV.4 100–9. While it is true that Christ is the ultimate sacrament, this truth does not necessarily reduce baptism to a mere ordinance. See, for example, W. Travis McMaken, *The Sign of the Gospel: Toward an Evangelical Doctrine of Infant Baptism after Karl Barth* (Minneapolis, MN: Fortress Press, 2013). For more details, see the discussion in Liston, *The Anointed Church*, chapters 4 and 6.
[21] Hunsinger, "Baptism and the Soteriology of Forgiveness," 254.
[22] Gunton, "Baptism," 212–13.

7.3 The Church as a Participant in Trinitarian Life

While the end result is equally rich, viewing ecclesiology from the control belief of the Trinity through the lens of the Spirit is more complex and requires significantly more nuance than the previous situation where Christology was used as a control belief. The reason for the increased complexity and nuance required is that in the former situation, both entities being discussed "include" divinity and humanity. In comparing the Trinity and the church, however, this similarity no longer holds. One entity is entirely divine, while the other is partially (and perhaps predominantly) human. Consequently, utilizing the analogy between the Trinity and ecclesiology requires determining the answers to two pertinent questions. The first question is "Which Trinity?" Not that there are many Trinities, but there are many doctrines of the Trinity, as evidenced in the disagreements about the *filioque*. The second question is exactly whether and how the Trinity can be analogically related to ecclesiology.

Regarding the first question of "Which Trinity?," this has already been addressed in Chapter 6, and the following analysis will proceed on the basis that Weinandy's "reconceived" characterization of the Trinity where "the Father begets the Son in or by the Holy Spirit"[23] is the understanding most consistent with Spirit Christology and God's overall economic revelation. Regarding the second question, quite a lot of effort has been devoted recently to establishing a coherent analogical link between the Trinity and the church. Attempts to engineer a viable bridge are often followed by theological quality-control inspectors, however, who argue that such links have flawed foundations and inadequately span the gulf between Creator and creature. This section briefly outlines an argument that TAT enables a viable analogical connection to be constructed, but results in an ecclesial understanding that is substantially different from those that utilize connection mechanisms that do not prioritize the Spirit.

---

[23]Weinandy, *The Father's Spirit of Sonship*, 17. See also Habets, *The Anointed Son*, 224. Habets has also extended his formulation of Weinandy's understanding. See Myk Habets, "Filioque? Nein: A Proposal for Coherent Coinherence," in *Trinitarian Theology after Barth* (ed. Myk Habets and Phillip Tolliday; Eugene, OR: Pickwick Publications, 2011), 161–202.

Consider first (as an important counterexample) Miroslav Volf's well-known characterization of the church as the Trinity's image or likeness.[24] The logic he uses to link the two doctrines is best described as reflective. Volf considers Trinitarian characteristics one by one and determines to what extent each of these characteristics can also be considered to apply to the church. Just as the Trinity is a relational community, with divine hypostases that cannot and do not exist in isolation from the Trinitarian community, so (in reflection) individual Christians form a relational community, and they cannot and do not live in isolation from the ecclesial community. The Trinity is an egalitarian, nonhierarchical community of persons; therefore, the church should be like this too. Volf's application of *perichoresis* is similar, although more limited. Volf argues that Trinitarian persons indwell each other as persons, while ecclesial persons merely indwell each other through the "mutual internalization of personal characteristics." He writes, "we give to each other a piece of ourselves, something of that which we have made of ourselves in communion with others, and from others we take not only something, but also a piece of them."[25]

A number of theologians, however, voice the opinion that Volf's reflective approach is fundamentally flawed. They maintain that a "reflective" model cannot work because the church is not an image of the Trinity at all. Perhaps the most influential voice of this group is Kathryn Tanner, who argues that "it would be better to steer attention away from Trinitarian relations when making judgments about the proper character of human ones."[26] Taking aim not just at Volf's work, but others such as Moltmann, Boff, Zizioulas, and LaCugna who adopt such a reflective methodology, she outlines four broad areas of concern.

First, she notes the decidedly ambiguous sociopolitical potential of applying Trinitarian theology to human relationships, arguing that Trinitarianism has to be interpreted quite narrowly for it to be maintained as a helpful social analogy. Think about what Trinitarianism *could* mean if indiscriminately applied to human interactions. The fact that Trinitarian persons are defined by their relationship *could* imply that people should be defined by their (often demeaning) social roles, for example. Second, she argues that making the Trinity directly applicable to social relationships

---

[24]Miroslav Volf, *After Our Likeness: The Church as the Image of the Trinity* (Grand Rapids, MI: Eerdmans, 1998).
[25]Volf, *After Our Likeness*, 211.
[26]Kathryn Tanner, *Christ the Key* (Cambridge: Cambridge University Press, 2010), 207–8. The following paragraph in the text briefly summarizes Tanner's argument in this chapter.

involves making unjustified theological moves. For example, to have social applicability, the Trinity must be viewed as equivalent to a society of human persons, with the clear implication of tritheism. Tanner's third concern centers on our limited knowledge of the Trinity's inner workings. This leads to the circular logic well documented by Karen Kilby, where something unknown in the Trinity is "filled out" from our human experience, only then to be presented as a resource to *inform* our human experience.[27] Fourth and finally, Tanner recognizes the infinite gap between creature and Creator, and she argues that to the degree that the Trinity either is or becomes like humanity, it can teach us nothing about human society, for we already know from experience what it means to be human. But to the degree that the Trinity remains distinct from humanity, we are inevitably powerless to imitate it. Humanity's finitude and sinfulness mean that Trinitarian imitation is thus reduced to an unreachable utopian goal. Tanner comments, "Turned into a recommendation for social relations, the Trinity seems unrealistic, hopelessly naïve, and, for that reason, perhaps even politically dangerous."[28] Tanner's solution to all of these problems is to replace the Trinitarian analogy with a Christological one. She claims that the incarnation provides much more insight into human relationships, and is a much better analogy for human communities to aspire to.

Applied specifically to the reflective methodology of Volf and others, Tanner's concerns, critiques, and conclusions are very persuasive. Indeed, they are so persuasive that several theologians argue that not just reflective analogical bridges like Volf's, but any and all analogical bridges joining the Trinity and the church are similarly flawed. For example, John Webster writes that "the connection of theology proper and ecclesiology is [not] best explicated … by setting out two terms of an analogy."[29] Such comments, however, go well beyond Tanner's explicit and implicit intent, and significantly too far in general, precisely because there exist viable analogical alternatives to the reflective methodology adopted by Volf and others.

What about an alternative analogical methodology that, in Gunton's words, "replaces a logical conception of the relation between God and the world with a personal one"?[30] What about an alternative approach that, rather

---

[27]Karen Kilby, "Perichoresis and Projection: Problems with Social Doctrines of the Trinity," *New Blackfriars* 81 (2000): 432–45.
[28]Tanner, *Christ the Key*, 228.
[29]John Webster, "In the Society of God: Some Principles of Ecclesiology," in *Perspectives on Ecclesiology and Ethnography* (ed. Pete Ward; Grand Rapids, MI: Eerdmans, 2012), 206.
[30]Gunton, "The Church on Earth," 60.

than looking at how the church is *like* the Trinity, examines the implications of the church being pneumatologically *in* the Trinity, participating in its very life? What if the similarities between divine and human relationships occur not because humans are somewhat like divinity, but because they are personally indwelt by the divine Spirit, and therefore united with the human Christ? If this approach is adopted, then the continuities between the Spirit's immanent identity and his ecclesial role could be utilized to inform our ecclesial understanding. And further, believers' pneumatological union with Christ would enable comparison between his identity as Son and our participatory filial role in the Trinity. Such a pneumatologically enabled but christologically conditioned approach would proceed by first determining the Trinitarian understanding that is most responsible to the biblical revelation. That understanding of the Trinity is then applied to the economy by observing how the immanent identities of the Son and the Spirit are reprised on a series of expanding stages, christologically in the hypostatic union between the human and divine natures of Christ, soteriologically in the mystical union between Christ and the church, and finally and most pertinently ecclesiologically in the ecclesial relation between individual church members. It is not too difficult to see that this kind of alternative analogical approach not only avoids Tanner's critiques and concerns, but also demonstrates that a Trinitarian perspective is needed to complement and enhance the christological analogy suggested by Tanner and exclusively commended by others.[31] The following discussion presents a brief overview of such a TAT approach to constructing an analogical bridge between the Trinity and the church.

As outlined previously, the first question to address is to which Trinity the church is analogously related. Chapter 6 of this volume argued not just that "Spirit Christology provides our best mode of access to the theology of the Trinity,"[32] but also that a Spirit Christology implies a "reconceived" understanding of the Trinity where "the Father begets the Son in or by the Holy Spirit [and] the Son is begotten by the Father in the Spirit and thus the Spirit simultaneously proceeds from the Father as the one in whom the Son is begotten."[33] Consider three key aspects of this Trinitarian understanding.

---

[31]For more detail, see Liston, *The Anointed Church*, chapter 8.
[32]David Coffey, "Spirit Christology and the Trinity," in *Advents of the Spirit: An Introduction to the Current Study of Pneumatology* (ed. Bradford E. Hinze and D. Lyle Dabney; Milwaukee, WI: Marquette University Press, 2005), 315.
[33]Weinandy, *The Father's Spirit of Sonship*, 17. See also Habets, *The Anointed Son*, 224; and Habets, "Filioque? Nein," 161–202.

First, both the Son and the Spirit originate from the Father in one single action with two distinguishable parts. Just as, in human speech, breath and word are logically distinguishable but existentially inseparable, so too is the Father's breathing of the Word. The immanent identities of the Son and Spirit are thus logically and chronologically synchronous. Second, each of the Trinitarian persons is truly personal, with an active and constitutive role in the Godhead. So the Father (the originating person), persons the Son (the personed person), by the Spirit (the personing person). What this leads to is a nuanced understanding of Trinitarian *perichoresis*, which is identified as the very begetting or spirating by which the hypostases are personed. And third, this personing is not a one-off activity, but an ongoing reality, which is the third feature of this "reconceived" understanding of the Trinity. There is no distinction between how the Trinity is and how the Trinity came to be; God *in fieri* is God *in facto esse*. In every moment of eternity, the Godhead is constituted and subsists as a relational ontology *through* the Father begetting the Son in the Spirit, and the Son returning the love of the Father through the Spirit of Sonship given to him.

Having characterized our Trinitarian understanding, the next stage is to apply this understanding to the economy by observing how the immanent identities of the Son and the Spirit are reprised on a series of expanding stages, the first of which is Christology. So, in an analogous manner to the Father begetting the Son by the Spirit, the Father sends the Son to become human by the Spirit. And in an analogous manner to the Son returning love to the Father by the Spirit, Jesus prays and worships the Father, giving all that he is and has to the Father by the Spirit as a loving response. The simultaneous nature of the immanent Trinity is elongated and spread, for the limitations of space, time, and Jesus' changing and growing humanity bring an inevitably sequential component. Jesus must grow and develop as a human in order to increasingly experience in an actualized relationship the Sonship that is his by nature. But the overall shape of the immanent identities remains. First, the Son and the Spirit *together* are sent out from and return to the Father. In the incarnation, like in the Trinity, there is no Jesus the Son without the Spirit and no Spirit without Jesus the Son. Second, it is through the Spirit that the Son is incarnated as a human and through the Spirit the human Son returns love to the Father. So, the Son and the Spirit reprise in time their immanent identities. The Son is again the personed person, or in this case the incarnated person, the Spirit is again the personing person, as the means by which the Son becomes incarnate and also the means by which the incarnate Son returns love to the Father. And following the third

Trinitarian feature, this gift and return is an ongoing activity. While there is a natural elongation in the pattern so that a distinction is needed between Jesus' status and experience of Sonship, it is nevertheless true that it is only through the continuing gift of the Spirit from the Father that the incarnate Son has and retains both his status and his growing human experience of Sonship.

The second stage on which the hypostases reprise their identities is soteriology. For as the incarnate Son loves and worships the Father by the Spirit, believers participate in Christ's filial relationship. We *enjoy the status* of Sonship because the incarnate Son in his vicarious humanity has responded to God on behalf of humans. And we *appropriate this status* of Sonship as an active experiential relationship *through the Spirit*. As Paul explains in Galatians, "Because we are God's children [our status], God sends the Spirit of his Son into our hearts, the Spirit who calls out 'Abba, Father' [our experience]" (Gal 4:6). The immanent identities of the Son and the Spirit are thus reprised not just in the hypostatic union but in the mystical union. Just as the Son was begotten in eternity *through the Spirit*; just as Christ was hypostatically united in the incarnation *through the Spirit*; so the church is adopted as sons and daughters of God in Christ *through the Spirit*. The Spirit continues to do what the Spirit has always done and will always continue to do … *person* sons and daughters of God in Christ. Recognizing necessary discontinuities, there are also significant continuities between the unions: what the Spirit does in eternity is what the Spirit does in the incarnation is what the Spirit does in the church. As Calvin asserts, "We are the sons of God because we have received the same Spirit as his only Son."[34] And the Son too reprises his immanent identity in the mystical union. So, the Son who is begotten in eternity, who is incarnated in creation, is embodied in the church, which consequently becomes his mystical body. Again, recognizing necessary discontinuities, there are significant continuities between the Son being *personed* in the Trinity, *personed* in the hypostatic union, and most pertinently here *personed in the church*. So now it is Christ who lives his life through us (e.g., Gal. 2:20). Calvin again: "we are *one* with the Son of God … because, by the power of the Spirit, he imparts to us his life and all the blessings which he has received from the Father."[35]

---

[34]John Calvin, *Calvin's Commentaries* (trans. John Pringle; 22 vols; Grand Rapids, MI: Baker Books, 2009), Gal 4:6; 23:120.
[35]Calvin, *Calvin's Commentaries*, John 17:21; 18:184.

So again, in this expansion into the mystical union, the same three immanent features appear. First, the Son and the Spirit are breathed out (the Son is the Word and the Spirit is the breath) and return to the Father together. Their roles are logically distinct but existentially inseparable. Second, the Spirit is again the personing person and the Son the personed person. It is by the Spirit that the church is personed as the mystical body of Christ, or to say the same thing in reverse, it is Christ who is embodied in the church by the Spirit. But third, this embodying is not a one-off activity but is continuously repeating. Tanner comments, "Son and Spirit are sent … in order to enable our return to the Father. But returned to the Father we are sent out with Son and Spirit again to do the Father's work of service to the world. The return brings with it another going out because in returning we are incorporated into the dynamic Trinitarian outflow of God's own life for the world."[36]

While it must be emphasized that this filial participation is primarily communal, something that we as a church enjoy together, similar affirmations can certainly be made regarding the relationship between Christ and each believer as an individual. Perhaps the key biblical image by which this communal and individual reality is conveyed is that of priesthood. Jesus is our great high priest, and through his life, death, and resurrection he offers us God's grace: grace that is precisely identified as neither more nor less than union with him through the Spirit, and consequently participation in his Trinitarian Sonship. All the other aspects of salvation follow as a consequence of this union. But the New Testament does not merely speak of Christ as the great high priest, but also speaks of each of us individually as priests, together forming a kingdom of priests, or a royal priesthood. Gerald O'Collins and Michael Keenan Jones comment, "While the priesthood of Christ is unique, it is also participated in, albeit differently, by all the baptized."[37] But if Christ's priestly gift of grace is the gift of union with him through the Spirit and therefore participation in his Trinitarian Sonship, then our participatory role as priests leads to the conclusion that we too offer others grace as we participate in Christ. Other believers' union with Christ goes not just through the Spirit, but through us. Other believers are personed not just by Christ's relationship with them through the Spirit, but by our relationship with them as well. Not only is Christ formed or personed

---

[36]Tanner, *Christ the Key*, 205.
[37]Gerald O'Collins and Michael Keenan Jones, *Jesus Our Priest: A Christian Approach to the Priesthood of Christ* (Oxford: Oxford University Press, 2010), 271.

in each believer through Christ's gift of the Spirit, but also, in a participatory way, we person each other as well. In this manner, the Trinitarian identities of Son and Spirit are not just extended *to* the church but *within* it, not just to the inter-ecclesial relationship the church enjoys in Christ with the Father, but also to the intra-ecclesial relationships between individual church members.

This ecclesial union can be characterized as follows. As a believer participates in Christ's life, they offer his love to other believers by the Spirit, and those other believers, by the Spirit given to them, return the love of Christ to the one who originally offered it. So once again in this intra-ecclesial union, the immanent Trinitarian identities are reprised. First, the work of the Son and the work of the Spirit are again inseparable but logically distinct from each other. It is only as we participate in the life of Christ that we can offer his love by the Spirit, and it is only as this love is received and returned by the Spirit that Christ is "personed" or "formed" in the receiver. Second, in this union, the Spirit again acts as the "personing person" constituting others as ecclesial persons in Christ through their receipt and response of love. And the respondent is intrinsically identified with Christ (the "personed person") for it is through the believer's response of love enabled by the offered Spirit that Christ is personed or formed in the believer, and that he or she shares Christ's ecclesial consciousness and thus participates in his life. In other words, it is through their Spirit-enabled positive response that Christ is formed in them. In the very act of reaching out with the love of Christ by the Spirit, both the one receiving the love and the one giving it are constituted as ecclesial persons. Third, this gift of the Spirit from one to another is not a single activity that is once done and then complete, but a continuing action. We are *continually* "personed" in Christ as he offers us the gift of the Holy Spirit and we return that love to him by the very Holy Spirit *continually* given to us, *and* moreover, we are continually personing *each other* in Christ as we offer the Spirit to others, and as they receive and return the love offered by the very Spirit continually given to them.

There are many and varied outworkings and implications of this ecclesial understanding. First and foremost, it enables a clear characterization of the church as existing in any and all relationships where, by the Spirit, the love of Christ is offered and returned. It identifies the church as being intrinsically relational, an event of intersubjectivity, characterized by mutual giving and receiving, where every believer is both mother and mothered. It recognizes the Spirit's foundational role, but argues that the Spirit does not indwell an individual but rather resides in relationship. And significantly it identifies the sacramental nature of fellowship. Each of these points could be expanded at length,[38] but the concluding section looks particularly at the practical implications this understanding has for the church's corporate worship.

7.4 A TAT Understanding of Worship

Perhaps the best way to illustrate the practical value of utilizing a TAT approach to ecclesiology is to contrast the practical implications it has for corporate worship with that of the ecclesiology derived by Volf and his directly reflective approach. Both understandings utilize the language of Trinitarian participation, but they use the concept in profoundly different ways. Such a comparison is the objective of the chapter's final substantive section.

Consider first, the fundamental difference between the two understandings. As Richard Bauckham recognizes, Volf's twin ideas of the church participating in Trinitarian life and the Trinity being a model for the church are compatible only "if we think of the Trinity as simply like a group of three friends who include us in the friendship as yet more friends. This means that the kind of relationship (i.e. friendship) enjoyed by the original group of three friends is the kind of relationship the new members of the circle have with each other, since what has happened is that the friendship circle has expanded."[39] In Volf's understanding, then, our Trinitarian participation is participation *with* the Trinity. We take on Trinitarian characteristics, and our relationship with them is similar to their relationship with each other.

In the alternative Trinitarian ecclesiology presented in this chapter, the church does not participate *with* the Trinity, but rather *in* it. We do not merely take on Trinitarian characteristics, we indwell the unique Trinitarian life. The reason such an understanding is enabled is because, unlike Volf's argument, our relationships with the Trinitarian persons and their relationship with each other are uniquely and permanently differentiated. Through the Spirit (who always is and acts as the personing person), we are united with Christ (who always is and acts as the personed person), so that we share Christ's

---

[38]For more detail, see Liston, *The Anointed Church*, chapter 10.
[39]Richard Bauckham, "Jürgen Moltmann's *The Trinity and the Kingdom of God and the Question of Pluralism*," in *The Trinity in a Pluralistic Age* (ed. Kevin J. Vanhoozer; Grand Rapids, MI: Eerdmans, 1997), 160–1. See also Paul S. Fiddes, *Participating in God: A Pastoral Doctrine of the Trinity* (London: Darton Longman Todd, 2000), 46–9.

unique status and experience of Sonship. Participating *in* Trinitarian life is incompatible with an egalitarian Trinity like Volf's (or Moltmann's), which allows changing relationships between the Trinitarian persons, as Ralph Del Colle recognizes: "Out of deep respect for Professor Moltmann I implore him to consider that the divine unity is indeed a perichoretic tri-unity (as he so strongly affirms) but that this tri-unity manifests itself now and in glory in the constitutive *distinction* of persons without which our participation in the divine nature could not occur, for our very persons are birthed anew by the Spirit to manifest the Son to the glory of the Father."[40]

What are the practical implications of such discordant understandings for the church's life of worship? Consider first Miroslav Volf's characterization. If, rather than participating in the Trinitarian life, we *reflect* it as if, in Bauckham's critical assessment of Volf's understanding, we are joining a group of friends, then worship is fundamentally a task *we* do. It is offered to the persons of the Trinity, certainly, and the Trinitarian persons may help, but ultimately it is sourced from ourselves as individuals. It cannot be *sourced* from the Trinitarian persons because it is *offered* to them, and we cannot have differentiated relationships with them, for they do not have differentiated relationships with each other. Thus, although Volf's understanding is intentionally Trinitarian, the effect on the church's worship is not dissimilar to that of the "Unitarian" model critiqued by J. B. Torrance. "No doubt we need God's help to do it [i.e., pray and worship]. We do it because Jesus taught us to do it and left us an example of how to do it. But worship is what *we* do before God."[41] Volf's understanding does not provide any practical assistance or insight to our worship beyond throwing us back on our own initiative. It is, at the very least, indicative that while Volf's monograph mentions prayer and worship when discussing Ratzinger's and Zizioulas's ecclesiologies, in his own explication of Trinitarian ecclesiology, prayer and worship do not merit a single mention.[42] The reflective model may give insight into ecclesial structures,[43] but even its protagonists have little to say about its impact on the church's life of worship.

---

[40]Ralph Del Colle, "A Response to Jürgen Moltmann and David Coffey," in *Advents of the Spirit: An Introduction to the Current Study of Pneumatology* (ed. Bradford E. Hinze and D. Lyle Dabney; Milwaukee: Marquette University Press, 2005), 346.

[41]James B. Torrance, *Worship, Community and the Triune God of Grace* (Downers Grove, IL: IVP Academic, 1996), 20.

[42]According to the index, see Volf, *After Our Likeness*, 312. It is recognized here that the argument from absence is the weakest of arguments. So while an indicative data point, this is a long distance from an irrefutable proof.

[43]Although, as has already been noted, these insights are questionable. See Hunt, "The Trinity and the Church," 215–35.

In contrast, the understanding of ecclesiology developed through a TAT sees worship simply as believers joining the dynamic immanent Trinitarian life, with all three persons actively and intimately involved. It is initiated by the Father, who through the Spirit directs Christ as to how we should worship, and Christ in turn directs us as we are in him (opening our lives to his reign in us) and in the Spirit (enabled to hear him guiding us). Then, because of our union with Christ, as we obediently follow the guiding of the Spirit, the Father accepts our worship as if they were from Jesus. Essentially, Jesus takes our worship and gives it to the Father as if they were his. It is he who loves, worships, and prays, and we do these things only in him. Sarot's comments accurately characterize this understanding: "We do not pray *to God*, but *in God*. It is only because the Christian community in prayer is the body of the Son that it has *through the Spirit* access *to* the Fatherhood *of the Father*."[44] In this "reconceived" understanding of the Trinity and its analogical application to ecclesiology, our worship is something of a soliloquy with God as source, life, and object.[45] The wonder is that he chooses us as intermediaries and participants. C. S. Lewis, who himself espoused a robust doctrine of Trinitarian participation,[46] expresses this well:

> They tell me, Lord that when I seem
> To be in speech with you
> Since but one voice is heard, it's all a dream,
> One talker aping two.
> Sometimes it is, yet not as they
> Conceive it, Rather I
> Seek in myself the things I hoped to say,
> But lo! The wells are dry.
> Then seeing me empty, you forsake
> The listener's role and through

---

[44]Sarot, "Trinity and Church," 44 (italics in original). Note that Sarot does not distinguish between different Trinitarian models or Trinitarian ecclesiologies in formulating this characterization of prayer.

[45]Not that human agency is denied, but it is a participating, corresponding agency. As Vincent Brümmer comments, "In this Trinitarian way, however, God's agency is not coercive but enabling and motivating and therefore does not deny the freedom, responsibility and personal integrity of the human agent through whose action God realizes his will. On the contrary, it is still up to human agents to do God's will ..." Vincent Brümmer, *What Are We Doing When We Pray? On Prayer and the Nature of Faith* (Burlington, VT: Ashgate, 2008), 75.

[46]See Myk Habets, "Walking in *mirabilibus supra me*: How C. S. Lewis Transposes Theosis," *Evangelical Quarterly* 82 (2010): 15–27. "For Lewis, all people are bound for immortality, not the sloughing off of human nature but a participation in the triune Godhead" (Habets, "Walking in *mirabilibus supra me*," 20).

My dumb lips breathe and into utterance wake
The thoughts I never knew.
And thus you neither need reply
Nor can; thus while we seem
Two talkers, thou art One forever, and I
No dreamer, but thy dream.[47]

---

[47]C. S. Lewis, *Prayer: Letters to Malcolm* (London: Fount, 1964), 71. *Letters to Malcolm* by CS Lewis © copyright 1963, 1964 CS Lewis Pte Ltd. Extract used with permission. Note that Lewis believes (accurately) that the word "dream" in the last line is too pantheistic.

8

Soteriology: Pneumatological Participation in the Life of God

8.1 Introduction: Salvation Today

Soteriology is the technical term for the doctrine of salvation, and it refers to a cluster of events that span the vast distance of space and time. Salvation acts as an umbrella term, and soteriology is a categorical heading for the work of God toward humans, both archaeologically and eschatologically. Standard treatments of soteriology distinguish between the chronological aspects of salvation and its logical aspects, but in general, soteriology starts in eternity past with the *pactum salutis*, or God's secret and hidden will to create and save human beings, and works through time to key points of human experience that includes regeneration, conversion, justification, sanctification, and final glorification. These various aspects of salvation are often termed the *ordo salutis* or the order of salvation. This *ordo* is then often packaged into one or another theory or model of salvation. Salvation, then, is far broader, richer, and more comprehensive than many immediately think.

What does a TAT have to offer to a discussion of soteriology? Not surprisingly, our answer is, a lot! The work of salvation is rightly and properly trinitarian,[1] and for that reason alone, it is rewarding to ask specifically about the work of the Holy Spirit in human salvation. When this question has been

---

[1] See, for example, Fred Sanders, *Fountain of Salvation: Trinity and Soteriology* (Grand Rapids, MI: Eerdmans, 2021), "the revelation of the triunity of God is tightly bundled with the fulfilment

asked in theology, the answers are often truncated or jaundiced accounts whereby the Spirit applies the benefits of Christ, or the Spirit comes after the real work has been done. To use a sports analogy, it often sounds like Christ is the triumphant team, and the Spirit is the cleanup crew responsible for ensuring the stadium is tidy for the next event. The real action seems to occur with Christ, and the Spirit offers a mere supporting role or afterthought. That is not the biblical way, of course. Other problems have crept into contemporary accounts of soteriology, including a near divorce between the incarnation and the atonement. Still, other issues are evident, most notably, the inability of many accounts of a theory of the atonement to provide a clear and compelling answer to the actual mechanism of atonement used by God to account for human salvation.

This chapter briefly addresses the issues already identified as problems in contemporary discussions of soteriology, and it will bring to the fore a coherent account of salvation from the perspective of the Spirit's work.[2] To achieve this, it will be argued that a Christian doctrine of *theosis* (deification/divinization), properly understood, provides the necessary foundation and framing for a pneumatological account of salvation and, on that basis, key accounts of our union with Christ, sanctification, and the centrality of the cross of Christ come into clearer focus. The chapter concludes with a discussion of one application of this theology: the believer's innate responsibility for their neighbor's salvation. Throughout the discussion, we will draw upon certain scholastic theologians such as Matthias Scheeben, and refer to the work of the Fathers, in order to further establish the fact that TAT is not a theological novelty in the Great Tradition, but is, rather, more of a retrieval of key aspects of orthodoxy that have been eclipsed in recent thought.

8.2 The Spirit and Salvation

As with Chapter 9 on anthropology, so too with soteriology; it has to be grounded in Christology (because it is trinitarian). Various writers have called the church back to this realization, that what we establish in our

---

of God's promises in the gospel, and it is the Father's sending of the Son and the Holy Spirit that accomplishes at the same time the revelation of God as Trinity and the particular salvation accomplished by these three as one, 1".

[2] No attempt to be comprehensive is offered, of course, as that is beyond the scope of this current project.

doctrines of the Trinity and Christology must be consistently applied in our soteriology.[3] Adam Johnson rightly informs us that "it is the business of the doctrine of the atonement to unpack the reality of God's triune life as basis for God's saving activity in Christ."[4] No one has said this as clearly, perhaps, as Khaled Anatolios, who cuts behind so-called atonement theories to locate the normative criteria that lie at the foundation of an understanding of the atonement. Anatolios writes, "One of the most significant manifestations of the way that modern soteriological discussion unmoors itself from doctrinal norms and drifts into an unregulated sea of free-floating images and 'models' is that there is typically no attention paid to how a given image or model can be articulated in terms of a two-natures, one-person Chalcedonian framework."[5] And further, when soteriology is attuned to Christology, the "cafeteria buffet of 'soteriological models'" is avoided.[6] The soteriological foundation for the early church was *theosis*, and in what follows, we claim this ancient and conciliar tradition as our foundation too, arguing it is most consistent with our doctrines of the Trinity and Christology, but also with the approach of TAT.[7]

In a work largely focused on Patristic dogmatics, Alexis Torrance writes, "deification is a corollary of the Incarnation and cannot be properly expressed in any other way without grave doctrinal risk."[8] Only Christ is properly divine, and so any talk of deification must take place in him. *Theosis* is, of course, always intimately connected to the work of the Holy Spirit, and so we can legitimately move from a Spirit Christology to a Christological *imago Dei* (anthropology), on to a full-orbed TAT, and into *theosis* as a way of speaking about a TAT soteriology. This works itself into conversion-baptism (or baptism-conversion for non-Baptists), and then into faith, works, sanctification, glorification, and the other aspects of the *ordo salutis*. All stages of the *ordo salutis*, however, are stages of deification, deification being the architectonic motif. This deification is literal, not merely

---

[3] Sanders is correct when he warns that there is "a great deal at stake for theology and the Christian life in grasping this relation correctly," Sanders, *Fountain of Salvation*, 2. He goes on to rightly warn about the dangers of a free-floating and irrelevant doctrine of the Trinity and doctrines of the atonement descending into human inventions captive to historical and cultural forces.
[4] Adam J. Johnson, *Atonement: Guide for the Perplexed* (London: Bloomsbury T&T Clark, 2015), 67.
[5] Anatolios, *Deification through the Cross*, 207.
[6] Anatolios, *Deification through the Cross*, 223.
[7] We are not making the argument that a TAT soteriology *must* adopt a doctrine of *theosis*, but only that a doctrine of *theosis* is the most obvious, compatible, and fruitful way to proceed.
[8] Alexis Torrance, *Human Perfection in Byzantine Theology: Attaining the Fullness of Christ* (Oxford: Oxford University Press, 2020), 32.

metaphorical, or rhetorical, and Torrance is quick to remind readers that *theosis* is as real in humans as it is in Christ: "To say that human deification is 'metaphorical' and never literal would be tantamount to saying that the incarnation itself was 'metaphorical' and not 'literal.' "[9] The incarnation and *theosis* are intimately connected, and they are as real as each other. Torrance explains this in a pro-Chalcedonian way, "Christ's humanity remains intact, even while being truly and *literally* deified by the hypostatic union. While the deification of the Christian is not a 'hypostatic union' in the same sense, it is nonetheless a grafting of the Christian by the grace of the Holy Spirit into the deified humanity of the God-man."[10]

Viewing the topic of salvation through a pneumatological lens brings the theme of union with Christ to the forefront. Indeed, from a pneumatological perspective, *theosis* is God's ultimate unifying goal and intent for humanity. This chapter explores these topics, with particular emphasis on the Spirit's role at the cross, and the implications a pneumatological understanding of salvation has for our present experience of participation in God's life. Viewing soteriology through the lens of the Spirit, perhaps even more than other doctrines, illustrates how each of the *loci* are intricately and intimately pneumatologically intertwined.[11]

Emphasizing the work of the Spirit in salvation, and this time drawing on a neo-Scholastic source, Matthias Scheeben offers a partial description of *theosis* as follows:

> But even this loving relationship of the Holy Spirit to creatures, which the term *donum* expresses, is brought out with far greater force and vividness in the all-embracing, significant name "Spirit." As spirit, as breath of God, we behold Him flowing forth from God's heart over creatures, and entwining a living bond about both. We see Him with all the warmth of His affection penetrating the creature, refreshing him, and filling him with ineffable rapture. We behold Him communicating the ardor of His love to creatures; and from the light of the Son from whom He proceeds we see Him transferring to creatures glowing sparks of divine knowledge, and fanning them to brilliant flame. We perceive Him flooding the creature with His own vital energy,

---

[9] Torrance, *Human Perfection in Byzantine Theology*, 33. It is equally clear in Scripture, the tradition, and in this work that this *does not* mean that humans literally become like the immanent Trinity or become full persons of the Godhead. That is heresy. Instead, the use of "literal" clearly indicates that the extent of Christ's deification is extended to those human creatures who participate in him. In Christ, we become "sons" too!

[10] Torrance, *Human Perfection in Byzantine Theology*, 34. (Italics in original.)

[11] For this reason, Sanders calls the doctrine of the atonement one of two "mega-doctrines" of the Christian faith (the other mega-doctrine is the Trinity). Sanders, *Fountain of Salvation*, 57.

freeing him from death and corruption, and filling him with immortal life. We recognize Him finally, in St. Bernard's words, as the *osculum suavissimum* [the sweetest kiss] in which God seals the bond of love with the creatures He has favored with His grace.[12]

Scheeben is here repeating a recurrent but largely forgotten theme of the tradition, that salvation, when viewed especially through the lens of the Spirit, emphasizes our total union with Christ such that the blessed exchange is operative: Christ became human so that humans might become divine. Scheeben elaborates on the point that salvation is theotic, because "the natural filiation of the Son of God, which is the exemplar, is at the same time God's motive for making us His adoptive children."[13] Furthermore, "the doctrine of the generation of the Son of God from the Father provides us with the key to the understanding of our elevation to the status of children of God."[14] Scheeben rightly, as established above, is careful to ground soteriology in the Trinity and Christology. To labor the point, Theology Proper (the doctrine of God) is to norm and form our soteriology.[15] Grounding salvation in the missions and processions of the Son and Spirit is crucial if soteriology is to keep its dogmatic shape. First, the mission of the Son is commensurate with his eternal procession from the Father. Because he is the eternal Son, his mission in the world is to make us adopted "sons" too. The incarnate Son unites us to himself and brings us before his Father in this salvific and beatitudinal move, we are recreated, regenerated, and renewed, crying "Abba, Father!" What is true of the Son eternal and by nature, is not true of believers by grace and adoption as we live and move and have our being in God (Acts 17:28), by which is surely meant, in Christ and the Spirit. In the words of Sanders, "all the long lines of the life in Christ reach up toward the life of God in himself."[16]

Because the processions and the missions of the Son and Spirit are thoroughly and necessarily coordinated, we cannot speak of one without speaking of the other. "The classical Christian view grounds the coherence of the economy in the coherence of the Trinity."[17] For this reason, *theosis/salvation* is not only established in the procession (and mission) of the Son but also the procession (and mission) of the Spirit:

---

[12] Scheeben, *The Mysteries of Christianity*, 110.
[13] Scheeben, *The Mysteries of Christianity*, 142.
[14] Scheeben, *The Mysteries of Christianity*, 142.
[15] The language of norm and form comes from Sanders, *Fountain of Salvation*, 89.
[16] Sanders, *Fountain of Salvation*, 90.
[17] Sanders, *Fountain of Salvation*, 95.

for this relationship essentially includes the procession of the Holy Spirit in whom the Father and the Son seal their unity, and is adequately knowable only in connection with this procession. Since the entire Trinity forms one single, indivisible organism, the significance which we ascribe to any one phase of it must be attributed to the whole, and consequently at least indirectly to the other phases.[18]

In fact, because salvation comes to creatures by way of gift and love, it has more in common with the spiration of the Spirit than the procession of the Son.[19] Gift and love are used here, of course, in reference to the "names" given to the Holy Spirit in the Tradition.[20] While Scheeben's point is surely correct, that salvation has as much to do with the Spirit's procession (and mission) as the Son's, his point has rarely been accepted or even developed. This has contributed to the eclipse of pneumatology in dogmatic discourse and is again, an impetus for the work of TAT.[21]

The Son's procession is by way of natural necessity "whereas we as adoptive children participate in that nature not by generation but through sheer love and grace."[22] In God, this is most clearly seen in the spiration of the Spirit. The Spirit communicates to the creature the love of God shared between the Father and the Son, and in that communication, the Spirit imitates his own spiration in our deification.[23] By analogy, *theosis* acts like a wax seal whereby the Son is the signet ring or the stamp, he is the original image of the owner or authority, and his image is recreated in others. The

---

[18]Scheeben, *The Mysteries of Christianity*, 143. Sanders refers to this same thing as a work of "triangulation," Sanders, *Fountain of Salvation*, 110.
[19]Scheeben, *The Mysteries of Christianity*, 143.
[20]While there is a prehistory to these names, they take their theological impetus from the work of Augustine in book 5 of his *De Trinitate*.
[21]For his part, Sanders repeatedly makes the point that the processions and missions of the Son *and the Spirit* are crucial for a proper trinitarian account of salvation, and yet in his chapter dedicated to the eternal procession of the Spirit, he mounts an argument against any form of TAT, arguing that the activity of the Spirit is (merely?) to deepen what we already know, in fact, "nothing changes, but everything is better when pneumatology is explicated last," Sanders, *Fountain of Salvation*, 125. TAT will have to repeatedly confront challenges such as those from Sanders, who argues, "the point is that while it is wrong to neglect the Holy Spirit, it is also wrong to belabor pneumatology in a distracting way, or to attempt to lay a pneumatological foundation in the first moves of systematic theology," Sanders, *Fountain of Salvation*, 126. We clearly disagree and offer the present work, among many others, as proof of concept.
[22]Scheeben, *The Mysteries of Christianity*, 143. John seems to allude to this very reality when in John 1:13 the rebirth of believers is in spiritual parallel to the supernatural birth of the Son in Matt 1:18. John connects these events in John 3:3 when speaking to Nicodemus about the need to be born again/from above.
[23]See Scheeben, *The Mysteries of Christianity*, 145.

Spirit is the fire making the wax melt and be receptive to the seal or image of the authority. The Father is the authority or owner, the one who wears the signet ring that bears his image and presence.[24] "When God graciously adopts us as His children and truly unites us to Himself in a most intimate manner by the grace of sonship which, as participation in the divine nature is a very real entity, He gives us Himself, His own essence, as the object of our delight."[25]

In our account of salvation as *theosis*, we are being consistent with what has been established in the doctrines of the Trinity and Christology, and on that basis, extending the discussion into soteriology. To further cite Scheeben, "In the Holy Spirit and through Him we embrace the Son and the Father, who had sent Him to us as the pledge of their love and happiness; with Him and through Him our thoughts and our love are raised to the enjoyment of those persons from whom He proceeds."[26] Further, "we shall perceive that by dwelling in our soul as a guest the Holy Spirit is in a most exalted and marvellous manner not only the efficient and exemplary cause, but in a certain sense also the formal cause of our supernatural sanctity, of our dignity as sons of God, and of our union with the divine persons."[27] This, Scheeben reminds us, is the consistent position of the church catholic, and what is so useful about Scheeben's work is the way he is able to highlight the specific work of the Spirit in the process. "We are made like the natural Son of God not only because we are conformable to Him, but most of all because we personally possess within ourselves the very same Spirit that He possesses; and our union with the heavenly Father is so glorious because of the fact that He has incorporated His own Spirit in us."[28] Even Sanders, no advocate of TAT, is able to affirm these same basic contours of a Spirit Christology, as seen, for instance, when he writes, "The Holy Spirit does more than tutor us in the way of Jesus. He bears witness to us about Jesus by dwelling in us as the Spirit of Christ. Because we have the Spirit, we have Christ and the promise of life in him."[29] Further, in his gloss on Rom 8:15 and our adopted sonship,

---

[24]The analogy was inspired by Scheeben, but it is not one he uses. Scheeben, *The Mysteries of Christianity*, 146.
[25]Scheeben, *The Mysteries of Christianity*, 159.
[26]Scheeben, *The Mysteries of Christianity*, 160–1.
[27]Scheeben, *The Mysteries of Christianity*, 167.
[28]Scheeben, *The Mysteries of Christianity*, 169.
[29]Sanders, *Fountain of Salvation*, 143.

Sanders states, "as sons, the Son includes us in his Spirit-anointed, Spirit-directed mission to draw all people to himself."[30]

The eclipse of the Spirit, as chronicled in the early chapters of this work, has effects well beyond the doctrine of the Trinity; it has distorted the entire theological narrative. TAT is a concerted attempt to get back to orthodoxy and, perhaps surprisingly, getting back to orthodoxy makes our theology remarkably contemporary! In summary fashion, Scheeben is once more a helpful guide when he writes,

> Thus the soul, joined by the Holy Spirit to the Son as sister and bride, and to the Father as child, is taken up by the same Holy Spirit into intimate communion, into the fellowship and company of both, into the wonderful fellowship of the Father and the Son, which St. John depicts as the purpose of the Incarnation [1 John 1:3].[31]

This is the overarching vision of salvation offered to us in the Good News of Jesus Christ. When we fail to incorporate a robust pneumatology into our soteriology, we end up with etiolated and functional accounts of salvation. What TAT offers is a relational, Christological, and trinitarian account of salvation that eschews the dualist and bifurcated theologies of contemporary Christianity; those that tend to separate the incarnation from atonement, separate the person from the work of Christ, and separate the work of the Son from that of the Spirit. As St. Symeon the New Theologian once expressed it, *theosis* is the reality, experience, and hope of being "wholly God" by communion with God through participation in Christ by the Spirit.[32]

8.3 The Spirit and Atonement

It is a constant temptation in discussions of soteriology to fall into one of two errors. The first error is to focus so much on the saving significance of the incarnation that the work of Christ on the cross is either glossed over or simply left out. The second error is to focus so much on the passion of Christ and the place of the cross that the saving significance of the life of

---

[30]Sanders, *Fountain of Salvation*, 143.
[31]Scheeben, *The Mysteries of Christianity*, 171–2.
[32]See St. Symeon the New Theologian, *Hymn* 50.184-202, cited in Torrance, *Human Perfection in Byzantine Theology*, 119.

Christ is either glossed over or simply left out. While a caricature, it is said that the Fathers tended toward the first error and the Reformers toward the second. Without adjudicating this debate in detail, it is our conviction that a robust incarnational soteriology must be the foundation for any account of the atoning work of Christ on the cross, and that has been the approach in this chapter.[33] We do, however, come to the point of speaking directly of the work of atonement and the place of the cross, with a special focus on the work of the Spirit in relation to the passion of Christ.

As with the person of Christ (a Spirit Christology), we need to develop a properly Spiritual theology of the atonement. As Sanders avers, "If the problem God poses in the Old Testament is, How can the Spirit of the holy God dwell among the sinful people? the answer of the New Testament is, incarnation and atonement."[34] Within the conditions of a fallen world and the corollary of that world, sinful creatures, God must not only become human so that humans may become divine; he must also atone for the sin that separates unholy creatures from an all-holy God. In Sanders's words, "atonement serves indwelling."[35] Still further, Sanders correctly states that "a trinitarian soteriology would be a two-handed doctrine of salvation that attended to the pervasive presence of the Son and the Holy Spirit across this whole span from the *historia salutis*, through the *ordo salutis*, to the shape of a Christian life that follows from them."[36] The shape the Christian life takes will be dealt with in the chapter on theological anthropology. What remains in this chapter is to sketch the contours of a TAT theology of the passion of Christ.

There is a near consensus in theological studies that we have too often been captive to one or another so-called theory or model of the atonement, and that has blinded us to the richness of the biblical testimony to the saving work of Christ.[37] Another near truism in biblical studies is that the biblical witness to the saving work of Christ clusters around a constellation of images and metaphors that seek to explain what Tom Greggs rightly calls the "breadth of salvation."[38] These motifs and metaphors cannot be reduced to a single

---

[33]Tom Greggs helpfully reminds us that while atonement models are good, we must remember that it is not the model itself that saves but "Jesus Christ in his self-sacrificial life, death, resurrection, and ascension is the basis of salvation," *The Breadth of Salvation: Rediscovering the Fullness of God's Saving Work* (Grand Rapids, MI: Baker Academic, 2020), 2–3.
[34]Sanders, *Fountain of Salvation*, 144.
[35]Sanders, *Fountain of Salvation*, 144.
[36]Sanders, *Fountain of Salvation*, 145.
[37]See Johnson, *Atonement: Guide for the Perplexed*.
[38]Greggs, *The Breadth of Salvation*.

atonement model as none is able to do justice to the whole.[39] This does not mean we are left with a collage of images that are mutually exclusive of each other or that are unable to come together to form a coherent whole.[40] Instead, the various models of the atonement are localized, specific, contextual comments relevant to a time and place, but they are not strong enough or broad enough to provide the foundations for the atonement edifice. Instead, what has been argued here is that Trinity and Christology are that broad and foundational base and upon these, we can see how specific aspects of the atonement found in the various models are able to be incorporated into the superstructure that is the atoning work of Christ.[41]

What, specifically, does a TAT add to the picture? Once more, at the risk of over-repetition, what is offered here, and in a TAT more generally, is a partial contribution to the dogmatic task of explicating and applying the biblical witness. Much could be said about justification by faith alone, or election and predestination, and so forth. These are important, but selectivity and focus are in order, and due to the constraints of this chapter we will focus only on those aspects of atonement most informed by a TAT perspective. A TAT soteriology highlights the work of the Spirit in the passion of Christ and then beyond that in its application and realisation in human lives, what has often been termed our *sanctification*. Sanctification is considered in the chapter on theological anthropology; the passion is considered here.

In relation to the Spirit and the passion of Christ, Thomas Smail insightfully notes that "Where this relationship has not been recognised and grasped … [people] rightly judge that anything, however experientially exciting, however edifying the gifts that it may have brought to light, which is not centrally anchored in Calvary and Easter is suspect in the extreme, and might well prove little more than a distraction and diversion from the main Christian concern

---

[39]See the historically sensitive and helpful work by Willian G. Witt and Joel Scandrett, *Mapping Atonement: The Doctrine of Reconciliation in Christian History and Theology* (Grand Rapids, MI: Baker Academic, 2022).

[40]This is essentially what Joel Green argued for when he proposed a "kaleidoscopic" model of the atonement! Joel Green, "Kaleidoscopic View," in *The Nature of the Atonement: Four Views* (ed. James Beilby and Paul R. Eddy; Downers Grove, IL: IVP Academic, 2006), 157–85. While popular, this fails to do justice to the biblical testimony and the ordered and wholistic work of Christ. Better, but still metaphorically wrong, is Joshua M. McNall, *The Mosaic of Atonement: An Integrated Approach to Christ's Work* (Grand Rapids, MI: Zondervan Academic, 2019).

[41]Johnson helpfully comments, "Perhaps atonement theories, rather than being seen as competing to offer a comprehensive and sufficient account of the work of Christ, are best understood as mutually complementary accounts of different aspects of the work of Christ, which together work to fill out the substance of the doctrine," Johnson, *Atonement: Guide for the Perplexed*, 5.

with the crucified and risen Lord."[42] Smail was talking about the Charismatic renewal, but he could just as easily have been talking about TAT. The same is true, today that many "raise questions about how this new emphasis on the Spirit is connected with the Saviourhood of Jesus."[43] The following offers a brief reply to such concerns, showing how the Spirit is intimately connected to the passion of Christ and that "a Spirit who could derogate from the glory of Christ crucified in order to promote a more dazzling glory of his own, who passes by the sufferings of Christ in order to offer us a share in a painless and costless triumph, is certainly not the Holy Spirit of the New Testament."[44]

The Gospel writers are of one accord in framing the account of Jesus' life and work within a pneumatological frame. Adopting what in Spirit Christology are termed "Messianic *kairoi*,"[45] Jesus' mission begins with his conception by the Holy Spirit and concludes with the crowning event of his coronation-exaltation when he sends the Spirit at Pentecost. The climax of that story is the Passion of Christ, and this, too, must be read in light of the framing and foundational work of the Spirit. Three events are especially important here: Gethsemane, the crucifixion, and the resurrection of Jesus. When these events are read with an awareness of the Spirit's presence in Jesus' life, we are led to reflect on what has been called a *pneumatological crucis* or a "pneumatology of the cross," which complements the more familiar *theologia crucis* developed by Martin Luther and many after him.[46]

The night before being crucified, Christ withdrew to the nearby Garden of Gethsemane, where he purposed to pray. Prayer, we know from the rest of the New Testament, is a Spirit-inspired and Spirit-enabled activity whereby we come before the Father. Jesus taught his disciples to pray the way he did, with the "our Father" prayer, applying his relationship with the Father by the Spirit to them as they participate in Christ. So here, in Gethsemane, Jesus prays in the Spirit to his Abba (Mark 14:36). Here in a Garden, Christ is reciprocating the Father's words from his Baptism, "You are my beloved Son," with the call of his beloved (Abba) Father. The Spirit is present in the garden, resting on Jesus, mediating the presence of the Father in his time of

---

[42]Thomas A. Smail, *Reflected Glory: The Spirit in Christ and Christians* (London: Hodder and Stoughton, 1975), 104.
[43]Smail, *Reflected Glory*, 104.
[44]Smail, *Reflected Glory*, 105.
[45]Habets, *The Anointed Son*, 118–85.
[46]For background comments and a detailed discussion, see Habets, *The Anointed Son*, 162–70. Also worth consulting is Carolyn E. L. Tan, *The Spirit at the Cross: Exploring a Cruciform Pneumatology: An Investigation into the Holy Spirit's Role at the Cross* (Eugene, OR: Wipf and Stock, 2019).

anguish and trouble (Mark 14:33). One can only presume that with the final prayer of Jesus in this text where he conforms his human will to that will of God (Matt 26:39, 42, 44), that he experienced that "peace that passes all understanding" of which Paul spoke (Phil 4:7); surely here, a gift of the Spirit (Rom 14:17; Gal 5:22).

It is hard to imagine the Gethsemane scene without considering Jesus' earlier conversation with his cousin John in Matt 11:2–15. On that occasion, John is about to lose his life in a gruesome and traumatic way for maintaining righteousness in the face of evil. Here, Jesus is praying and spending time with some of his disciples in isolation, and he is working hard to bring his own will into conformity with that of his Father. He knows what he must do, and he knows he will do it, but he needs a word of pastoral reassurance. I hope this sounds familiar. Here, with John the Baptist, we see the same situation Jesus faces in Gethsemane: John is about to lose his life as an innocent victim, and the death will be gruesome and traumatic, he is with his disciples in isolation (he is imprisoned), he is praying, and he is conforming his human will to the Father's. John sends disciples to Jesus to ask if he is the Messiah as he needs a pastoral word of reassurance. John knows Jesus is the Messiah; he has testified to it, he has baptized him, and he has witnessed the inauguration of Christ's public ministry. He knows; now he wants to know again. Jesus replies to John's disciples, "Go and report to John what you hear and see: the blind receive sight and the lame walk, the lepers are cleansed and the deaf hear, the dead are raised up, and the poor have the Gospel preached to them, and blessed is he who does not take offence at me" (Matt 11:4–6). John's disciples reported to him these words, and what John undoubtedly heard was: Yes. Yes. Yes! I am the Coming One, the Messiah, the Suffering Servant, the One! And John, I am sure, went to his death not in happiness but with the "peace that passes all understanding" (Phil 4:7). So too with Jesus as with John. He is aware of the intimate connection he has with his Abba, the Spirit mediates to him the presence of the Father, and he is settled, "not my will but yours be done" (Mark 14:36). The next day, Jesus, I am sure, went to his death not in happiness but with the "peace that passes all understanding" (Phil 4:7). The Gethsemane account concludes with Jesus' declaration, "the hour has come, behold the Son of Man is being betrayed into the hands of sinners" (Mark 14:41). Without the Spirit, Gethsemane could have gone very differently. Instead, the Spirit prepares Jesus for the task ahead.

Textual clues to the Spirit's presence, empowering, and operation in the passion of Christ are numerous and include at least the following: Luke 12:50

and the metaphorical use of baptism for his passion alluding back to his Spirit baptism in the Jordan; Rom 8:26 and the intercession of the Spirit in our weakness; Heb 9:14 and the explicit association of the Spirit with the Passion; 1 Cor 15:35 where Christ is said to live in the life-making Spirit; Rom 8:11 the Spirit raised Christ from the dead and gives life to our mortal bodies; 1 Cor 15:45 where, in his resurrection, Christ became a life-giving Spirit; 2 Cor 13:14 wherein the Spirit is the bond of fellowship and participation between Christ and creatures; and Eph 1:14 which teaches believers are sealed by Christ with the Holy Spirit that sealed Christ in the first place. But these are not all. When we start looking, the evidence mounts up.

In 1975, Thomas Smail outlined a catena of texts that frame the cross in a pneumatological light.[47] First, Smail focused on the Gospel of John and noted the following. In John 7:37-39, Jesus calls the thirsty to come and drink and receive rivers of living water, after which "the author breaks in with a remarkable editorial insertion, in which he seems to futurise and relocate the promise … by explaining that its fulfilment belongs … to the ministry of the ascended Lord" when he would pour out the Holy Spirit upon believers. This will happen as a consequence of the cross (John 16:7) after Jesus has been "lifted up" (John 3:14; 12:32, 34). As Smail concludes, "all three terms [glorification, going away, lifted up] refer to the whole series of events—cross, Easter, ascension, his being lifted up on the cross to die, his being lifted up from the grace to live, his being lifted up to the Father to reign—and it is upon the completion of that series of events that the release of the Spirit depends."[48] John 16:7 affirms the same thing, "the fruit of the cross is the coming of the Spirit."[49] John 19:30 records the cry of Christ from the cross, "it is finished," after which Jesus bows his head and dies as the Spirit leaves him. For Smail, this is significant. *Paredoken to pneuma*—"he gave up his Spirit"—is odd language. Smail, with others, sees in this language a reference to Jesus passing on or handing over his Spirit to the disciples, specifically Mary and John, who were at the foot of the cross. Linking this episode with the earlier words of Jesus in John 7:37-39, the rivers of living water that Jesus would impart is "pictured" at the cross in the wound Jesus sustains from the soldier who pierced his side and blood and *water* flowed forth, "water and the Spirit are one."[50]

---

[47]Smail, *Reflected Glory*, 106-12.
[48]Smail, *Reflected Glory*, 106.
[49]Smail, *Reflected Glory*, 106.
[50]Smail, *Reflected Glory*, 108.

Many more texts can be appealed to in order to make the same point.[51] Smail cites John Taylor by way of summary, and so do we:

> What was the Holy Spirit doing at Calvary? First, in a mystery that we cannot plumb, he must have been about his eternal employ between the Father and the Son, holding each in awareness of the other, in an agony of bliss and love that must for ever lie infinitely beyond our understanding. For Jesus this included both the forsakenness and the ultimate trust … But, beyond the inwardness of the Trinity, the Spirit of communion spilled out into other awareness; his concern for others, surpassing the pain, and their deepening perception of him. The thief's and the centurion's recognition … was the start of a turning of eyes that has been going on ever since.[52]

Finally, for our purposes, we note the resurrection and how the Spirit is the power of the resurrection and the empowering presence of God released also by the resurrection of Christ. In Rom 8:11, the Spirit is the power of Christ's resurrection and the resurrection of those who believe in Christ; 1 Cor 15 is, of course, the *locus classicus* on the resurrection—there the work of the Son and Spirit are perfectly coordinated (1 Cor 15:45). Christ here becomes the "life-giving Spirit" (*pneuma zoopoioun*), the creative source of life for others, the one who can impart the Spirit beyond measure, in fulfillment of the Old Testament prophecies. Christ, raised by the Spirit, now raises others into a new spiritual birth and then, eventually, into a bodily resurrection. Christ's risen body has become, in the words of Smail, "completely plastic to the operations of the Spirit, has become 'spiritual,' *pneumatikon*, restored to the incorruptibility and immortality which were God's original design for it."[53] Christ is now, and we too will one day be, that oxymoron, a *pneuma somatikon*, a spiritual creature, made like Christ, fit for the kingdom, infused with the Spirit, and able to participate in the divine life (*theosis*).[54] Between now and then, between salvation inaugurated and salvation consummated, we, as Eph 1:14 makes clear, are "sealed with

---

[51] For his part, Smail includes a brief discussion of Pauline texts that support this same reading, including Gal 3:13–14 and Rom 8. Smail, *Reflected Glory*, 110–12.

[52] Smail, *Reflected Glory*, 114–15, citing John V. Taylor, *The Go-Between God* (London: SCM, 1972), 102.

[53] Smail, *Reflected Glory*, 121.

[54] This idea, and language close to it, comes from Clive S. Lewis, *A Grief Observed* (London: Faber and Faber, 1966), 61, where he writes that God's grand plan is "To make an organism which is also a spirit; to make that terrible oxymoron, a 'spiritual animal.' To take a poor primate, a beast with nerve-endings all over it, a creature with a stomach that wants to be filled, a breeding animal that wants its mate, and say, 'Now get on with it. Become a god.'"

the promised Holy Spirit, which is the first instalment (*arrabōn*) of our inheritance, until we acquire possession of it."

The empowering presence of the Spirit in Jesus' life becomes the paradigm for the presence of the Spirit in the salvation of others. When attuned to the work of the Spirit in salvation, the doctrine of union with Christ is a natural emphasis. Spirit baptism, too, looms large, as does sanctification, as mentioned earlier. For each part of the rich narrative of salvation, the Spirit works with the Son to achieve the Father's good and gracious purposes in creation. As believers participate in Christ by the Spirit, they experience salvation. The Spirit is, as others in the tradition have noted, the *Spiritus sanctus vivificans!*—the life-giving Holy Spirit![55]

8.4 The Weight of Our Neighbor's Glory

In one of his magisterial sermons, C. S. Lewis applied the rich, orthodox, and compelling doctrine of *theosis* to his wartime congregants, where he held out to them the astounding, almost blasphemous promise of the Good News that we are created to be "like God," to be like Christ, to become gods and goddesses—so glorious that, "if you saw it now, you would be strongly tempted to worship … There are no ordinary people. You have never talked to a mere mortal … But it is immortals whom we joke with, work with, marry, snub, and exploit."[56] I am sure this came as both a shock to their "proper Christian sensibilities," as it likely does to some readers of this work, but also a salve to their anxious and depressed state (as we, too, hope our work is for many today). And so, it should have! But Lewis did not merely teach the doctrine of *theosis* as a comfort to people, although it is surely that. He went on to make the important point that we too want to make, that when we existentially experience the truth of Rom 8:38–39, that is, when we too are "convinced that neither death nor life, neither angels nor demons, neither the present nor the future, nor any powers, neither height nor depth,

---

[55]For example, Hildegard of Bingen's Psalm antiphon for the Holy Spirit, D 157r, R 466v (http://www.hildegard-society.org/2014/11/spiritus-sanctus-vivificans-antiphon.html, and https://hlbrm.digitale-sammlungen.hebis.de/handschriften-hlbrm/content/pageview/450567; date of access: March 13, 2023).
[56]Clive S. Lewis, "The Weight of Glory," in *Faith, Christianity, and the Church*. C. S. Lewis Essay Collection (ed. Lesley Walmsley; London: HarperCollins, 2020), 105–6.

nor anything else in all creation, will be able to separate us from the love of God that is in Christ Jesus our Lord," then we too, like Paul, will feel the passionate burden to share the Good News with others.

Worship is the impetus to evangelism, and the more we realize how glorious our salvation is, the more we want to share that with others. And so, Lewis spoke of "the weight of glory" the doctrine of *theosis* creates and how this weight is felt by believers as a burden to share the Good News with others. And so, it should be. Paul was "compelled" to preach the Good News (1 Cor 9:16); "constrained" to pass on the Gospel (2 Cor 5:14–15); he "presumed to not speak of anything except what Christ had accomplished through him" (Rom 15:18); he boasted" only in the Lord (2 Cor 10:17); grace was his motivation to reach others (Eph 3:8); he felt under obligation (an obligation of love, not works!) to preach to the Gentiles (Rom 1:14); and so it goes. Other apostles and disciples could equally be referred to, but in each situation the message is clear, Good News cannot be contained. While evangelism is not the unique terrain of a TAT, a TAT does emphasize the work of the Spirit in Christ recreated in believers and passed from believers to others. Lewis's idea of the weight of glory and the emphasis in TAT that the Spirit is the impetus for all mission are closely related and as such, Lewis's mediation on the weight of our neighbor's glory fits nicely with the approach of TAT.

When Jesus gave the Great Commission (Matt 28:19–20) to go and make disciples, it was not so much a military command to reluctant soldiers as it was an invitation to eager volunteers. Appealing to Lewis, again, he knew this principle well and applied it to the Gospel. "We are told to deny ourselves and to take up our crosses in order that we may follow Christ; and nearly every description of what we shall ultimately find if we do so contains an appeal to desire."[57] Lewis knew that when we receive good news we can't resist passing it on, be it a winning prize, a good diagnosis, a birthday, or receiving a present. Lewis noted that "all enjoyment spontaneously overflows into praise,"[58] and that "just as men spontaneously praise whatever they value, so they spontaneously urge us to join them in praising it: 'Isn't she lovely? Wasn't it glorious? Don't you think it magnificent?' The Psalmists in telling everyone to praise God are doing what all men do when they speak of what they care about."[59] And in true Lewis fashion, he distills these observations

---

[57]Lewis, "The Weight of Glory," 96.
[58]Clive S. Lewis, *Reflections on the Psalms* (Collins, MS: Fount Paperbacks, 1961), 80.
[59]Lewis, *Reflections on the Psalms*, 81.

down into a principle, namely, "I think we delight to praise what we enjoy because the praise not merely expresses but completes the enjoyment; it is its appointed consummation."[60] This is precisely what we see in Scripture and what we need to see again in contemporary Christianity.

Knowing, experiencing, and living into the reality of our union with Christ, being full of the Spirit, and being conformed to the image of Christ from glory to glory should naturally compel those who call themselves Christians to evangelistic activity, to praise, worship, and witness. As the Spirit empowered Jesus' ministry and mission, so too he empowers us to participate in what Christ is doing now in his work in the world. And in response, we, with the angels, clap our hands across our mouth and worship: holy, holy, holy is the Lord God almighty!

A Spirit-saturated soteriology is one that attends to the needs of our neighbor. To the extent that we love one another, we witness God's love for us (1 John 4:7–8). Love for others is the fruit of salvation as sure as the triune God of grace and glory is the fount of salvation. The Spirit, the Other Paraclete given by Christ at Pentecost as part of his great coronation is the divine agent of eschatological hope and realization, at once witnessed in the Eucharist and in the eucharistic lives of the saints on a daily basis. What the Spirit did with and through Christ then, in his life and passion, is what the Spirit does now, in the present, in and through believers. "Now is the time of God's favour, now is the day of salvation" (2 Cor 6:1).

---

[60] Lewis, *Reflections on the Psalms*, 81.

9

Anthropology: The Spirit Reveals and Releases Our True Humanity

9.1 Introduction

Chapter 8 considered the broad contours of a TAT approach to salvation, where the argument was made that *theosis* is the shape a soteriology should take. A second claim was also made, that soteriology and anthropology must be grounded in Christology. Following on from the insight of Spirit Christology that Christ is the clearest revelation to us of what it means to be truly human, this chapter argues that just as it was through the Spirit that Christ's true humanity was both revealed and released, so it is with our humanity. Indeed, our humanity is a pneumatological participation in Christ's humanity. We agree with the conclusion Marc Cortez offers, "if the *Imago* is thoroughly christological, and if Jesus cannot be understood apart from the Spirit, then the *imago* should be thoroughly pneumatological."[1] This chapter explores the pneumatological implications for our humanity, noting particularly what it means to be made in God's image, what true spirituality is, and how ongoing personal transformation occurs. In the words of Tom Smail,

> [Christ] died not just "that we might be forgiven" (our justification), not just "to make us good" (our sanctification), not just "that we might go at last to heaven" (our salvation), but that, in and with all these we might in our new

---

[1] Marc Cortez, "Idols, Images, and a Spirit-ed Anthropology: A Pneumatological Account of the *Imago Dei*," in *Third Article Theology: A Pneumatological Dogmatics* (Minneapolis, MN: Fortress Press, 2016), 281.

humanity be called and equipped to take up his mission and to be witnesses to the drawing near of his kingdom.²

A focused discussion on mission is the subject of Chapter 10. For now, we share Tom Greggs's prescient comment:

> There is a need for the horizontal work of God's salvation to be considered more fully, for a broader account of the continuing work of salvation which the Spirit is undertaking in the time between the ascension of Christ and his return. This is the time of the patience of God; it is the time of God's work of reconciling us to one another; it is the time of the church. God's work of sanctifying us (making us holy in conforming us to Christ Jesus) is a salvific act that reverses the effects of the fall by returning humans to communion, not only with God in Christ, but simultaneously with each other through the saving work of the Holy Spirit.³

Anthropology is not another topic, technically speaking, but is, instead, a further extension of Christology and soteriology with a focus on human life and experience. Sanctification is the term most often associated with this discussion, and we, too, shall take up this theme as part of the discussion. Before this, however, we must establish how anthropology is grounded in Christology and what a TAT adds to this picture. We will conclude the chapter with a brief consideration of how this approach can helpfully inform our considerations of identity. The focus on Christology in the first part of the chapter is deliberate and necessary for the pneumatological implications that follow. In following this Christ-centered approach, we remain consistent with the stated methodology of TAT in Chapter 3, specifically with criteria 6 and 7 that a TAT is focused on Jesus and that his redemptive mission is central to the story of Scripture.

9.2 What Anthropology

Theologians have traditionally not looked to the mass of humanity as the primary means to define what it means to be human.⁴ Seeing

---

²Smail, *Reflected Glory*, 107.
³Tom Greggs, *The Breadth of Salvation: Rediscovering the Fullness of God's Saving Work* (Grand Rapids, MI: Baker Academic, 2020), 41.
⁴See the work of Christian Smith, *What Is a Person? Rethinking Humanity, Social Life, and the Moral Good from the Person Up* (Chicago: University of Chicago Press, 2010), 2–9. Smith's work operates out of a robust Critical Realism.

humanity as fallen, as living east of Eden and faulty, even totally depraved, the phenomenological study of humanity can only result in a partial understanding of who we are, and it cannot address the question of what we are meant to become. Instead of looking at humanity to define human beings, theologians have rightly looked first to Christ and defined actual human beings by his humanity, and only after that have they moved to other forms of anthropological studies. Christ is the archetype of humanity, its creator, template, image, and perfection.[5] In short, it has consistently been argued that anthropology is simply Christology in a minor key. Put more articulately, anthropology must be founded upon Christology. "Theological anthropology is a gift of Christology,"[6] writes Alexis Torrance. Further, "At root, theological anthropology is concerned with the question of the human ideal, an ideal uniquely to be found in and through the person of Jesus Christ."[7] Further still, Torrance rightly identifies problems with starting with other foundations than Christ, for example, the Trinity, when he writes, "absent a thorough Christological orientation to anchor itself, such thinking is at risk of disintegrating into a sentimental application or projection of worldly and hazy concepts of personality and 'community' to both the Godhead and the people of God."[8] Along with the clear testimony of the New Testament and endorsed by the Tradition, with Torrance, we want to "underscore the need for theological anthropology to be methodologically grounded in Christology."[9]

In a Christological anthropology, Jesus Christ is uniquely the image of God—*imago Dei*—and all other humans are images of that image—an *imago Christi*. This is foundational to any formal understanding of theological anthropology.[10] The Son is the eternal image of the Father (Phil 2:6), the Father's radiance and glory (Heb 1:3). With the Son's assumption of an

---

[5]We continue to hold that Christ is the *Archetype* and not, as some suggest, our *Prototype*. A prototype is merely the first model, normally improved upon in successive generations. An archetype is not simply the first but the best or complete, or, in this case, mature instantiation of what it means to be human.
[6]Torrance, *Human Perfection in Byzantine Theology*, 1.
[7]Torrance, *Human Perfection in Byzantine Theology*, 1.
[8]Torrance, *Human Perfection in Byzantine Theology*, 10.
[9]Torrance, *Human Perfection in Byzantine Theology*, 11.
[10]The case for Christological anthropology has been comprehensively argued for by Marc Cortez over the course of several key works, including: *Theological Anthropology: A Guide for the Perplexed* (London: T&T Clark, 2010); *Christological Anthropology in Historical Perspective: Ancient and Contemporary Approaches to Theological Anthropology* (Grand Rapids, MI: Zondervan, 2016); and *Resourcing Theological Anthropology: A Constructive Account of Humanity in the Light of Christ* (Grand Rapids, MI: Zondervan, 2017).

anhypostatic human nature, he becomes incarnate as Jesus the Christ. As such, Christ is the true instantiation of what a human person is most fully like (Col 1:15; Phil 2:7–8). The Son takes to himself a human nature from the (fallen) stock of Adam,[11] and he redeems that nature, turning it back to the will of the Father, through a lifetime of perfect obedience, worship, and sacrifice (Luke 2:52; Heb 5:8).[12] In the resurrection, he genuinely receives a renewed human nature, a perfected one that has new capabilities, not least of which is the capacity to be fully endowed with and pervaded by the Holy Spirit, able to stand in the presence of the triune God accepted and unmediated, gloriously reflecting God's radiance in human form.[13] Jesus is thus the archetype of our humanity and its completion; he is the Alpha and the Omega, the last Adam (1 Cor 15:45), and the person all humans were created to be conformed to, from glory to glory (1 Cor 15:20, 42–44).

When anthropology is viewed in this way, as a subset of Christology, if we can put it that way, then the biblical narrative makes more sense than when Christians attempt to define what being human is with recourse to a generic idea of community or some such. The first parents, Adam and Eve, were proleptically created in the image of Christ and were charged to grow into the maturity of the incarnate Son (the *Logos incarnandus*). Because Christ is the incarnate Son of God (the *Logos incarnatus*), he is the only one perfectly able to image God in human nature, and so he shows us what it means to be a human, fully alive and mature, in right relationship with God, with creatures, with creation, and with himself. Now, all people are to be conformed to his image and in that conformation, we image God. We, however, image God as the body of Christ (*imago Christi*), of which Christ is the head; Christ images God as "the image of the invisible God" (*imago Dei*), the one of whom it "was the Father's good pleasure for all the fullness to dwell in him" (Col 1:15, 19).

What of the Spirit? As a full, genuine, and mature human person, Christ relies on the Spirit at all points of the incarnation; we, too, must do the same. It is the Spirit that gives physical life (Gen 2:7; Matt 1:18), it is the Spirit that

---

[11] See Habets, "The Fallen Humanity of Christ," 18–44. The assumption of a fallen human nature is not required in a TAT, but it is conducive to it.

[12] See Habets, "Spirit Christology and the Power of Jesus."

[13] The argument is not developed here; we simply note that for many who argue that Christ assumed a perfect(ed) human nature, a pristine nature unaffected by the fall, it is hard to see how they can affirm a genuine resurrection of Christ, and not simply some form of resuscitation. However, if Christ does assume a fallen human nature and redeems it through his life and death, then he is genuinely resurrected and is the first fruit of our resurrection to come, as Paul promised (1 Cor 15:20).

gives spiritual life (John 3:3,5), and it is the Spirit that gives resurrected life (Phil 3:21; 1 Cor 15:42). And in between, we live our lives in the Spirit (Rom 8:9-11; Gal 6:8). The Holy Spirit is essential to Jesus' life (Spirit Christology) and hence, essential to ours too as *imago Christi*. We owe the Spirit our physical, spiritual, emotional, psychological, and new life. The Pentecostal outpouring of the Spirit on the church is the means by which believers can live in Christ and become like Christ. To be Christlike is to be filled with the Spirit (Eph 5:18) and display the fruit of the Spirit (Gal 5:22–23), enabled by the gifts of the Spirit (1 Cor 12:4–11).

One further point to be made is the relationship between *theosis*, Christ, the Spirit, and the believer. In the chapter on salvation, we made a case for theotic soteriology; here, in anthropology, that same theme is extended into the concrete particulars of a life that is being deified. We have already considered Christ's life (Spirit Christology) here that is extended to believers as they participate in Christ by the Spirit and are made like the Son (Rom 8:29); as we are transformed into his image from glory to glory (2 Cor 3:18), in mind (Rom 12:2; Col 3:10), body (1 Cor 15:49), and life/activity (Eph 1:4). In numerous places in Holy Scripture, we are promised that we shall become like the incarnate Son. The extent of our likeness to Christ has been debated, but it seems clear that we should take a maximal view of this teaching and assert that we will become as receptive to God in our humanity as Jesus was (and is) in his. This means that our selves, our bodies, and rational souls are increasingly made porous to the Holy Spirit, receptive to his empowering presence, changing us from the inside out.

One telling episode that lays out this promise in startling ways is the transfiguration of Christ (Matt 17:1–8//Luke 9:28–36//Mark 9:2–8).[14] We are no doubt familiar with the transfiguration of Jesus on the mountain, but we often miss the important detail, highlighted in Luke 9:34, that the three disciples also entered the cloud of God's presence on the mountain. This was no virtual event. They were not simply aloof, far off, and separated. They entered the transfiguration act itself. No longer sleepy observers, they became active participants. Here, we have a prophetic enactment. In the disciples being taken into this event, into the glory cloud of God's presence, we see the anticipation of the church—each of us together—being taken into Christ by the Spirit, and in Christ by the Spirit, we are brought before the

---

[14] On the theological significance of the transfiguration, see Thomas G. Weinandy, *Jesus Becoming Jesus: A Theological Interpretation of the Synoptic Gospels* (Washington, DC: Catholic University of America Press, 2018), 227–39.

Father and made children of God, adopted, heirs (co-heirs with Christ!), acceptable, and loved. And our only response, like the disciples, is to fall prostrate and worship, and then to rise and extend that worship into good works. In Jesus' exodus through the cross to the resurrection and into the Kingdom of God, we, too, find our place. In Christ, as the risen Son, we will enter the new covenant relationship with the Father, empowered by the Spirit, to obey the new law written on our hearts, and we will happily abide within the Kingdom of God. As the disciples were drawn into the cloud of God's glory and presence, so too the Spirit draws us into Christ and his Father, into glory, and into the kingdom that will never end.

A final word on theological anthropology in general, as it relates to a specific TAT agenda, has to do with the notion of "transcendental determinism." The term was coined by Thomas F. Torrance and is meant to communicate the fact that humans are created with an inbuilt trajectory for growth and maturity into the fullness of Christ.[15] In Torrance's work, as here in ours, transcendental determinism is a correlate of *theosis* and functions as a way to describe the elevation of humanity from infancy to maturity, from human being to genuine human personhood. Echoing themes found already in Irenaeus, humans are created as infants whom God fully intended to develop into mature, Christlike adults.[16] The essential key to transcendence is the presence and work of the Holy Spirit, who "impels the human movement toward God," a movement adequately "characterised as *theosis*."[17] Throughout the life of the believer, the Spirit is recreating people and conforming them to the person of the incarnate Son. This is our anthropology (true nature), *theosis*, our salvation, and the character of the Christian life. Anthropology, or being human, is, according to TAT, the work of the Spirit making believers Christlike. What follows is a brief reflection on part of that process, typically termed sanctification, followed by a reflection on identity.

---

[15] See Thomas F. Torrance, "The Soul and Person in Theological Perspective," in *Religion, Reason, and the Self: Essays in Honour of Hywel D. Lewis* (ed. S. R. Sutherland and T. A. Roberts; Cardiff: University of Wales Press, 1989), 103–18. For a discussion of the concept, see Myk Habets, *Theosis in the Theology of Thomas F. Torrance* (Farnham: Ashgate, 2009), 39, 41, 44.

[16] For Irenaeus' elevation-line anthropology, see his *On the Apostolic Preaching*, St. Vladimir's Popular Patristics Series No. 17 (trans. John Behr; Crestwood: St Vladimir's Seminary Press, 1997), 47, 48, where humanity at creation is described as "very little," "infant," having an "innocent and childlike mind."

[17] Habets, *Theosis in the Theology of Thomas F. Torrance*, 37. Where people do not move toward God due to their sinful decisions, transcendental determinism is replaced by self-determinism.

9.3 Sanctification: Or, toward Becoming a *soma pneumatikon*

While the biblical teaching on sanctification is not entirely consumed with the progressive aspects of a believer becoming holy, that is the concern of this section. Don Payne has convincingly pointed out that "our theology of growth and transformation, both conceptually and practically, will be only as good as our theology of accomplished sanctification."[18] This section takes for granted our accomplished sanctification and keeps together, as Calvin so clearly argued, the *duplex gratia* or double grace of justification and sanctification, such that the life of good works and conformity to Christ is established in Christ by the Spirit, and it is subsequently worked out by grace through faith. As Calvin wrote, "sanctified by Christ's Spirit we may cultivate blamelessness and purity of life."[19] Any discussion of the Christian life has to be based on this solid foundation of the finished work of Christ and the believers' participation in that ongoing ministry of Christ by the Spirit if it is not to fall into either the heresy of Pelagianism (and the various categories of semi-Pelagianism) or its opposite, lawlessness (cheap grace). Payne helpfully reminds us that "sanctification is far more than, and far more robust than, a repackaged version of moral improvement, a weight that makes followers of Jesus sag and sigh when reminded of it. It is more than deepened spiritual impulses, inclinations, and sensibilities. It is integral to God's overall work of redemption."[20] Through our union with Christ, believers live their lives in intimate relationship with Christ and the Spirit to the glory of the Father.

Because anthropology is grounded in Christology, the Christian life is also grounded in Christ's life. As such, Christ's sanctification is the basis for the believer's sanctification. "The sanctification of all disciples depends on Jesus's sanctification," writes Payne, reflecting on John 17:17–19, "because he assumed our humanity and made the way—in every conceivable and necessary way—for us to be restored to God. He is the Sanctified One with

---

[18]Don J. Payne, *Already Sanctified: A Theology of the Christian Life in Light of God's Completed Work* (Grand Rapids, MI: Baker Academic, 2020), 5. With Payne, we acknowledge that *sanctification* may not be the correct technical term to describe the Christian's progress in growth and holiness; however, we use the term here for two reasons. First, pragmatically, this is the term that we have inherited; and second, *sanctification* still correctly signals our being made holy, and so it is appropriate to use, with qualifications, for a believer's growth and transformation.
[19]Calvin, *Institutes of the Christian Religion*, 3.11.1 (725).
[20]Payne, *Already Sanctified*, 71.

whom believers are united through the Holy Spirit and, therefore, benefit from a sanctification that is both participative and derived."[21] Christ asks nothing of us that he has not already accomplished himself. Paul informs us in 1 Cor 1:30 that Christ is our sanctification, and we must take that seriously.[22]

Further developing the foundations of our sanctification in Christ, Thomas Torrance applies these insights to believers in his well-known theology of the vicarious ministry of Christ and the Spirit. Atoning reconciliation includes "the whole of our Lord's incarnate life from his cradle to his grave in which, as one of us and one with us, he shared all our experiences, overcoming our disobedience through his obedience and sanctifying every stage of human life, and thereby vivified and restored our humanity to communion with God."[23] Through Christ's sanctification, we, too, find our sanctification in him as the Spirit unites us to Christ. In Christ, the Spirit was perfectly receptive and operative, empowering Christ for a life of obedience, worship, and service to the Father such that "God highly exalted him" (Phil 2:9).

With Torrance, we too say, "Here let Gregory Nazianzen speak for Nicene theology," before citing his *Theological Orations*:

> Let us become like Christ, since Christ became like us. Let us become divine for his sake, since he for ours became man. He assumed the worst that he might give us the better; he became poor that we through his poverty might be rich; he took upon himself the form of a servant that we might receive back our liberty; he came down that we might be exalted; he was tempted that we might conquer; he was dishonored that he might glorify us; he ascended that he might draw us to himself, who were lying low in the fall of sin. Let us give all, to him who gave himself a ransom and reconciliation for us.[24]

In Christ's perfect obedience, joyous service, sacrificial death, and glorious exaltation, believers find their lives, their selves, and their stories. Christology is foundational for anthropology, no less in sanctification than in any other area of the Christian life.

The specifically pneumatological, hence TAT, contribution to the sanctifying transformation of believers revolves around the need not to instrumentalize the Spirit's work, as if he were only there to apply the benefits of Christ to the believer. Instead, the Spirit, active in the life of

---

[21] Payne, *Already Sanctified*, 75.
[22] See Payne, *Already Sanctified*, 76–7.
[23] Torrance, *The Trinitarian Faith*, 166–7.
[24] Torrance, *The Trinitarian Faith*, 180–1, citing Gregory Nazianzen, *Orations* 1.5.

Christ, is equally active in the life of believers, empowering them in union with Christ to become what they are declared to be, holy and acceptable to the Lord. The presence of the *Holy* Spirit is what makes believers holy, and the ongoing work of the Holy Spirit is what continues to make believers holy. The ethical imperatives of the New Testament only make sense when they are the result, not condition, of the believer's already declared (justification) and initially realised (sanctification) status before God as a family member (Gal 4:6–8). Without the Holy Spirit, the vital life connection between being declared righteous and actually becoming so is lost. "The Spirit is the explicitly stated agent of sanctification" in texts such as 1 Pet 1:2, where "transformation is a fruit of sanctification."[25] More than this, Payne makes clear that the indwelling presence of the Spirit "touches and transforms our deepest desires toward God," such that, "a Spirit-sanctified vision of God feeds our desire for God and thus changes us specifically toward and into the likeness of Jesus Christ (2 Cor 4:4; Col 3:10) as the Spirit exposes us to God's glory through Jesus (2 Cor 3:18)."[26]

The Holy Spirit, the Spirit of Christ, the Spirit of Pentecost given to believers is the perfecting person of the Godhead, active in creation to bring things to their proper ends. "It is thus through this work of the Spirit that salvation in Christ acquires a fully trinitarian profile,"[27] writes Ian McFarland. Connecting our sanctification to the work of Christ and, through that, to the Divine identity, McFarland affirms that "from all eternity the Son rejoices in the life of the Father through the power of the Spirit. But in taking flesh the Son now lives out that relationship in time and space, so that just as the Sprit has joined the Son's life to that of human beings through the Incarnation … so now human beings may through the gift of that same Spirit share the Son's life as children of the Father."[28] The Spirit empowers Jesus to be the Messiah, the one anointed with the Spirit beyond measure, and thus able to give the Spirit beyond measure to others. David deSilva echoes this theme when summarizing Paul's message of good news as follows, "God offers you the means to become reconciled with him and to become a new person who will want and love and do what is pleasing to him because the Spirit of his Son will live in you and *change* you. The result of God's kindness and activity is that you will live a new kind of life now and, after death, live forever with

---

[25]Payne, *Already Sanctified*, 132.
[26]Payne, *Already Sanctified*, 132.
[27]Ian A. McFarland, "The Saving God," in *Sanctified by Grace: A Theology of the Christian Life* (ed. Kent Eilers and Kyle C. Strobel; London: Bloomsbury T&T Clark, 2014), 71.
[28]McFarland, "The Saving God," 72.

him."²⁹ Believers are united to the incarnate Son, and they too are baptized with the Holy Spirit, the Spirit of Christ, and out of that baptism, they are empowered, in Christ and by the Spirit, to live lives holy and pleasing to the Lord.

9.4 Identity and the Spirit: Me, Myself, and the Spirit

As with other chapters, this one concludes with an applied example. In 2022, Joshua Rothman wrote a fascinating little piece for the *New Yorker* entitled: "Are you the same person you used to be?"³⁰ In the article, he reflected, and I quote at length:

> The question of our continuity has an empirical side that can be answered scientifically. In the nineteen-seventies, while working at the University of Otago, in New Zealand, a psychologist named Phil Silva helped launch a study of a thousand and thirty-seven children … In 2020, four psychologists associated with the Dunedin study … summarized what's been learned so far in a book called *The Origins of You: How Childhood Shapes Later Life*.³¹ …
>
> The authors of *The Origins of You* … suggest [human beings] are like storm systems. Each individual storm has its own particular set of traits and dynamics; meanwhile, its future depends on numerous elements of atmosphere and landscape. The fate of any given Harvey, Allison, Ike, or Katrina might be shaped, in part, by "air pressure in another locale," and by "the time that the hurricane spends out at sea, picking up moisture, before making landfall." … We change, and change our view of that change, for as long as we live.³²

Studies such as those found in *The Origins of You* are more than interesting; they are important reminders that we are each on a journey of maturation, growth, and spiritual development, and the Holy Spirit is at work in the midst of it all. The image of a storm system used by Rothman is

---

²⁹David A. DeSilva, *Transformation: The Heart of Paul's Gospel* (Bellingham, WA: Lexham Press, 2014), 2. (Emphasis in original.)
³⁰Joshua Rothman, "Are You the Same Person You Used to Be?" *The New Yorker* (October 3, 2022), https://www.newyorker.com/magazine/2022/10/10/are-you-the-same-person-you-used-to-be-life-is-hard-the-origins-of-you.
³¹Jay Belsky, Avshalom Caspi, Terrie E. Moffit, and Richie Poulton, *The Origins of You: How Childhood Shapes Later Life* (Cambridge, MA: Harvard University Press, 2020).
³²Rothman, "Are You the Same Person."

redolent with the biblical images of the Spirit as *ruach/pneuma*—the breath or wind of God. It is the Holy Spirit, God's empowering presence, that is at work in human beings actualizing their transcendental determination to be conformed to the image of Christ. Todd Billings makes the link between sanctification and our personal identity when writing of believers' "new life of sanctification in which the Spirit calls and empowers Christians to live into their adopted identity."[33] We are created by God with a unique identity, and we are called to live into that identity over time and throughout life. A basic conviction of the Christian faith is that God knows us because he created us, and he created us with purpose, with calling, and with a life of activity planned carefully beforehand (Eph 2:8–10). Evoking the metaphor bequeathed by Irenaeus, that God works in the world by his two hands, the Son and the Spirit, along with the metaphor bequeathed by Basil of Caesarea, that the Spirit is the perfecting cause in creation, we look to the Spirit of God to recreate in us the life of Christ in all its fullness and flourishing.

In our own day, we need to hear the clear message that we are to be obedient to the identity God has given us no less than with any other God-given gift. And that identity protection, development, and stewardship can often come at great cost. DeSilva reminds us of Paul's obedience to Jesus and how this cost him, when reflecting on Phil 3:8–11. In that passage, Paul writes (to use deSilva's translation):

> On account of Christ I have written off everything as a loss and consider it all to be sewage in order that I may win Christ and be found in him, not having my own righteousness attained on the basis of the Torah but attained through trusting Jesus—God's righteousness attained on the basis of trust—in order to know him and the power of his resurrection and the fellowship of his sufferings, being reshaped in connection with him (*symmorphizomenos*) into the likeness of his death, if somehow I might arrive at the resurrection from the dead.[34]

DeSilva makes two specific points about this text. First, to become like Jesus is a process of being "*morphed* into the self-giving obedience Jesus displayed in his own obedience unto death." And second, this process is integral to sharing in Christ's resurrection. In short, without transformation

---

[33] J. Todd Billings, *Union with Christ: Reframing Theology and Ministry for the Church* (Grand Rapids, MI: Baker Academic, 2011), 10, cited in Payne, *Already Sanctified*, 135.
[34] DeSilva, *Transformation*, 11.

into Christlikeness, no one will see the Lord.³⁵ Whether it is Phil 2:5–11; Rom 6:1–23; Gal 2:19–20; 4:19 or any number of other texts, Paul is adamant that salvation consists in the life of Christ taking form or shape within the believer as the Spirit works within us from the inside out. In deSilva's words, the Gospel is "primarily about working with people to surrender themselves to this work of God, this deep and fundamental transformation whereby their lives cease to be what they *were* and begin to be an extension of *Christ's own* willing, being, and doing."³⁶ Transformation into Christlikeness by the Holy Spirit is the essence of the Gospel and is at the heart of a believer's identity.

One of the defining social issues of our day concerns personal identity. In the clamor of rhetoric over identity, the LGBTQI+ agenda threatens to overwhelm public discourse and cancel the voices of those who might have other perspectives to offer on human identity and personal flourishing, voices such as those coming from the churches. What might a TAT perspective on theological anthropology have to offer this discussion? Working with the concepts we have identified above, we suggest that instead of rushing to the issues that are keenly debated—homosexuality, transgenderism, and so forth—it would be better to locate such specific discussions within the broader narrative sweep of Scripture and the dramatic theology it recommends, and then look to see how the parts of a topic are related to the whole.³⁷ In short, the approach of narrative ethics to issues of personal identity can help Christians find clarity around addressing some of the contested social issues of our day. The following does not seek to resolve such issues but merely to provide a sketch of how the approach of TAT might help.

There are many ways to faithfully tell the story of Scripture, of course, but fundamental to the wholistic narrative scope of the Bible is the centrality of Christ and the identity of believers in relation to him. The Spirit is at work in the world, transforming people to the image of Christ and in Christ, we are brought before the Father in worship. This is the primary identity of believers, as children of God: created by him, loved, filled, empowered, and becoming like Christ as they live into the life of the Spirit. From the Garden of Eden to the City of New Jerusalem, from Genesis to Revelation, from

---

³⁵ DeSilva, *Transformation*, 12.
³⁶ DeSilva, *Transformation*, 12. (Emphasis in original.)
³⁷ On narrative theology and the turn to drama, see Myk Habets, "'The Dogma Is the Drama': Dramatic Developments in Biblical Theology," *Stimulus* 16 (2008): 2–5.

infancy to maturity, from human *being* to human *personhood*, the story of Scripture is one of conformity to Christ. We move from the order of creation to the disorder of the fall and sin, into the reordering of the world brought about by Christ and in the hope of the coming transformation of order in the renewed heavens and earth. Throughout the various stages of redemptive history, God is at work in the world, by the Spirit, to transform and conform people into Christ's image and in that image, we find our true selves.

Helpful in framing some of the foundational issues of identity in regard to the contemporary LGBTQI+ discussions is the work of Mark Yarhouse. Yarhouse has developed what he terms two "scripts" that are useful in this discussion, the "Gay Script" and the "Identity in Christ Script." Yarhouse uses the term "script" as an apt metaphor for the internal narratives that inform the way we live out the drama of identity. As Yarhouse puts it, "Actors read from scripts all the time. They use scripts to determine how their character thinks and feels and relates to others. Young people similarly look for scripts to read from to make sense of who they are. And young people who experience same-sex attraction similarly look for a script to read from."[38] Yarhouse then presents what he calls the Gay Script, namely:

- Same-sex attractions signal a naturally occurring or "intended by God" distinction between homosexuality, heterosexuality, and bisexuality.
- Same-sex attractions are the way you know who you "really are" as a person (emphasis on discovery).
- Same-sex attractions are at the core of who you are as a person.
- Same-sex behavior is an extension of that core.
- Self-actualization (behavior that matches who you "really are") of your sexual identity is critical for your fulfillment.[39]

As Yarhouse notes, this is a compelling script, and it is a powerful one in today's social context. Does it fit with a TAT anthropology, however? Not entirely, precisely because the fundamental commitments inherent to this script are not biblical (regardless of what position one takes on LGBTQI+). What is the alternative? Yarhouse has developed what he terms the "identity in Christ script." Yarhouse admits there are likely many other scripts people can live their lives in accordance with, but this response to the gay script is based on his empirical studies and his own theological commitments. The "identity in Christ script" looks like this:

---

[38] Mark A. Yarhouse, *Homosexuality and the Christian* (Minneapolis, MN: Bethany House, 2010), 48.
[39] Yarhouse, *Homosexuality and the Christian*, 49.

- Same-sex attraction does not signal a categorical distinction among types of person, but is one of many human experiences that are "not the way it's supposed to be."
- Same-sex attractions may be part of your experience, but they are not the defining element of your identity.
- You can choose to integrate your experiences of attraction to the same sex into a gay identity.
- On the other hand, you can choose to center your identity around other aspects of your experience, including your biological sex, gender identity, and so on.
- The most compelling aspect of personhood for the Christian is one's identity in Christ, a central and defining aspect of what it means to be a follower of Jesus.[40]

Comparing the two scripts, we see the key differences between them coalesce around those who "made their beliefs and values line up with their identity and behavior," as opposed to those who "made their identity and behavior line up with their beliefs and values."[41] It is our conviction that a proper theological anthropology, and certainly the one developed here as part of a TAT, adopts the second set of commitments, seeking to align identity and behaviour with biblically formed beliefs and values.

Personal identity is primarily formed by our relationship with Christ and the Spirit and the decisions we make considering that relationship. Being obedient to Christ often comes at great cost as we take up our cross daily to follow him, and the leading, guiding, equipping, convicting, and consoling mystery of the Spirit empowers us to put our identity in Christ first, above all other competing claims to identity. In his studies, Yarhouse finds that "young adults who have been able to respond positively to the Scriptures and the Christian sexual ethic have felt genuinely convicted by the Holy Spirit. They are convinced that they should say no to what they experience as a natural desire and longing for connection in favor of saying yes to a personally fulfilling life in Christ."[42] These types of decisions are not limited to the issues facing LGBTQI+ people, of course, but they are illustrative of the types of decisions we each have to make on a daily basis to choose to have our identity formed in Christ by the Spirit, over any other

---

[40] Yarhouse, *Homosexuality and the Christian*, 51.
[41] Yarhouse, *Homosexuality and the Christian*, 51.
[42] Yarhouse, *Homosexuality and the Christian*, 126–7.

competing claims. Yarhouse goes on to present a kind of practical theology of sanctification, making it explicit that reliance upon the Holy Spirit is the only way to press into our true identity in Christ, and that this takes the concerted effort of a community of faith in support. This looks like "a curriculum of Christlikeness" and commitment to spiritual disciplines.[43] Specifically regarding the Holy Spirit, Yarhouse writes, in light of Dallas Willard's work, "the function of the Holy Spirit appears to be 'to move within our souls, and especially our minds, to present the person of Jesus and the reality of his kingdom.' Put differently, the Holy Spirit is active and plays a vital role in shaping our lives and the acts that come to reflect the nature of our inner lives."[44]

Based on Rom 6:2–11 and a host of supporting texts, deSilva is correct in his affirmation that "Paul is setting *conditions* on entering into the 'life' of the resurrection: it is necessary to allow God's Spirit to become the driving force in one's life and to cease to live for oneself. Continuing to feed the passions and drives of self-centred, self-directed living … shipwrecks God's work of transformation and deliverance."[45] These are sobering words. But, again, these words apply to all people, facing all manner of self-centered temptations. But the Good News again comes in at just this point, "yielding ourselves to the transformation God desires to work within us through God's precious gift of the Holy Spirit," writes deSilva, "allows God to complete the work of deliverance begun in us in our coming to faith. One must be '*led* by the Spirit' to be in fact a 'child of God' (Rom 8:14)."[46]

The Gospel is good news precisely because it provides the relational context—the church—and the causal power—the Spirit—to transform each of us into the persons God has created us to become. Our identity is given by God and is developed by God, and in reliance upon the Spirit, we can truly become the people God has designed us to be. We conclude this chapter with deSilva's conclusion to his short book on transformation in Paul's epistles:

> The "good news" is that redemption, inclusive of the entire *kosmos* currently gone awry, will indeed happen. When the new humanity formed in Christ is transformed from mortality to immortality, creation itself will participate in

---

[43] Yarhouse, *Homosexuality and the Christian*, 168, where Yarhouse is citing Dallas Willard.
[44] Yarhouse, *Homosexuality and the Christian*, 169.
[45] DeSilva, *Transformation*, 20.
[46] DeSilva, *Transformation*, 20.

the glorious liberation of the children of God from all the forces of death … For now the new humanity in Christ must hope—and this not passively as people waiting, but actively as people longing, who are themselves investing fully in embracing the transformation God is working out as the way forward to the resolution of all present ills.[47]

---

[47]DeSilva, *Transformation*, 113.

10

Missiology: The Spirit as Present and Active in the World

10.1 Introduction

Although their explorations only rarely spring explicitly from a Spirit Christological base, or use the language of Third Article Theology (let alone the rigorous methodological approach explained in the early chapters of this volume), many scholars have nevertheless examined and exploited the commonly recognized close association between the Spirit and mission (cf., Acts 1:8). The aims of this chapter are first to briefly mention some of these missiological investigations that intentionally adopt a pneumatological perspective, give a descriptive outline of one as a pertinent and illustrative example, and then finally to explore ways in which a specifically TAT approach can extend beyond the pneumatologically focused missiological investigations seen to this point. This final section will also include a discussion of some practical implications for mission, exploring how each point discussed can be worked out in the everyday life of Christian individuals and communities.

For many decades, and particularly since the publishing in 1972 of John V. Taylor's *The Go-Between God: The Holy Spirit and the Christian Mission*,[1] there have been many analyses that adopt an intentionally pneumatological approach to mission. They can be divided, very roughly, into three overlapping groups, each of which is briefly listed below and illustrated

---

[1] Taylor, *The Go-Between God*.

with a couple of pertinent examples. The first grouping are Pentecostal or charismatic scholars, who, following their traditional emphasis on the Spirit, explore the connection between the pneumatological focus and the missional approach of the movements. This group includes such scholars as Andrew Lord, who in *Spirit-Shaped Mission* attempts to develop a "holistic charismatic theology of mission, shaped by the Spirit, rooted in Christ, and seeking to embrace more of the fullness of God's working in the world."[2] Amos Yong's similar collection argues that "only a pneumatological imagination can secure the Trinitarian vision that empowers missional performance amidst the many tongues of the many missionary contexts."[3] Yong has also more recently developed a monograph length theological interpretation of Scripture utilizing the lenses of both pneumatology and missiology, combining the three *loci* of Scripture, Spirit, and mission into an interpretative triad.[4]

A second grouping, which overlaps with the first, has emerged from within the missional church movement. Following the observation of retired missionary Lesslie Newbigin that Europe and North America have become mission fields in themselves, this movement explores and emphasizes the intrinsically missional nature of the church. While there are many within the movement that recognize the pivotal role of the Spirit in mission, a subset have taken the subsequent step of exploring in depth the interaction of the church's missional role with pneumatology. Examples include Gary Tyra, whose volume *The Holy Spirit in Mission* outlines a missional pneumatology, surveying what "the Bible as a whole has to say about the Holy Spirit's apparent penchant for involving God's people in the fulfilling of God's purposes in their churches and neighborhoods by inspiring them to engage in prophetic speech and action."[5] Perhaps particularly pertinent within this grouping, given that it explicitly uses the grounding of Spirit Christology, is Lucy Peppiatt's PhD thesis, "Spirit Christology and Mission." Peppiatt argues that Spirit Christology, through its emphasis on the Spirit's role in Christ's humanity, provides a helpful model to understand the church's existence and task as a Spirit-anointed colaborer with God in his

---

[2] Andrew Lord, *Spirit-Shaped Mission: A Holistic Charismatic Missiology* (Milton Keynes: Paternoster, 2005). This work will be explored in more detail in Section 10.2.
[3] Amos Yong, *The Missiological Spirit: Christian Mission Theology in the Third Millenium Global Context* (Eugene, OR: Cascade Books, 2014), 15.
[4] Yong, *Mission after Pentecost*.
[5] Gary Tyra, *The Holy Spirit in Mission: Prophetic Speech and Action in Christian Witness* (Downers Grove, IL: Intervarsity Press, 2011).

mission to the world, and in applying this model she adopts a particular focus on Western culture.[6]

A third grouping explores the relationship between pneumatology and missiology, but rather than explicitly addressing its application and insights within the Western world and its post-Christian culture, they focus on the majority world, and how the Spirit informs and transforms missiological activity in these less commonly examined cultural arenas. Examples include Kirsteen Kim's initial PhD thesis and subsequent work. In her original contribution, *Mission in the Spirit*, Kim suggests that the "Indian contribution to mission pneumatology has been above all to connect mission and spirituality."[7] Kim has continued to explore these themes through subsequent research, and argues quite convincingly in a recent work that a shift from a focus on the *Missio Dei* to a *Missio Spiritus* has emerged from pneumatological examinations within traditionally pluralistic settings such as India.[8] Other authors have also explored the relationship between pneumatology and Christian mission in a variety of cultural contexts.[9]

While the above examples and groupings are no more than indicative, they do illustrate that there has been considerable interest in examining the interaction of pneumatology and missiology. The next section chooses one particular example of this scholarship to explain in detail.

10.2 Andrew Lord's *Spirit-Shaped Mission*

In his volume, *Spirit-Shaped Mission: A Holistic Charismatic Missiology*, Lord asks the question, "what would mission look like if we start with the work of the Spirit?"[10] In illustrating this pivotal question, Lord makes the distinction between the "the Spirit of mission" and the "mission of the Spirit." The former

---

[6]Peppiatt, "Spirit Christology and Mission." See also Sánchez's summary of Peppiatt's work in Sánchez M., *T&T Clark Introduction to Spirit Christology*, 157–64.
[7]Kirsteen Kim, *Mission in the Spirit: The Holy Spirit in Indian Christian Theologies* (Delhi: ISPCK, 2003), 241.
[8] See, for example, Kirsteen Kim, "The Shift from *Missio Dei* to *Missio Spiritus* in Recent Mission Thinking: The Indian Contribution," in *The Holy Spirit and Christian Mission in a Pluralistic Context* (ed. Roji T. George; Bangalore: SAIACS Press, 2017), 152–64.
[9]See, for example, Roji T. George, ed., *The Holy Spirit and Christian Mission in a Pluralistic Context* (Bangalore: SAIACS Press, 2017).
[10]Lord, *Spirit-Shaped Mission*, 8.

refers to an approach that starts with an understanding of mission and then explores the question of what the Spirit's role is within it. In contrast to this, Lord argues that an alternative and better approach is to ask the question of who the Spirit is and what the Spirit is doing in the world, and then, from that basis, allow an understanding of mission to arise. This emphasis precisely matches the approach of TAT and its methodology of prioritizing pneumatology. In unpacking these movements of the Spirit, Lord notes two key tensions that need to be recognized. The first is a tension and movement between the particular (focusing on specific individuals and communities) and the universal (embracing all of creation, and beyond this eschatologically in both time and space). Lord argues that an understanding of missiology in which the work of the Spirit is prioritized will balance both poles and enhance our understanding of the Spirit's movement between them. The second tension is between the twin realities of blessing and yearning. Lord argues that a Spirit-driven missiology will recognize both the great blessings that come from the Spirit as the wonders of God are proclaimed and experienced, together with the great yearnings that emerge as we participate in the Spirit's groaning for a world that is presently experiencing exile from the kingdom life that is still to come. From the basis of these tensions, and after a review of prior Pentecostal and Charismatic missiologies, Lord goes on to suggest that a Pentecostal theology of mission needs to address five key themes: holistic mission, experience, context, community, and spirituality. Exploring each of these themes while adopting a pneumatological priority clearly illustrates these tensions between particular and universal, and between blessing and yearning, and provides a coherent and compelling understanding of contemporary mission.

By recognizing holistic mission as a key theme within charismatic missiology, Lord emphasizes the intrinsically eschatological nature of mission. He argues that mission's eschatological grounding implies that mission should be seen as the bringing back of heaven's core features to the present time—including healing, justice, unity in diversity, creation set free, praise and worship, love, fellowship, and above all the centrality of Jesus. Most importantly, Lord recognizes that the Spirit is "the means by which the eschatological blessings are brought to life."[11] Consequently, the Spirit's missional work goes beyond the traditional Pentecostal emphases of prophecy and power. Other aspects included in the broad vision of mission

---

[11] Lord, *Spirit-Shaped Mission*, 66.

that emerges are ethics and salvation, among many others.[12] Lord even argues that this perspective reveals that evangelism has a certain kind of priority in mission, precisely because of the priority and centrality of Jesus in the eschatological kingdom.[13] He writes, "'Holistic evangelism' is about the 'holistic centrality of Christ' to all mission in this world."[14]

The recognition of the eschatological nature of mission and the Spirit's role in bringing back characteristics of the coming kingdom does not lead Lord to a triumphalistic understanding of mission, however. He argues that Jesus and his discipleship in the Spirit provide a model for our lives, and that just as Jesus endured suffering, so too will the contemporary church. He introduces Begbie's musical metaphor as one way of explaining this reality, noting that in a similar manner to how music is marked "by multi-levelled patterns of equilibrium, tension, and resolution"[15] so the church's missiological journey at various levels will echo the same kind of tension and release motifs that characterize the overarching story of salvation history itself. It is precisely this multilayered reality that allows both the blessings of the Spirit who brings back anticipations of the life to come to be experienced concurrently with the yearnings that emerge when the coming kingdom is not yet fully experienced. Such yearnings occur not merely through suffering, but also in the opposition the church faces in its missional outworking. A pneumatological perspective on this subject requires adopting a holistic approach to opposition, holding together aspects that derive from both heavenly and earthly sources. "What is needed is a model that allows for the 'multidimensionality of the demonic' within which evil opposition to mission can take a variety of forms as the heavenly and earthly interact in a multitude of ways … I am arguing for a holistic approach to opposition which reflects a holistic approach to mission."[16]

Lord's holistic understanding of mission outlined in the previous paragraphs, where the future traits of the kingdom are brought back to the present, needs to be complemented by a movement from the present reality to the eschaton. Mission needs to move from the particular to the universal, as well as from the universal to the particular. Consequently, Lord argues that for a fully rounded understanding, the universal aspect of holistic mission must be partnered with the particular aspect of experiential mission.

---

[12]Lord, *Spirit-Shaped Mission*, 67–8.
[13]Lord, *Spirit-Shaped Mission*, 66.
[14]Lord, *Spirit-Shaped Mission*, 66.
[15]Jeremy S. Begbie, *Theology, Music and Time* (Cambridge: Cambridge University Press, 2000), 98.
[16]Lord, *Spirit-Shaped Mission*, 72.

Indeed, without such an experiential emphasis, the missional understanding developed would not be charismatic, because "charismatic mission is not something thought about but something experienced ... the experiential prayer 'Come, Holy Spirit' can be seen to sum up charismatic missiology."[17] But it is a directed experiential mission that is needed, says Lord. The focus needs to be not just on how the Spirit is present and at work in all life (and therefore in each individual and community), but how through working in each individual and community, the Spirit works in "ever expanding circles that embrace individuals, communities, nations and the whole of creation."[18]

Lord further develops this necessary tension by reflecting on the themes of transcendence and the immanence in mission. Noting Moltmann's close association of the two through terminology such as immanent transcendence, Lord recognizes that while the Spirit has to be identified closely with creation, there still needs to be a distinction between the two, given that the Spirit "is free to interrupt and confront creation."[19] But there is an opposite pole advocated by some Pentecostal scholars where the Spirit is seen as only active in creation through particular transcendent experiences, most commonly those associated with the Charismatic and Pentecostal movements. Lord sees experience as being the core issue at play here, with Moltmann stressing that our experience of God is of his transcendence experienced through his immanence, while Pentecostal scholars emphasize our immanent experience of God through transcendent experiences. Moltmann's resulting understanding of mission thus focuses on the universal reality of God, while Pentecostal scholars stress particular and unique signs and wonders. Lord recognizes the value in both positions and argues that the tension here between the universal and the particular is not a contradiction but a polarity. The Holy Spirit is involved in both ... the transcendent and the immanent, the universal and the particular ... but it is in the Spirit's movement between the two that mission occurs. Movement in both directions is enabled by the Spirit, and movement in both directions needs to be included in a complete understanding of pneumatological mission. Lord even goes so far as to suggest that the way forward, which brings the universal and particular together, is through considering a Spirit

---

[17]Lord, *Spirit-Shaped Mission*, 75.
[18]Lord, *Spirit-Shaped Mission*, 81. Lord illustrates the two movements of the Spirit through examining a recent dialogue between Moltmann and Pentecostal scholars. See Lord, *Spirit-Shaped Mission*, 75–81.
[19]Lord, *Spirit-Shaped Mission*, 83. This distinction is based on the work of Macchia, but Lord appears to at least partially endorse it in this chapter.

Christology ... "placing Christology in the context of the Spirit's global operations."[20]

Lord recognizes that to address the current diverse reality, the model of mission he is proposing, which moves from both the particular to the universal and the universal to the particular through the movements of the Spirit, needs to explicitly consider the way in which mission is affected and altered within different cultures. He thus adds the theme of contextual mission to the themes of holistic and experiential mission already examined. He suggests that the role of the Spirit has received limited treatment in current examinations of contextualization and argues that a Charismatic and Pentecostal mission must be contextual precisely because the Spirit works in and through particular experiences—experiences located within particular cultural settings. While speaking in tongues was initially seen as the key to contextualization in Pentecostal settings, "experience, enlightened and empowered by the Spirit, is still at the heart of Pentecostal missiology."[21] Lord does not directly address the question of how to determine which aspects of culture to affirm or reject, but he does note the general tendency within these movements is to have a more negative view of culture than is perhaps warranted.

No topic more clearly illustrates the challenges of contextualization than a Christian understanding of other religions. Lord examines the work of Pinnock and Yong in this area. He notes that while both propose a more universal understanding of the Spirit's work than is common, Pinnock privileges Christology, arguing that Jesus is the key criterion of salvation, while Yong argues that the Christological concerns should be pushed back to allow the common and universal understanding of the Spirit to develop and grow. Lord's resolution of this difference in approach is to return to his understanding of the movement of the Spirit from the particular to the universal. He argues that at a universal level, everything in creation is *both* influenced *and* challenged by the Spirit. (Lord thinks that Yong does not sufficiently emphasize the Spirit's challenge, and presumably that Pinnock does not sufficiently emphasize the Spirit's influence.) At the particular level, the Holy Spirit is personal, his influence and challenge is shaped around Christ, and the intensity of his work relates to people's response to Christ.

---

[20]See Pinnock, *Flame of Love*, 82. This phrase is also quoted in Lord, *Spirit-Shaped Mission*, 88. Lord does not appear to develop this connection with Spirit Christology to any great degree though.
[21]Lord, *Spirit-Shaped Mission*, 95.

What this means (I presume) is that the Spirit is always at work, even in other religions, but the Spirit's movement and intensity is heightened as the reality and Lordship of Christ is increasingly acceded and acknowledged.

The themes of holistic mission, experience, and contextualization Lord has examined to this point could perhaps be viewed individualistically. To correct this false assumption, Lord adds community mission as a fourth theme. The community is the primary bearer of mission, he argues. "When the Spirit breaks into our experience we will naturally find ourselves drawn together with others who share something in the Spirit."[22] The Spirit is thus the former, sender, and uniter of communities in mission. Moreover, a pneumatological focus can help communities to avoid the divisions and disputes that plague the mission world. Lord's logic in this chapter is clear, and matches the majority of the work that is done exploring the communal nature of the missionary endeavor. The first step is to develop an understanding of what mission is, and then on the basis of that, to explore what the character of the community is, which can fulfill this missionary task.

The particular perspective Lord adopts of prioritizing the Spirit (a TAT approach although not using that terminology) leads him to characterize mission as primarily populated by volunteers ("it is the Holy Spirit, working in the hearts of individual believers, that brings them together for the work of Christian mission"[23]) but he adds to this a charismatic flavor that is also based on a pneumatological motivation (including a focus on experience, signs, and wonders, an emphasis on those on the margins, and the empowering of indigenous communities). So, the characteristics of charismatic missionary communities include a reliance on the Holy Spirit to guide and send, a deliberate seeking of encounters with God, the promotion of every member mission, an intrinsically community oriented approach to mission, an intentionally diverse but united community, and an approach to mission that it is intentionally grounded in the local culture. He points out the common tendency of missionary-motivated communities to overorganize God rather than rely on his Spirit and also argues that while the community can work in isolation, a desire for partnership with other communities that "reflects the Spirit's yearning for unity"[24] needs to be encouraged.

Lord's final theme, mission spirituality, emphasizes the important recognition that mission is not a separate activity from the day-to-day life of

---

[22]Lord, *Spirit-Shaped Mission*, 95.
[23]Lord, *Spirit-Shaped Mission*, 108.
[24]Lord, *Spirit-Shaped Mission*, 120.

the Christians and communities in the world, but integrates into it—mission can and should be seen as a framework for life in the Spirit. Lord characterizes this as a missionary movement of the Spirit that works from God through particular individuals and communities into all the world and then back again to God. Lord explores these themes through starting universally with an attractive holiness, working particularly through to a patient waiting, and then moving back again to God through intercessory prayer. In this way, our missional lifestyles echo the missional movement of the Spirit from universal to particular, and particular to universal, which has already been outlined. Lord links attractive holiness with the coming kingdom. It is about the whole created order being transformed into the patterns of God, reflecting his purity, unity, and grace. While this is an almost utopian ideal, Lord recognizes that the consequent mission that emerges from this is not about frantic activity. Rather, the missional outworking of this universal ideal, at the particular level of individuals and communities, is a call to wait for the Holy Spirit. "This waiting on God for the blessings brought by the Spirit may be characterised by yearnings as we are more aware of the needs than the fulfilment."[25] The ways this reality moves from the particular back to the universal is many and varied, but Lord focuses on the importance of grounding this return movement in prayer. Prayer moves us outwards in line with the Spirit, he argues. "Given the presence of such prayer that moves us outwards in mission into the world, ministry is a response to the call of God discerned in prayer, a way of serving God and others that cannot rest until God's blessings are shared by all and are brought together under Christ's Lordship."[26]

Lord's pneumatologically inspired charismatic missiology provides an excellent example of the valuable work being done by those who are exploring the doctrine of missiology through the lens of the Spirit. While it does not use the terminology of TAT, the clear prioritization of the Spirit leads to some valuable conclusions about the nature of mission. In particular, his recognition of the movement of the Spirit from both the particular to the universal, and from the universal to the particular, and the way that works itself out through the themes of holistic mission, experience, contextualization, community, and spirituality is very helpful. Similarly, his broad characterization of both the blessings and yearnings that emerge from an analysis of mission through the lens of the Spirit means that his work is

---

[25] Lord, *Spirit-Shaped Mission*, 130.
[26] Lord, *Spirit-Shaped Mission*, 133–4.

both grounded and aspirational. Overall, Lord's work provides an excellent example of the value of exploring missiology through the lens of the Spirit, even if he does not explicitly use the rigorous methodological approach outlined in the early chapters of this volume. The question naturally arises, though, what further insights could be gained if the methods and methodology of those original chapters were used? The next section explores just one potential area where the beginnings of an extension or alternative approach provides equally valuable and complementary insights to those developed by Lord and others.

10.3 Pneumato-Ecclesiology and Pneumato-Missiology

While a pneumatological approach to examining missiology such as that adopted by Lord and others is undoubtedly profitable, as the above section amply demonstrates, the question that arises is whether utilizing the full methodological scope of TAT can add anything to the pneumatological insights into missiology already gained. This section provides just one example of how adopting the full methodology of TAT not only affirms the insights observed above, but also allows us to reach beyond them. In order to illustrate this extension, consider the relationship between missiology and ecclesiology. In the example of Lord's work given above, the fourth theme he examined was community mission, and Lord's approach to determining what a missional church should be was clear. His first step was to pneumatologically develop an understanding of what mission is, and then on that basis, his second step was to pneumatologically explore what the character of the community is that can fulfill this missionary task. While such an approach is undoubtedly valid, is such an understanding of Christian community entirely determinative? Many missional church authors argue that this is the case. For example, Frost and Hirsch argue that ecclesiology is entirely determined by mission.[27] For them, structure follows strategy, or more accurately, identity follows function. Frost and Hirsch suggest the church should adopt a chameleon-like identity depending on how it can best

---

[27]Michael Frost and Alan Hirsch, *The Shaping of Things to Come: Innovation and Mission for the 21st-Century Church* (Peabody, MA: Hendrickson, 2003), 201–23. More specifically, Hirsch comments that "Christology determines missiology, and missiology determines ecclesiology." Alan Hirsch, *The Forgotten Ways* (Grand Rapids, MI: Brazos Press, 2006), 142.

fulfill its mission in the world. "Our Christology informs our missiology, which then in turn determines our ecclesiology."[28] Guder comments similarly that "the witness to which we are called is an all-encompassing definition of Christian existence."[29] Recognizing that comments like these from missional authors are often made more in a pragmatic than a purely theological sense,[30] the approach is nevertheless unsatisfactory. The end result of determining ecclesiology entirely from mission is an emaciated understanding of both the church and her mission. As Clark comments, "This completely separates the person of Christ from the body of Christ in mission and relegates the church to a completely instrumentalised tool for individuals."[31] Such an approach places the value of the individual over and above the community. Further, it "reduces the church to a project, a means to a functional end."[32] The biblical vision of ecclesiology is much richer than sheer functionality and goes well beyond collectivized individualism. Indeed, Fitch argues that making mission constitutive of ecclesiology is individualistic not just soteriologically, but also epistemologically.[33] He points out the modernist assumptions underpinning the approach, noting that mission only makes sense within the framework of a community that embodies the gospel narrative which we witness. Fitch concludes that "putting missiology before ecclesiology [will] eventually lead to the contextualising of the church into oblivion."[34] Put simply, the primary underlying reason that missiology cannot determine ecclesiology is that the church extends beyond its world-facing mission. Of course, to say that mission does not *determine* ecclesiology does not imply that mission does not *inform* ecclesiology, but rather that its foundational essence is not intrinsically determined only by its outward-facing purpose.

---

[28]Frost and Hirsch, *The Shaping of Things to Come*, 209.
[29]Darrell L. Guder, *Be My Witnesses* (Grand Rapids, MI: Eerdmans, 1985), 233.
[30]See, for example, Frost's response to those who question this priority as noted in Michael Frost, *Your Fixed Idea of Church Is Turning You into a Marketer, Not a Missionary*; available from https://mikefrost.net/fixed-idea-church-turning-marketer-not-missionary/; accessed February 28, 2024. In making these comments, Frost, Hirsch, and Guder's primary concern is those who have not just a previously decided ecclesiology, but also a previously decided outworking of that ecclesiology. But like others before them, their justified correction of a deformity in the church is itself deformed by its opposition to that which it seeks to correct.
[31]Jason Swan Clark, "Just Go to Church" (paper presented at the Society of Vineyard Scholars Conference, London, 2019), 10, n. 15.
[32]Patrick S. Franklin, "The God Who Sends Is the God Who Loves: Mission as Participating in the Ecstatic Love of the Triune God," *Didaskalia* 28 (2017): 77.
[33]David Fitch, *Missiology Precedes Ecclesiology: The Epistemological Problem*; available from https://www.missioalliance.org/missiology-precedes-ecclesiology-the-epistemological-problem/; accessed February 28, 2024.
[34]Fitch, *Missiology Precedes Ecclesiology*.

The basis on which many missional church authors argue that missiology entirely determines ecclesiology centers on the now ubiquitous catchphrase of the *missio Dei*. While different authors use this phrase in different ways, most often the key point being made through it is that mission is primarily God's and not just ours. If we affirm the *missio Dei*, though, we must also affirm the *ecclesia Dei*. If it is primarily God's mission, it is also primarily God's church. Trinity and Christology can also be used as vantage points from which to determine what the church is, and this understanding of ecclesiology can and should inform the nature of missiology. So, rather than missiology determining ecclesiology (or ecclesiology determining missiology), we must adopt an understanding where missiology informs ecclesiology, and ecclesiology informs mission. Such an approach fits very well with the Wolterstorffian methodology adopted in this book and commonly used within TAT. Sometimes mission can be the control belief, and ecclesiology examined as the data belief. Other times the roles can be swapped, with ecclesiology as the control belief, examining mission as the data belief. It is through examining the coherence and consistency between both doctrines that the closest approximation to true reality can be approached.

The question of how the insights of missiology can be applied to ecclesiology has been thoroughly examined by missional church authors and others. Lord's work above provides a coherent example of some insights that arise when such a pneumatologically enabled approach is taken. But what about the insights going in the other direction? How can the insights from ecclesiology be applied to missiology? Paralleling Lord's work going in the other direction, such an approach would comprise two clear steps. The first is to develop a coherent understanding of a pneumato-ecclesiology. The second is to use that understanding to pneumatologically inform missiology. So, in the first step, ecclesiology is utilized as a data belief, while the doctrines of Christology, Trinity, and eschatology are used as control beliefs. In the second step, ecclesiology is used as a control belief, while missiology (and particularly ecclesial mission) is used as a data belief. In each of these steps, though, pneumatology forms the integrative link. All the doctrines are connected pneumatologically.

This section overall, and the following three subsections in particular, explore the insights that arise from exploring this particular connection from pneumato-ecclesiology to pneumato-missiology. The first step of pneumatologically exploring the church from the perspective of other doctrines is one that a TAT of ecclesiology directly addresses, and that has already been discussed in Chapter 7. So, TAT argues that the constituent features of a pneumato-ecclesiology can be determined by examining the church through the lens of the Spirit from the vantage point of other theological *loci*. For example, viewing ecclesiology from the vantage point of Christology illuminates the reality that it is the Spirit that forms the church as the body of Christ (1 Cor 12:13). Viewing ecclesiology from the vantage point of the Trinity emphasizes that it is by the Spirit that we join in the Son's communion with the Father.[35] Further (as will be discussed in the following chapter), viewing ecclesiology from the vantage point of eschatology enables the understanding that it is the Spirit that makes the church the proleptic anticipation of the coming kingdom. All these vantage points provide insight into the constituent features of the church's nature. The rationale behind developing a TAT of mission is to take these insights and extend them into the church's world-facing missional activity. The next three subsections briefly and indicatively outwork these three connections between ecclesiology and missiology. It takes pneumatological insights about the church derived from the Christological, Trinitarian, and eschatological vantage points and applies them to ecclesial mission. Even further, though, for each area of application we also conclude the discussion by outlining practical implications for how mission can and should be accomplished.

10.3.1 The Christological Connection

Regarding the first Christological connection, the initial pneumatological insight noted in Chapter 7 is that the Spirit forms the church as the body of Christ. Viewed through the lens of the Spirit, the church is intimately connected to Christ, and reflects Christ as the incarnation's sequel. The terminology here is indicative.[36] Just as sequels have a continuous, discontinuous, and asymmetrical relationship with their original, so too is the church related to Christ. Continuity arises from the church being Christ's body, his physical presence on earth. But the church is not a mere repetition or extension of the incarnation. The discontinuity between the two means that rather than adding to or replicating Christ's completed

---

[35] See, for example, Torrance, *Worship, Community and the Triune God of Grace*, 31.
[36] For a detailed explanation, see Liston, *The Anointed Church*, 85–9. Also, see Section 7.2 of this book.

work, the church is called primarily to witness to and enjoy him. And the relationship is intrinsically asymmetrical. Christ is the source and life of the church, but he exists independently of it.

Applying this Christological ecclesiology to missiology begins with recognizing how Christ was empowered and guided by the Spirit both to reveal God to the world, and to draw the world to God through his obedient suffering. The church in its continuity as the body of Christ, anointed and empowered by the Spirit, has an analogous role. In other words, it is as the church obediently suffers that she both reveals Christ to the world and draws the world to Christ. In terms of the revealing, Torrance explains it like this: "wherever the Church shows forth His death until He comes and presents its body a living sacrifice, there the image of Christ is to be seen and His Body is to be discerned in the Church."[37] Eugene Peterson illustrates this concept using the word "inscape."[38] He notes how some painters or photographers merely capture the reality in front of them (landscapes). Others, however, convey the inner truth of what is really going on (inscape). Applying this to theology, there are some who looked at Jesus, for example, and seeing only a human, decided there was nothing there worth noticing.[39] But there were a small number who saw through the human component (inscape!) and recognized something of immeasurable worth, God himself. In a similar manner, the church is intrinsically human. Some who look at the church see only the human side, and conclude that there is nothing there of importance. But that is merely the external, landscape point of view. There are those who see through the human component (inscape!) and so recognize something in the church of immeasurable worth. The church through her obedient suffering reveals Christ to the world.

Extending this ecclesiological parallel to missiology involves recognizing that the church does not just *reveal* Christ in and through obedient suffering, it *draws* the world to Christ through suffering as well. Certainly, it is true that Christians suffer, and that we should expect to.[40] And certainly, it is true that Christ suffered for us and suffers with us. But the biblical witness goes well beyond this. Because of the Spirit's presence, our suffering is not the end. The theology of the cross means our story extends

---

[37]Thomas F. Torrance, "Atonement and the Oneness of the Church," *Scottish Journal of Theology* 7 (1954): 259.
[38]Eugene Peterson, *Practise Resurrection* (London: Hodder & Stoughton, 2010), 141, 142, 146.
[39]See Isa 53:2, for example.
[40]See 1 Pet 4:1–2, for example.

beyond suffering and death. And as we endure suffering while living in the light of that bigger story, it witnesses to Christ and draws people to him. As people see us suffer, and remain obedient in suffering, they realize the extent of the story we are participating in. As Peraud says, "The thrust of the theology of the cross is missional."[41] Perhaps the most obvious example of this is the suffering of the martyrs. Holwerda argues that "Martyrdom is not what it appears to be. It appears to be the cruel cessation of witness, but actually it is its empowerment because martyrdom is the example par excellence of how God's kingdom of peace overcomes the violence of empires and ideologies opposed to Christ."[42] The disciples recognized Jesus through his scars, the world will recognize Jesus in us in the same way.

Viewed through the lens of the Spirit, there are important continuities between Christ and the church's respective missional roles. But there is a necessary discontinuity and asymmetry as well. The church reveals and draws people to Christ, only because Christ does so. The church's pneumatologically enabled missional role in the world asymmetrically parallels the missional role of Christ.

In terms of practical implications, it is vitally important to recognize that the ecclesial reality and missiological necessity of inscape—that by the Spirit we can look through the church and see Christ—is foundationally important not just as a theological affirmation, but as a practical skill. This is perhaps the core reality that marks out a church as truly Spiritual and intrinsically supernatural. A church that intentionally prioritizes the Spirit consists of people who have intentionally and practically become skilled at looking through the church and seeing Christ there. And mission occurs precisely as we allow this Christ-light within us to shine more and more brightly and clearly. The more we can learn to use pneumatologically enabled eyes to deliberately and intentionally see that Christ is present and at work in our Christian communities, and the more we can make this vision of Christ within us clearer and more distinct to those observing us from the world, this is fundamentally what sets the church apart from all other merely human institutions.

---

[41] Winston D. Persaud, "The Theology of the Cross as Christian Witness: A Theological Essay," *Currents in Theology and Mission* 41 (2014): 15.
[42] David E. Holwerda, "Suffering Witnesses—to What End?: A Sermon on Revelation 11:1–14," *Calvin Theological Journal* 41 (2006): 131–2.

10.3.2 The Trinitarian Connection

Regarding the second Trinitarian connection, the key pneumatological insight here is that it is by the Spirit that the church joins the Son's communion with the Father. Through the Spirit, the church participates in Trinitarian life. Extending this insight to missiology involves exploring how what the Spirit does in eternity is repeated in time, in the church, and in us as individuals, and particularly in our missionary activity.[43] The picture is seen most clearly by starting with the Trinitarian union and then working outwards.

As was noted previously in Chapter 6, the Trinitarian union is not lifeless or static. In the Trinity, there is an ever-present dynamism. But this life or dance is not random. It has an inherent pattern to it—a pattern of breathing in and breathing out. The Father breathes out the Word by the Spirit of love, and then through this Spirit given to him, the Son returns love to the Father. And that breathing out and breathing in is ongoing constantly. The Father constantly breathes out the Son by the Spirit, and then love is returned from the Son through the Spirit of love and Sonship given to him.[44]

But this pattern occurs not just in eternity, but also in time. The same pattern of breathing out and breathing in gets repeated on a new stage. The Father incarnates the Son in time as the human Jesus Christ by the Spirit, and then, by the Spirit the human Jesus returns love to the Father, a human love that the Father gratefully receives. This is the hypostatic union.

The pattern repeats again, not just in eternity or in time, but in human community—in the church. God the Father breathes the Spirit on the church through the Son, and as he does that, Christ is formed in our communities. And then, through this Spirit that has been given to us, together, we breathe out our love to the Father. As Calvin says, "We are the sons of God because we have received the same Spirit as his only Son."[45] Through this Spirit of Sonship, we pray, worship, and give everything back to the Father. And this giving and receiving, this breathing in and breathing out is constantly going on. The Son is embodied in the church through the Spirit. This is the mystical union.

---

[43]This repeated activity of the Spirit is explained in detail in Liston, *The Anointed Church*, 273–301. The objective of this section is to extend the logic of this understanding to the missional activity of the church.

[44]Note that this is a particular understanding of the Trinitarian relations as suggested in Weinandy, *The Father's Spirit of Sonship*.

[45]Calvin, *Calvin's Commentaries*, Gal 4:6; 23:120.

Not just in eternity, in time, and in the church, but in each of us individually, the pattern repeats. As we participate in Christ's life, we reach out with love to others in the church community through the Spirit of love given to us from the Father. And other believers, by this very same Spirit, respond to us in love. It is through this offering and receiving of love, through bearing one another's burdens, through learning to live with each other's differences that we are grown and shaped into who Christ made us to be, people who reflect Christ himself. The Father directs us to love others within the church (breathing out), but others accept that love and return it (breathing in) and it is through this breathing out and breathing in that Christ is formed in us, both individually and as a community. The church of God exists exactly and only "where the love of Christ is found."[46] This is the ecclesial union.

Working through the spheres of eternity, time, the church, and individual believers, leads finally to the aspect of mission. The key recognition here is that the same pattern occurs. The same breathing in and breathing out reality that was seen in ecclesial community happens in ecclesial mission. Because God, of course, does not just direct the church to love others within the church, but to love others beyond it. Just as the church exists exactly and only where, by the Spirit, the love of Christ is offered and returned, mission occurs wherever by the Spirit the love of Christ is offered, and salvation comes wherever that love is returned. So, there are two aspects to our missional activity. We breath out by showing love to the world and those around us, but then we breathe in by gathering again, centering ourselves, and allowing Christ to be formed in us and in our community. And this breathing out and breathing in, going out and coming in, it does not just happen once, it happens constantly, again and again, over and over.

While this trinitarian connection between ecclesiology and missiology is very rich indeed in terms of its implications, this overview is restricted to mentioning just two practical insights. Many missional church authors present the church as being all about what happens out there in the world. Certainly, this is important, but as this analysis points to, it is like constantly breathing out. People and churches cannot last when breath is only being expelled. In contrast, the opposite error is a church that is primarily inwardly focused.[47] But constant intake of breath is just as hazardous. What

---

[46]Gregory J. Liston, "Where the Love of Christ Is Found: Toward a Third Article Ecclesiology," in *Third Article Theology: A Pneumatological Dogmatics* (ed. Myk Habets; Minneapolis, MN: Fortress Press, 2016), 321.

[47]Newbigin's characterization here is apt, saying that such a "Church becomes an introverted body, concerned with its own welfare rather than with the Kingdom of God, and—even if successful

is required are churches and individuals who reach out and reach in, who breath out and breath in. Achieving a balance between these two is not just about creating an approach to mission that is sustainable, although it does have that outcome. More importantly, this approach to mission is about pneumatologically and practically participating in the life of God who in his very trinitarian nature breathes in and breathes out, and continually does both.

10.3.3 The Eschatological Connection

Having addressed the pneumatological insights into ecclesiology when it is viewed from the vantage points of Christology and the Trinity, and the missiological implications that emerge from both of these perspectives, the third and final connection to explore is eschatological. Viewed from an eschatological vantage point through the lens of the Spirit, the church is illuminated as the proleptic anticipation of the coming kingdom.[48] Moreover, this viewpoint provides a nuanced picture of how the Spirit is transforming the church through time. Using this understanding as a control belief to examine the data belief of mission leads to exploring not just the Spirit's intra-ecclesial transformative work, but how the Spirit wields the church as a transforming institution, creating systemic change in the communities and environments that it engages.

Like the other connections, the analysis begins with the development of a pneumato-ecclesiology. Looking at the church through the lens of the Spirit from the vantage point of eschatology reveals how the Spirit draws back features of the coming kingdom to be a part of what we experience now. It is through bringing the future back to the present that the Spirit transforms the church. Four key aspects are illustrative. So the coming kingdom is firstly a place where truth reigns. For in the coming kingdom Christ is king, and Christ is the truth. The Spirit, in part, brings that kingdom reality back to become a part of our present ecclesial existence now. He is the Spirit of truth, leading the church into all truth (John 16:13). Second, the kingdom is a place of justice—no more poverty, no more inequality, no more oppression. And

---

missionary work is carried on by others—the Church will be no fit home for those who are gathered in." Lesslie Newbigin, *One Body, One Gospel, One World: The Christian Mission Today* (London: Wm. Carling & Co., 1958), 26.

[48]For a description of this aspect, see Gregory J. Liston, "The Church's Journey through Time: Toward a Spirit Eschatology," *Pneuma* 41 (2019): 43–60.

the Spirit, in part, brings that kingdom reality back to our reality. He is the Spirit of freedom, leading the church toward freedom, to an existence where righteousness and justice flourish (2 Cor 3:17). Third, the kingdom is a place of love, no more divisions, all are one in Christ. The Spirit, in part, brings that kingdom reality back to our current ecclesial existence. He is the Spirit of unity, transforming us from a divided people into a single, united, loving community (Eph 3:17–18). And finally, the kingdom is a place of eternal life, where there is no more death or disease or suffering. And the Spirit, in part, makes that kingdom reality part of our present reality. He is the Spirit of life, the Lord and giver of life, leading the church toward a fulfilled existence and a renewed creation (John 6:63). Truth, freedom, unity, life—each of these is indicative of how the Spirit is transforming the church.[49]

Utilizing this eschatologically inspired understanding of ecclesiology as a control belief from which to examine the data belief of missiology, and particularly ecclesial mission, the initial affirmation is that a core part of the church's mission is simply to live this reality in the world. In other words, a core aspect of the church's mission is to be a sign of the kingdom,[50] showing by its very existence and the way it goes about living in the world the journey the Spirit is taking the church on toward truth, freedom, unity, and life.[51] The implications for missiology go beyond this initial affirmation, though. If ecclesiology informs missiology, then the church cannot restrict itself to simply being an institution that is "being transformed" by the Spirit, it has to be a "transforming" institution. The Spirit works in the world through the church. What is it that the Spirit does for the world through the church? The Spirit continues to be the Spirit of truth, freedom, unity, and life. The Spirit brings all these gifts to the world, and he does it, at least in part, through the church. So it is an aspect of the church's mission to speak public truth. It is a part of the church's mission to liberate those who are oppressed. It is a part of the church's mission to unite people and draw them together. And it is a part of the church's mission to preserve life and bring healing to humanity and to all of creation. These are essential parts of the church's mission, because our ecclesiology informs our mission. The church has to act in the world in a way that is consistent with the reality of who the church is.

---

[49] See further Gregory J. Liston, "Eschatology and Munus Triplex: The Threefold Anointing of the Spirit in Time," *Journal of Reformed Theology* 14 (2020): 323–43.

[50] See, for example, Grenz, *Theology for the Community of God*, 472–9.

[51] As Hauerwas maintains, "the first social ethical task of the church is to be the church." Stanley Hauerwas, *The Peaceable Kingdom* (Notre Dame, IN: SCM Press, 1983), 99.

In terms of practical implications, the most important aspect emerging from this eschatologically inspired perspective is recognizing the sheer breadth of mission. Beyond just evangelism or social justice, the missional task of the church is broad and all-encompassing. Our concern is not restricted to merely one or two aspects of life but encompasses all of human reality. As a missional community, we are to seek the peace and prosperity of the community of which we are a part (see Jer 29:7). But equally important is the recognition that we need to missionally impact the community from the basis of who we are as the church. The imperative therefore lies very much with our own church communities to begin with. We must ensure that our own communities are places of truth, freedom, unity, and life, and that it is on the basis of the work that the Spirit is doing and has already done in our churches that we can missionally impact our communities. This provides a helpful complement and corrective to the volunteer principle outlined by Lord above. Certainly, mission will always require those who choose to volunteer to impact their local community, but they volunteer not just because they are called as individuals but because they are called by the churches of which they are a part. Moreover, and even more importantly, these volunteers have been formed and fashioned by their involvement in these churches to be kingdom people. They are people who live and breathe the characteristics and qualities of the kingdom of God, and on that basis, they extend the work of the Spirit from these churches to the communities in which they reside.

The two major sections of Chapter 10 have taken some initial steps toward the development of a TAT of mission. The first major section (10.2) utilized a pneumatological lens to explore what mission is, and then (at least partly) asked what kind of community the church would need to be to undertake this pneumatologically anointed and inspired role. The second section, in contrast, began with a pneumatological understanding of the church, and then asked how this community could live as a missional body in the world in a way consistent with what God has created them to be. Three connections between ecclesiology and missiology were examined. First, looking at mission from a Christological ecclesiology connection revealed how the church's mission has both a revealing and a drawing aspect to it. Guided by the Spirit in and through its obedient suffering, the church both reveals God to the world, and draws the world to God. Second, a Trinitarian ecclesiology revealed that the church's mission reflects God's existence in having a breathing in and breathing out rhythm to it. We breathe out, directed by the Father to love the world through his Spirit, and then we breathe in, gathering to allow Christ to be pneumatologically formed in us. And finally, an eschatological ecclesiology revealed that the church's mission is not just about being a sign of the kingdom, but also about being its purveyor, at least in part. The Spirit wields the church in order to transform the world, bringing to it truth, freedom, unity, and life. Engaging with all three of these connections results in a wide, grounded, and balanced understanding of the church's mission. Combining the insights from these three connections with the insights from the first section provides a broad and vast view of our missionary activity. This first section noted that pneumatological mission is holistic, experiential, contextual, communal, and spiritual. It noted that mission involves both blessings that are anticipations of the life to come, and yearnings as we await for that full reality. And it noted that mission involves movement in the Spirit from both the particular to the universal, and the universal to the particular. It is as the church lives out the full breadth and depth of this mission that the world sees the church for what it truly is, much more than a mere human institution, but a group of people defined and enlivened by the presence of the Spirit of God.

11

Eschatology: The Spirit as Transforming and Perfecting Presence

11.1 Introduction

Eschatology has not yet been as rigorously examined through the lens of the Spirit to the same extent as many of the other theological doctrines. This is well illustrated in that the most recent comprehensive edited volume of dogmatic developments in TAT contained sections and articles on Christology, Trinity, soteriology, ecclesiology, anthropology, and public theology (among others), but none focused on eschatology.[1] The limited initial investigations into this *loci* that have already occurred have nevertheless yielded some pertinent results, though. Namely, just as Spirit *Christology* has enabled a more nuanced understanding of Christ's growth and development as a human to emerge, so a pneumatologically focused Spirit *eschatology* enables the development of a nuanced understanding of the church's situation and journey through time. Consequently, this chapter investigates the value arising from exploring the doctrine of eschatology through the methodology of TAT, and particularly its implications for our current ecclesiological journey.

It is worthwhile hinting, even if only in very general terms at this point, about the reason for pursuing such a pneumato-eschatological

---

[1] Habets, ed., *Third Article Theology*. Habets notes that he wasn't aware of anyone utilizing a Third Article Theology methodology to explore eschatology up to the point of publication. Since that time, the monograph *Kingdom Come* has been published, which explicitly addresses this topic. The following chapter leverages on and summarizes the work in that volume. See Gregory J. Liston, *Kingdom Come: An Eschatological Third Article Ecclesiology* (London: T&T Clark, 2022).

approach.[2] Typically, theologians have introduced a pneumatological ecclesiology to counteract a purely Christological understanding of the church. Such a Christological emphasis typically leads to an understanding of the church that is excessively institutionalized or hierarchical, as if the church simply *is* what it *is* and what it *does* or how it goes about doing what it does is of less importance. The problem is that reactive and excessively exclusive pneumatological eschatologies and ecclesiologies often trend too far in the opposite direction, where the church's identity is tied too closely to the specific activities occurring within the church. In contrast to Christological approaches, an excessively pneumatological approach suggests that what the church *does* is all that matters and the church has no existence or independent reality outside of its actions. Similarly, a purely Christological understanding of the church can lead to an eschatological ecclesiology that is too triumphalistic, one that emphasizes the church's *eternal* existence and neglects to focus on its chronological journey through time, one where the discontinuity between our present existence and the coming kingdom is overly exaggerated. Such theologies often acknowledge the present reality of the kingdom, but all too often the church's present transformational journey through time is neglected. Reactive responses aim to focus on the purposes of the kingdom of God here and now, but unfortunately often end up simply replacing an eternal, Christologically focused ecclesiology with a timebound approach, where the continuities between the church and coming kingdom are dramatically overemphasized, and minimal recognition is given to the church's current sinful and fallen state.

The TAT approach to eschatology (and its application to ecclesiology) outlined in this chapter is distinguished from these excessive and unhelpful tendencies in two distinct ways. First, rather than attempting to develop an understanding that deliberately *contrasts* with the Christological eschatologies that have previously been developed, it intentionally utilizes and retains the great benefits they have achieved. The approach outlined below deliberately goes *through*, and not *around* Christological understandings. It builds on and complements their great strengths, in the same way that a Spirit Christology properly construed builds on and complements the great strengths of a Logos Christology. In other words (as noted in the methodological criteria in Chapter 3), it intentionally complements and

---

[2]Note that the very generalized explanation of the next two paragraphs is given needed nuance and specificity in Liston, *Kingdom Come: An Eschatological Third Article Ecclesiology*, 25–42.

doesn't contradict First and Second Article Theologies. Second, rather than simply developing an isolated pneumatological ecclesiology or an isolated eschatological ecclesiology, this approach deliberately ties both alternative approaches together, intentionally developing a *pneumato-eschatological* approach to ecclesiology, where eschatology is the vantage point from which ecclesiology is observed, and pneumatology is the lens utilized to connect the two doctrines. Such a connection between eschatology and pneumatology is both biblically and traditionally justified. From a biblical perspective, for example, Jesus explicitly viewed the work of the Spirit as a clear and unambiguous sign of the kingdom's presence (Matt 12:28; Luke 11:20).[3] And from a traditional perspective, both eschatology and pneumatology were intentionally combined together within the Third Article of the Apostles Creed.[4] There is quite some reason, therefore, for expecting such a combined approach to reap significant rewards in terms of developing an insightful, nuanced, and balanced understanding of ecclesial transformation.

Initially, Section 11.2 explores how TAT can be applied to eschatology, making the Spirit's foundational role in eschatology primary and explicit. This leads to an even more pivotal investigation in Section 11.3, exploring how such a Spirit eschatology provides a nuanced picture of the church's growth and development through time. As Yong comments, "the more important matter ... concerns how eternity's beckoning cuts into each present moment of existence."[5] The resulting portrait is one where the Spirit guides the church on its journey toward its future *telos* through its cruciform shape and actions. The final section of the chapter (11.4) then applies the insights gained from both the developed Spirit eschatology and its application to ecclesiology to the ecclesial sacrament of communion. This final section explores how we can align and partner with the Spirit's ongoing transforming and perfecting presence.

11.2 Developing a Spirit Eschatology

The aim of this first section is to view eschatology from the vantage point of Christology, using the mediating lens of pneumatology. Using Wolterstorff's

---

[3] For a more detailed biblical analysis of the connection between pneumatology and eschatology, see Liston, *Kingdom Come: An Eschatological Third Article Ecclesiology*, 28–35.
[4] See Pelikan and Hotchkiss, eds., *Creeds and Confessions: Early, Eastern and Medieval*, 669.
[5] Amos Yong, *Renewing Christian Theology: Systematics for a Global Christianity* (Waco, TX: Baylor University Press, 2014), 55.

terminology, Spirit Christology is the control belief, eschatology is the data belief, and all other doctrines are background beliefs.

In Chapter 3, it was argued that one of the key methodological criteria of TAT is that it complements and does not compete with First and Second Article Theologies.[6] Such a complementary approach is adopted here. Consequently, this section argues that just as Spirit Christology complements Logos Christology in demonstrating the Spirit's foundational role in Christ's incarnation, so a Spirit eschatology complements a Christologically focused eschatology by explicitly acknowledging the Spirit's foundational eschatological role.[7] The theological approach of exploring the eschatological relationship between eternity and time through a Christological lens without significant reference to the Spirit can be labeled "Logos eschatology" (paralleling the terminology of Logos Christology). The pivotal insight of Logos eschatology is (through analogy) to see eternity as corresponding to Christ's divine nature, and time as corresponding to his human nature, so that eternity and time can be related in a similar manner to Christ's divine and human natures. Such a Second Article Theology approach is exemplified in the work of Barth and T. F. Torrance among others and has proved to be exceedingly fruitful.[8] Many argue, however, that it undervalues the Spirit's role, and consequently results in an excessively static account of ecclesial development. For example, Balthasar argues (perhaps a little exaggeratedly) that Barth "avoids all talk about those things that would provide for a real ongoing history between man and God in the sphere of the temporal and the relative. ... nothing really happens in his theology of history, because everything has already taken place in eternity."[9]

Thomas F. Torrance's eschatology provides a mature and developed example of a Second Article Theology approach to the subject. The following discussion uses Torrance's work as an exemplar to demonstrate not just the

---

[6]See Section 3.2, point 4.
[7]Similar to the situation in the Christological *loci*, there are scholars who seek to replace a focus on the Son with a focus on the Spirit within other fields. Examples include Robert Jenson, John Zizioulas, and Reinhard Hütter, among others.
[8]Many resources expound the fruitfulness of this approach. See, for example, Stanley S. Maclean, *Resurrection, Apocalypse, and the Kingdom of Christ: The Eschatology of Thomas F. Torrance* (Eugene, OR: Pickwick Publications, 2012).
[9]Hans Urs von Balthasar, *The Theology of Karl Barth* (trans. John Drury; New York: Holt, Rinehart and Winston, 1971), 277. These are common critiques of Barth and won't be expanded further. For a more extended discussion, see Adrian Langdon, *God the Eternal Contemporary: Trinity, Eternity and Time in Karl Barth* (Eugene, OR: Wipf & Stock, 2012). Also, Wolfgang Vondey, "The Holy Spirit and Time in Contemporary Catholic and Protestant Theology," *Scottish Journal of Theology* 58 (2005). Particularly pp. 397–8. And Colin Gunton, "Salvation," in *The Cambridge Companion to Karl Barth* (ed. John Webster; Cambridge: Cambridge University Press, 2000), 143–58.

strengths and weaknesses of Logos eschatology, but also how constructing a complementary Spirit eschatology corrects its weaknesses without losing these strengths.[10] Recognizing the presence of both continuity and discontinuity in the relationship between the church and the coming kingdom, Torrance argues for a "Chalcedonian" relationship between the two, helpfully suggesting that the kingdom and the church are related "inconfusedly, unchangeably, indivisibly, inseparably."[11] Torrance argues that a "Chalcedonian" analogy can be utilized between church and kingdom because eschatology can and should be characterized Christologically. He writes "eschatology properly speaking is the application of Christology to the Kingdom of Christ and to the work of the church in history."[12]

From a TAT perspective, Torrance's approach is accurate, yet incomplete. For Christ's incarnation itself (let alone its eschatological application) cannot be understood except through the lens of the Spirit. If we affirm the Chalcedonian definition's understanding that in Christ, divine and human natures are hypostatically united, this requires an equal affirmation that this union happens through the Spirit. As was discussed and quoted in an earlier chapter, "Our Lord Jesus Christ is fully and uniquely the person of the Son *and fully and uniquely anointed by the Spirit.*"[13] Any explanation of the hypostatic union that does not explicitly include the Spirit's mission leads to a flawed Christological understanding, for it is through the Spirit that the divine and human are united in Christ.[14] Just as a simplistic understanding of Christology without pneumatology will end up imbalanced, a simplistic application of Christology to eschatology without acknowledgment of the Spirit's constitutive role will end up equally imbalanced.

Utilizing this Chalcedonian analogy, and launching from what Torrance labels the primary eschatological insight of the twentieth century—Barth's realization that the Word became a spatiotemporal being (becoming "time"

---

[10] Given that Torrance's characterization of eschatology is utilized only at a high level in this section, it is described without significant critique. For a helpful and critical analysis that goes into more depth, see Andrew Purves, "The Advent of Ministry: Torrance on Eschatology, the Church, and Ministry," in *Evangelical Calvinism: Volume 2* (ed. Myk Habets and Bobby Grow; Eugene, OR: Pickwick, 2017), 95–127. Also, Maclean, *Resurrection, Apocalypse, and the Kingdom of Christ*, 190–203.
[11] Pelikan and Hotchkiss, eds., *Creeds and Confessions: Early, Eastern and Medieval*, 181.
[12] Thomas F. Torrance, *Royal Priesthood: A Theology of Ordained Ministry* (Edinburgh: T&T Clark, 1993), 43.
[13] Liston, "A "Chalcedonian" Spirit Christology," 76. (Italics added.) For a full justification of this point, see Liston, "A 'Chalcedonian' Spirit Christology," 74–93.
[14] See, for example, Frank D. Macchia, *Jesus the Spirit Baptizer: Christology in the Light of Pentecost* (Grand Rapids, MI: Eerdmans, 2018), 11–14. Also, Sánchez M., *Receiver, Bearer and Giver of God's Spirit*, 86–109.

in the same way he became "flesh"[15])—Torrance draws out the implication that there are three "times" to be considered: "old" or "fallen" time (what humans currently experience in their fallen condition), eternity (God's time), and "new" or "redeemed" time (the time Christ experiences, which reconciles "old" or "fallen" time in union with eternity). The relationship between these three can be expressed through a Christological analogy. "Here too we may think of there having taken place in the Incarnation as it were a hypostatic union between the eternal and the temporal in the form of new time."[16]

The application of a TAT approach to Torrance's original chain of logic leads beyond this to the recognition that eternity and time are joined *through the Spirit*. Certainly, it is "in" Christ that time and eternity are intertwined, but the point that is often neglected in a Logos eschatology, and that is explicit and foundational in a Spirit eschatology, is that this happens "through" the Spirit. The relationship between time and eternity is Christologically situated, as Torrance ably notes, but it is also pneumatologically enabled. Eternity indwells time in Christ *through the Spirit*, and time is taken up into eternity in Christ *through the Spirit*. This is precisely why (with nuanced qualifications) the Spirit can take the past reality of Jesus' work and apply it to our present situation. But it is also precisely why (again, with nuanced qualifications) the Spirit can take the future benefits of Jesus' coming kingdom and apply them to our current reality. Through the Spirit (and in Christ), all times are this time. Just as through the Spirit (and in Christ), all places are this place. As Yong comments, "Not only does Luke say that the *time* of the last days has begun with the coming of the Spirit, but he also says that the *place* of the kingdom is now being redeemed by the Spirit."[17]

But Torrance, of course, is concerned not just with the relationship between time and eternity, but also with the relationship between old (fallen) and new (redeemed) time. "We must think ... of fallen time as having perfected itself through the Cross and resurrection into the abiding triumph of a perfection in God which both consummates the original purposes of creation and crowns

---

[15]See, for example, Barth, *Church Dogmatics*, III.2, 437–42.
[16]Thomas F. Torrance, "The Modern Eschatological Debate," *Evangelical Quarterly* 25 (1953): 224. See also Thomas F. Torrance, *Incarnation: The Person and Life of Christ* (Downers Grove, IL: InterVarsity Press, 2008), 334–6. And Thomas F. Torrance, *Space, Time and Resurrection* (Edinburgh: T&T Clark, 1976), 98–9.
[17]Amos Yong, *In the Days of Caesar: Pentecostalism and Political Theology* (Grand Rapids, MI: Eerdmans, 2010), 331. (Italics added.)

it with glory."¹⁸ The result is that there are two tensions to be considered—an "eschatological" tension between "new" (redeemed) and "old" (fallen) time and an ultimate "teleological" tension between the eternal and temporal. For Torrance, the first is equivalent to the tension between the new creation and the fallen world, while the second is equivalent to the holiness/sinfulness tension. Torrance essentially envisions time as two separate lines running in parallel (new and old time), both of which are positioned within the constant background and framework of eternity, with new time being the Christological union of old time with eternity.

But here again, we need to recognize not just the reality of what has been achieved in Christ, but the pneumatological manner through which it was achieved. For both the cross and the resurrection occurred *through the Spirit*. Not only was Jesus' life pneumatologically empowered, but it was through the Spirit that he offered himself to God on the cross (Heb 9:14), and it was by the Spirit that he was raised from the dead (Rom 8:11).[19] If, then, we think of fallen time as having perfected itself through the cross and resurrection (as Torrance says), we ought to also think of the means through which this happens—through the Spirit. It is in the Spirit that we who exist in fallen time participate in Christ's new redeemed time, and it is in the Spirit that Christ's past, present, and future in this new redeemed time are brought to bear on our present reality.[20] Essentially, what happens is that through the Spirit, all times in Christ's new time are brought to bear on the single moment we currently inhabit in old time.

It is at this point that the value of adopting a *complementary* approach to Spirit eschatology becomes particularly clear. The alternative of *replacing* a focus on the Son with a focus on the Spirit fundamentally alters the understanding of new and old time running in parallel that was developed through a Logos eschatology.[21] When the ecclesial mission of the Son is subsumed into that of the Spirit, the Spirit cannot be identified as a distinct person within the church leading us into the (logically distinguishable) life of the Son. Rather, the Spirit is simply the risen Christ drawing us gradually to himself. With only one active participant, there is only one place the

---

[18] Torrance, "The Modern Eschatological Debate," 224–5.
[19] See, for example, Studebaker, *From Pentecost to the Triune God*, 80–7.
[20] See particularly the detailed discussion of the interaction between God's time and our time in Matthew K. Thompson, *Kingdom Come: Revisioning Pentecostal Ecclesiology* (Dorset: Deo Publishing, 2010), 109–27.
[21] This tendency can be seen in several eschato-ecclesial approaches that replace a focus on the Son with a focus on the Spirit.

Spirit can act (within the church and its practices) and only one dimension along which the church can be transformed (continuously in fallen time toward its future teleological reality). The result is that, in direct contrast to the Logos eschatologies of Barth and Torrance that undervalue the church's development through time, these replacement Spirit eschatologies essentially merge new and old time together, giving our present experience of fallen time an undeserved precedence. Such an approach ignores the ontological separateness of Christ from the church, confusing and merging the two.

A complementary Spirit eschatology, in contrast, does not alter the broad framework connecting time and eternity developed through a Logos eschatology approach. Redeemed and fallen time are still understood as existing and evolving in parallel. In addition to these insights arising from a Logos eschatology, however, a complementary Spirit eschatology also enables a dynamic understanding of the church's transformation within fallen time (as explored in detail in the next section). Further, it ensures that the full interaction between the two times is considered. Using a complementary TAT approach, all of redeemed time, from its beginning with Christ's resurrection through to its culmination in the coming kingdom, interacts with the present moment we exist in within fallen time. Looking through the lens of the Spirit ensures that we do not minimize the relationship between the two parallel times by restricting it to just bringing forward Christ's past work, or just acknowledging the presence of Christ with us through the Spirit. But through the Spirit, the past, present, and future reality of Christ in new time impacts us at the present moment we are experiencing in ecclesial time. Christologically focused attempts to connect fallen and redeemed time often focus on specific aspects of redeemed time and neglect other aspects, rather than pneumatologically spanning the entire spectrum of Christ's existence in new time, and its relevance to us now. Barth's analysis, for example, focuses on bringing forward to us Christ's past work, and has a noetic focus. This aspect can be likened or appropriated to Christ's prophetic role, bringing forward the knowledge of our salvation in Christ through the Spirit. Torrance, without losing Barth's noetic understanding, has an ontic focus, exploring Christ's present heavenly session, and how we participate through the Spirit in Christ's present and ongoing vicarious humanity. This can be likened or appropriated to Christ's priestly role, effecting our salvation through standing in the gap between humanity and divinity, and between time and eternity. But what both Barth and Torrance both arguably undervalue (to differing degrees) is the telic aspect, the Spirit's role in bringing back to us (in part) the reality of Christ's future kingdom, a connection that can be likened or appropriated to Christ's kingly role. It is precisely this role that will be explored in the next section.

11.3 Applying a Spirit Eschatology to Ecclesiology

This section explores how the kingly connection between new and old time complements and extends Barth and Torrance's work (which explore the prophetic and priestly connection). It describes how the reality of Christ's future in new time is brought to bear on the church's present reality. The most obvious move in exploring this connection would be to leverage recent scholars who have intentionally adopted a future-oriented approach.[22] While there is creativity and value in this work, simplistically utilizing it to explore the kingly connection between new and old time proves intractable. First, because most often these chronologically oriented approaches do not distinguish between new and old time, and as such adopt an approach that intrinsically diverges from the framework, connections, and insights outlined above. Instead, they collapse the distinction between these two times, giving fallen time an undeserved precedence and priority, and consequently ignore the ontological separateness of Christ from the church.[23] A second challenge is that these approaches rarely acknowledge the practical reality of the future kingdom impacting present time. As van der Kooi acknowledges, "even where today the notion of God's kingdom is acknowledged as a holistic idea, there is still immediate hesitation, for example, if it involves healing. The theologies of Jürgen Moltmann and Wolfhart Pannenberg are examples of this position. Both scholars defend the idea that the future is already present here, but instead of becoming concrete, they remain stuck in generalities, if not obfuscations."[24]

The objective of this section, then, is to concretely explore how Christ's kingly reign is present in the church and how, by means of the Spirit, this impacts our current existence in fallen time. For the Spirit doesn't just prophetically bring forward Jesus' past work (the aspect Barth emphasizes), or in a priestly manner enable us to share in Christ's present vicarious

---

[22] Examples include Hütter, Pannenberg, Zizioulas, and Moltmann, among others.
[23] As discussed in the previous section.
[24] Van der Kooi, *This Incredibly Benevolent Force*, 16.

humanity (which is Torrance's area of focus). The Spirit also draws back into our current time features of the coming kingdom so that they become a part of our present ecclesial experience. Even more, this pneumatologically transposed experience of the future kingdom drives us forward, empowering our development and transformation. This section demonstrates these connections through outlining how four interrelated characteristics of the coming kingdom—truth, life, justice, and love—are pneumatologically brought back into our current time to become characteristics of our present ecclesial existence, and further how the Spirit transforms the church to more completely reflect these characteristics. In Scripture, these four qualities stand out as essential and often repeated features of the eschatological life. Each of them provides a concrete data point for how the future kingdom is pneumatologically anticipated in our present ecclesial experience. An examination of all four qualities allows common patterns to emerge. This section examines each of these data points in order to recognize the systematic patterns through which the coming kingdom pneumatologically impacts our present existence. The resulting picture outlines the kingly connection between new and old time.

That the coming kingdom is a place of truth, where every hidden reality is revealed and every falsehood is unmasked, is implicitly illustrated through God's ever-present revealing light (Rev 21:23–24) and explicitly noted through the absence of misleading evildoers (Rev 21:8, 22:15). The captivating descriptions in Rev 21–22 paint a picture where every remnant of falsehood and darkness has been swept away by God's all-encompassing truth and light. There is an ultimate connection between truth and holiness here, for the unalloyed presence of truth and righteousness necessarily means the holy removal of error and evil. Truth reigns in the coming kingdom because Christ reigns and Christ is the truth (John 14:6). But the Spirit, in part, brings that kingdom reality of truth back to become a reality in our ecclesial existence now. For not only has Christ's kingdom truth been revealed to us in the Spirit (1 Cor 2:9–12), but the Spirit is the Spirit of truth (John 16:13), who continuously leads us into all truth (1 John 2:26). Empowered by the Spirit, then, the church should not only oppose all mistruths that reject Christ and keep people from knowing God (1 Cor 10:4–5), but should also proclaim Christ's kingdom truth with all the wisdom that has been given to us, relying on Christ's power present within us to do so (Col 1:28).

Abundant life is perhaps the most insistently repeated characteristic in the depictions of the coming kingdom in the final chapters of Revelation. Its inhabitants are named in the book of life (Rev 20:12), and two central geographic features are a river (filled with the water of life) and the tree of life (Rev 22:1–2), whose leaves provide a healing so potent that the coming kingdom has no more death, sorrow, crying, or pain (Rev 21:3). This kingdom life goes well beyond biological existence (bios) to spiritual life (zoe)—life truly lived and lived to the fullest—a life that finds its true source in the resurrected Jesus (John 20:31), the lamb on the throne from which flows the water of life (Rev 22:1). Abundant life is consequently the reigning reality in the kingdom because Christ reigns, and Christ is life (John 14:6), and our life is found in him (John 1:4). But the Spirit, in part, brings that kingdom experience of abundant life back to become a reality in our ecclesial existence now. For not only has participation in Christ's resurrection life been given to us at the present time through the Spirit (John 7:37–39), but the Spirit is the Spirit of life (Rom 8:2), leading the church toward an abundant existence and a renewed creation (John 6:63). Empowered by the Spirit, then, the church should not only proclaim words of physical, emotional, and spiritual healing over those who are suffering (1 Cor 12:9),[25] but we should intentionally live out abundant lives, finding in our present existence true fulfillment and increasingly abundant joy in the pneumatological presence of the resurrected Christ (John 10:10).

Justice is the third characteristic of the coming kingdom, for it is a place where there is no more poverty, no more inequality, and no more bondage. From its earliest precursors through to its final descriptions, justice is explicitly noted as a primary characteristic of the Son's kingdom (e.g., Isa 9:6–7; Rev 19:11). There is a connection between justice and liberty here, for the judge who judges justly brings freedom to all those who are unjustly oppressed (Luke 4:18–19; John 8:34).[26] God's coming kingdom is consequently a place where freedom reigns—freedom from tyranny and oppression, certainly, but even more than that freedom from death, decay, and sin. Indeed, it is not just God's children who experience such justice and liberty, but creation itself that is rightly released from its unwelcome captivity to corruption (Rom 8:21–22). But the Spirit, in part, brings that kingdom reality of justice and freedom back to be experienced in our ecclesial existence now. For through the Spirit we have already been given a "foretaste of future glory" (Rom 8:23), being freed from the power of sin (Rom 8:1) and justified through the work

---

[25]See, for example, the profound discussion of healing in van der Kooi, *This Incredibly Benevolent Force*, 112–15.

[26]There is similarly a connection between truth and freedom (e.g., John 8:32), but that is perhaps more specifically seen as a freedom from evil and error, rather than a freedom from oppression. The two are clearly interrelated, as are all the characteristics of the coming kingdom.

of Jesus (Rom 3:21–26). That future declaration of righteousness from the final judgment has now, at the present time, been proclaimed over us, so that the justice of God in Christ might be truly seen. But the Spirit does not just declare the justice of God in our current time but grows us increasingly into becoming a just and liberated community. He is the Spirit of liberty, leading the church toward freedom, to an existence where righteousness and justice flourish, increasingly reflecting the character of our king (2 Cor 3:17–18). For one of the primary signs through which the Spirit's presence is evident within an individual (Luke 4:18–19) or a community (Acts 2:45, 4:32–34) is that they increasingly embrace the neglected and prioritize the poor.

The final characteristic of the coming kingdom addressed in this section is love, for all those who live in God live in love (1 John 3:16). Just as justice pervades the descriptions of the kingdom from beginning to end, so too does love (e.g., Isa 16:5; 1 John 3:1–7). Indeed, love is the greatest, most enduring, and primary defining trait of the future kingdom, for God is love (1 John 4:8). The coming kingdom is infused with love because Christ the king loves us (Rev 1:5) and has demonstrated this love through his sacrificial death (John 15:13). There is a connection between love and unity here, for Christ's loving sacrifice has broken down the dividing wall of hostility (Eph 2:14–16), so that the future kingdom is a place where all the diversity of humanity (Rev 8:9) and creation itself (Isa 11:6) dwell together in loving harmony. But the Spirit, in part, brings that kingdom reality of love and unity back to be experienced in our ecclesial existence now. This is why Paul can use a pneumatological argument to demonstrate that all divisions within the church are theologically impossible (1 Cor 12:13).[27] Just as the Spirit is the bond of love between the Father and Son, so too is he the bond joining Christians together in unity (John 17:20–26). But the Spirit does not just declare our loving unity, he leads us toward becoming a loving and united Christian community. He is the Spirit of unity (Eph 4:4), leading the church toward love and unity. Through the Spirit, our hearts are filled with love for each other (Rom 5:5, 15:30), and as our love grows more perfect, we lose our fear of judgment and look forward to the coming kingdom with longing (1 John 4:17–18).

---

[27]"This text affirms that the visible ritual of initiating diverse human beings through the power of the Spirit into a single local assembly is meant to point to the invisible bond of love by which the *Spiritus Congregator* renders them one in mind and heart as members of the universal Body of Christ." Philip J. Rosato, "The Mission of the Spirit within and beyond the Church," *Ecumenical Review* 41 (1989): 391.

All four of these examples reflect a common pattern. First, the qualities of truth, life, justice, and love that characterize the kingdom do so because of Christ's kingship. It is only because Christ is king that his character is reflected so perfectly in the coming kingdom. Second, through the Spirit, these kingdom characteristics are brought back to be a part of our ecclesial reality now. Their occurrence among us can be attributed to Christ's genuine presence with us as king. In other words, Christ dwells among us as king by his Spirit, and so our communities are places of truth, life, justice, and love. Of course, our ecclesial reality is not completely characterized by these qualities, because the fullness of the kingdom is still coming and has not yet arrived.

But Christ's kingly presence has ecclesial implications. This is the third feature in the pattern, for the Spirit leads our communities increasingly into these kingdom realities. In other words, in bringing back to us the presence of Christ the king, the Spirit leads and drives us on toward the coming kingdom, so that the presence of these kingdom qualities and Christ's kingly reign itself are increasingly apparent among us. The presence of Christ as king through his Spirit has consequences—it not only affects who we are, but who we are becoming. The Spirit's work goes beyond transforming our communities, however. The fourth and final feature of the pattern is that the church becomes not just the recipient of, and characterised by, these kingly qualities, but the purveyors of them. The Spirit continues his work as the Spirit of truth, the Spirit of life, the Spirit of liberty, and the Spirit of love, and he does this through the church. Just as Christ the king brings truth, freedom, unity, and life to the kingdom and to the church, so the Spirit uses the church to bring these qualities to the world. This is our vice-regency—as united with our king, we act on his behalf. So it is an aspect of the church's mission to speak public truth, to liberate those who are oppressed, to unite people and draw them together in love, and to preserve life and bring healing to humanity and creation. These are essential parts of the church's mission because the church's royal ministry role reflects Christ's kingly office. The relationship is not merely one of union, though, but of differentiation and asymmetry. The difference is that our royal ministry is not intrinsic but representative—we are Christ's ambassadors (2 Cor 5:20) who are working in enemy territory (2 Cor 4:5)—so we have no intrinsic authority to insist or compel, only the winsomeness to persuade. And the asymmetry comes from the fact that it is only because Christ has given us truth, life, justice, and love that we have the opportunity to be purveyors of these qualities to the world.

To summarize, this connection between the future of new time and our present moment in old time has three key features. First, it is a kingly connection. It is Christ's future reign as the true king of his coming kingdom that is pneumatologically anticipated in our present ecclesial communities. Second, it is a telic connection. The presence of the king transforms our communities toward our ultimate telos. Christ's pneumatologically enabled presence not only allows the kingly traits of truth, life, justice, and love to be evident and growing among us, it encourages and enables us to act as purveyors of these traits to the outside world, not forcefully through intrinsic authority, but through persuasion as kingly representatives living in a foreign land. Third, it connects the culmination of Christ's existence in new time with our present moment in old time. It denotes a connection between the coming kingdom and our present time. For these three reasons, this connection can be represented as an arrow from the culmination or "future" of Christ's new time through to our present moment in old time; an arrow labeled as both telic and kingly. These three features do not by any means exhaust the theological richness of this kingly connection. Many questions remain. They do, however, illustrate and outline the value of exploring the pneumatological connection between the coming kingdom and the present church, and the rich potential it offers to understand how the Spirit acts as a transforming and perfecting presence.

11.4 Application to Communion

Given the analysis above outlining how the Spirit both draws back to the present church characteristics of the coming kingdom and acts as a transforming and perfecting presence driving the church onward to its future *telos*, the natural question that emerges is how we can align ourselves with the Spirit's actions. How can we partner with the Spirit's transformational work among us? In order to make the following descriptions of how this occurs as concrete as possible, we choose one particular example of church life to focus on and explore how the Spirit works through that particular practice to transform the church. As the *centralis agere* in the life of the church, and the defining aspect of our ongoing worship, the eucharist is an obvious choice.[28] As Torrance characterizes it,

---

[28]The words eucharist, Lord's Supper, and communion are used interchangeably in this section.

the emphasis upon the once and for all union of God and man, of the eternal and the temporal falls most heavily upon the sacrament of Baptism, while in the eucharist or sacrament of holy communion we have the emphasis most upon the continuation of that in the contradictions and abstractions of fallen time. ... If at Baptism we think of our union with Christ as *opus dei*, work of God which takes place in and for its own sake, at communion we think of the same union inserted into our flesh and blood, into time and history as by faith we partake of Christ's flesh and blood.[29]

Like the church itself, the eucharist has three aspects, relating to its past, present, and future respectively. The past aspect of the eucharist is based in the meal's remembrance of what Christ has done: "do this *in remembrance of me*" (Luke 22:19) (italics added). The present aspect of the eucharist is derived from it being a meal of fellowship and communion, both with God and with other believers: "I have earnestly desired to eat this Passover meal *with you*" (Luke 22:15) (italics added). The future aspect of the eucharist is that the meal anticipates a coming celebration of the full and final union and communion between God and humanity: "From now on I will not drink of the vine *until the kingdom of God comes*" (Luke 22:18) (italics added). It is this latter aspect of the eucharist that is most obviously underemphasized in today's (particularly Protestant) church practice. For example, Craig Blomberg writes, "As for temporal emphases of the Lord's Supper, the church in general today seems best at stressing the backward look to the cross. The most neglected is our anticipation of the heavenly banquet. Somewhere in between falls our focus on present fellowship with God and others."[30]

Further, it is this future aspect of the eucharist that most clearly and directly influences the church's transformation through the passage of time. This section broadly and briefly sketches out the overarching aspects of how a pneumatologically and eschatologically enabled eucharistic celebration empowers the church's transformation. It argues that such transformation occurs through the intersecting interplay of imagination, presence, and practice.

---

[29]Torrance, *Incarnation*, 339.
[30]Craig L. Blomberg, *1 Corinthians* (Grand Rapids, MI: Zondervan Academic, 2009), 238. See also I. Howard Marshall, *Last Supper and Lord's Supper* (Vancouver: Regent College Publishing, 1980), 153.

11.4.1 Imagination

The first eschatological and pneumatological phenomenon considered in this analysis of the eucharistic celebration is the creation and stimulation of our imaginations. Through participating in the eucharist, we increasingly see ourselves as people of the kingdom, foreigners living in a strange world, an exiled community whose true home is distinct from the place and time in which we currently reside (Phil 3:20; 1 Pet 2:11). As an anticipation of the Lamb's wedding supper, the eucharist paints a picture for us of reality as it should and will be, a place and time where Christ is truly and completely king and we as the church are truly and completely united to him as his bride. Participating in the eucharist develops within our communities a foretaste, a picture, and a deep desire for such a reality, and it is these aspects that give significance and meaning to our participation in the eucharistic celebration and our lives beyond it. Moreover, pneumatological transformation is enabled through this created and stimulated eschatological imagination that occurs during the eucharist, a "renewing of our minds" (Rom 8:2).

Imagination, as the term is being used here, must be sharply distinguished from mere wishful thinking or fantasy. In contrast, it aligns with the type of construct Charles Taylor describes through the phrase "social imaginary."[31] Imagination in this sense provides the fundamental understanding of who we are as a community, how we relate to one another, and what our common life should be like. It is the framework through which we make sense of our existence and actions. While such imagination clearly has an intellectual component, it reaches well beyond this. It is pre- (and post-) cognitive, instinctual, embodied, aspirational, and affective. The theological imagination that is developed in the church through participating in the eucharist is much more than just an intellectual "worldview."[32] It is a way of seeing, understanding, and doing life that defines and characterizes who we are.

Perhaps the key word to associate with the creation and stimulation of such an eschatological imagination, then, is "longing." An "imagination" of the future that is based on Christ's death and resurrection and the anticipation that brings of the coming kingdom produces longing, and

---

[31] See, for example, Charles Taylor, *Modern Social Imaginaries* (Durham, NC: Duke University Press, 2004), 23–30.
[32] See James K. A. Smith, *Desiring the Kingdom: Worship, Worldview, and Cultural Formation* (Grand Rapids, MI: Baker Academic, 2009), 63–5.

through that longing, the church community both recognizes that the future is not currently realized in its completeness (with appropriate angst and groaning [e.g., Rom 8:29]), while simultaneously experiencing the reality that through Christ's current pneumatological presence as king the future kingdom is at least partially but nevertheless genuinely present and evident in the eucharistic feast. A church can only be the church if it both anticipates the quality of life that is planned and prepared for it in the coming kingdom, and also simultaneously realizes that to a great degree that quality of life and communion currently eludes it. As Neuhaus comments, "The Biblical statements about the Church … are either false or nonsense, unless they are understood as statements of a future hope anticipated in the present."[33]

Closely associated with the affections that this longing represents is the profound recognition that any extent to which the church does anticipate the future kingdom occurs not through human effort, but through a miraculous, pneumatological, and eschatological invasion. The foretaste of the kingdom comes from the outside, and not from within. "If the all-too-human church can be considered divine, it is as the institutional community that … anticipate[s] in its life and ministry the dawn of the new creation."[34] It is for this reason that the pneumatologically inspired imagination engendered through participating in the eucharist is not sufficient but must be partnered with genuine experience of the divine presence.

11.4.2 Presence

For at least the last five centuries, arguments about the exact manner of Christ's presence in the elements have pervaded and consumed discussions about the eucharist.[35] While these debates are not unimportant, such sustained attention to the manner of Christ's presence has to a large degree diverted the church from the more significant truths of the reality and impact of his presence. Leithart characterizes this emphasis as having a

---

[33]Richard John Neuhaus, "Wolfhart Pannenberg: Profile of a Theologian," in *Theology and the Kingdom of God* (ed. Richard John Neuhaus; Philadelphia: Westminster, 1969), 42.
[34]Scott MacDougall, *More Than Communion: Imagining an Eschatological Ecclesiology* (London: T&T Clark, 2015), 179.
[35]See, for example, Russell D. Moore, I. John Hesselink, David P. Scaer, and Thomas A. Baima, *Understanding Four Views on the Lord's Supper* (Grand Rapids, MI: Zondervan, 2007). For a more detailed history of eucharistic theology, see Paul H. Jones, *Christ's Eucharistic Presence: A History of the Doctrine* (New York: Peter Lang, 1994). Also, Gary Macy, *The Banquet's Wisdom: A Short History of the Theologies of the Lord's Supper* (New York: Paulist, 1992).

"zoom" like effect so that our attention is focused exclusively on functional (exactly what happens with the bread and the cup) and individualistic (what is the benefit to the individual participant) understandings of the eucharist, missing the ontological and communal aspects that are even more pivotal and significant.[36] Leithart argues that the more central and pressing issue is not the manner but the "doctrine of the real presence. ... The eucharist shapes the church because Christ is present at the meal by his Spirit, and therefore she is ... changed by communion with her husband. The Supper makes the church the church because the communion that takes place at the Supper makes the church like Christ."[37]

While our understanding regarding the exact nature of Christ's presence at the table is closest to the Reformed perspective, we maintain that the exact manner of Christ's presence does not affect to any great degree the points made in the following discussion about the pneumatological and eschatological transformation occurring in the eucharist. What is pertinent is not the specific manner but the genuine reality of Christ's presence. The foundational truth from which the eschatological and pneumatological understanding of transformation emerges is that Christ is genuinely present in the eucharistic celebration and that our celebration of the meal together intrinsically involves genuine communion with him. This is a point upon which virtually all viewpoints concur.[38]

While Christ's eucharistic presence necessarily includes all three of his offices of prophet, priest, and king, viewed from an eschatological perspective, the emphasis falls particularly on his kingly office. The Christ with whom we commune, the Christ whose wedding supper we are anticipating, this is Christ the king—the Lord of all creation. As was noted in the previous chapter, in bringing the future the presence of Christ the king back to us from, the Spirit leads and drives us on toward his coming kingdom, so that the presence of these kingdom qualities and Christ's kingly reign itself are increasingly apparent among us. In particular, the presence of Christ as king through his Spirit has ontological consequences, fundamentally affecting who we are as people. It is Christ's presence through the Spirit that writes the laws of the king on our hearts and minds. It is his Spirit living within us that moves us to follow his kingly decrees (Ezek 36:27).

---

[36] Peter J. Leithart, "The Way Things Really Ought to Be: Eucharist, Eschatology, and Culture," *The Westminster Theological Journal* 59 (1997): 159. Geoffrey Wainwright makes a similar argument. See Geoffrey Wainwright, *Eucharist and Eschatology* (London: Epworth Press, 1971), 1–2.
[37] Leithart, "The Way Things Really Ought to Be," 175.
[38] The only exception would perhaps be a hyper-extreme memorialist understanding.

To suggest this divine transformation happens intrinsically and automatically through partaking in the eucharist is to make the mistake of too greatly melding and confusing human and divine action. As Leithart comments, "the eucharist does not shape the church and its members by ceremonial manipulation, as if repetition of the rite, by putting words in our mouths and making us go through the motions of ecclesiastical unity, performs a kind of sacred brainwashing."[39] But we similarly cannot make the mistake of focusing only on divine action and ignoring, neglecting, or minimizing the human aspect. Divine action from the creator needs to be complemented by human action in a manner appropriate to the creature. And so the first pneumatological phenomenon (the creation and stimulation of our eschatological imagination), and the second (the eschatological presence of Christ in us through his Spirit), must be complemented and completed by a third pneumatological phenomenon (which is empowered human practice).

11.4.3 Practice

In the eucharist, we do not merely "imagine" the coming kingdom, and we do not merely enjoy communion with the coming king, we "practice" genuinely being part of the kingdom. Using the vocabulary of the Spiritual Disciplines movement, in the repeated performance of communal practices we are led into the righteousness of the kingdom through "indirection." By doing what we can do (taking the bread and the cup together in communion), we receive from God the resources to do what we cannot do (live virtuously as true subjects of the kingdom).[40] As we "practice" what it means to genuinely live as if the kingdom has already come, we are gradually transformed by the Spirit to become the kind of people and the kind of community who genuinely belong and fit within that coming kingdom.[41]

---

[39]Leithart, "The Way Things Really Ought to Be," 175.
[40]The language in this sentence adjusts Foster's words to directly address this context. See Richard Foster, "Foreword," in *The Spirit of the Disciplines* (London: Hodder and Stoughton, 1988), 14.
[41]On this topic, see particularly Sánchez's groundbreaking work on the transformative role of the Holy Spirit, based on Spirit Christology, Sánchez M., *Sculptor Spirit: Models of Sanctification from Spirit Christology*. The primary distinction between his work and this analysis is that his book is focused on how *persons* are formed by the Spirit into the image of Christ, while the focus here is particularly on how ecclesial *communities* are pneumatologically transformed into Christ's image. The intentionally eschatological approach used here also distinguishes it from Sánchez's methodology. The two approaches are complementary, of course. For a briefer summary, see Leopoldo A. Sánchez M., "Sculpting Christ in Us: Public Faces of the Spirit in God's World," in *Third*

The kingdom is both a present and a coming reality. The eucharist is therefore a celebration where we presently practice being a part of the coming kingdom, because (in one sense) we are already a part of the coming kingdom. "At the Supper, we eat bread and drink wine together with thanksgiving not merely to *show* the way things really ought to be, but to *practice* the way things really ought to be."[42] It is through acting as if the future were already here and that we are genuinely a part of it (which is partly but not completely true) that transformation occurs. In short, through the Spirit, as we take the eucharist together, we increasingly become like what we (in truth, but only in part) already are: genuine citizens of the kingdom, and true and loyal subjects of the king.

In characteristically forthright and helpful fashion, C. S. Lewis outlines the essence of this concept in *Mere Christianity* by describing our practices (and practice) as "pretending." Focusing specifically on the ecclesial practice of prayer, Lewis notes that the very first words of the Lord's prayer are "Our Father." He goes on to explain:

> Do you now see what those words mean? They mean quite frankly, that you are putting yourself in the place of a son of God. To put it bluntly, you are dressing up as Christ. If you like, you are pretending. Because, of course, the moment you realise what the words mean, you realise that you are not a son of God. You are not a being like The Son of God, whose will and interests are at one with those of the Father: you are a bundle of self-centred fears, hopes, greeds, jealousies, and self-conceit, all doomed to death. So that, in a way, this dressing up as Christ is a piece of outrageous cheek. But the odd thing is that He has ordered us to do it. Why? … the pretence leads up to the real thing. … Very often the only way to get a quality in reality is to start behaving as if you had it already.[43]

While Lewis explains the essence of this concept well for an introductory book on Christianity, there is obviously more nuance needed. When it comes to being God's sons and daughters, for example, we are living in a simultaneous state of both being and becoming sons and daughters. We are "becoming" sons and daughters of God in the sense that as we grow and develop through time, we are increasingly transformed by the Spirit to achieve greater communion with Christ, fully realizing this potential for

---

Article Theology: A Pneumatological Dogmatics (ed. Myk Habets; Minneapolis, MN: Fortress Press, 2016), 297–320.
[42]Leithart, "The Way Things Really Ought to Be," 175. (Italics in original.)
[43]Lewis, *Mere Christianity*, 187–8.

ontological union and identification at the eschaton. We are "becoming" sons and daughters of God in the sense that we are being prepared for that day. But simultaneously, we already "are" sons and daughters of God as Christ has already united himself to us, with the promise of fuller and greater communion to come. Just as the "not guilty" verdict of the final judgment is enacted "at the present time" (Rom 3:26), our future union with Christ and adoption as true sons and daughters of the Father is (in a nuanced sense) enacted at this moment, through the *arrabōn* (deposit) of the Spirit.[44] So the pretending is not mere pretence. But neither is it the entire reality. Being and becoming exist together.

Turning to the eucharist and its relationship with the coming kingdom, the situation is similar. Through the enacted and lived out practice of participating in communion, not only are the ways in which we are currently living a kingdom reality strengthened and solidified, but the intentional and unintentional areas in which we are *not* living out the reality of the kingdom also become increasingly clear to us. And having had these areas brought to our attention by the Spirit through our eschatological practice, we then lean on the Spirit's empowering to gradually transform us as individuals and as a community to live in a way that is more consistent with the coming kingdom that is our true home.

Using the eucharist as a significant and prototypical example, then, this section has explored how the Spirit transforms the church through the interplay of imagination, experienced presence, and empowered practice. Regarding the first aspect, the Spirit's work in our imaginations is primarily noetic, although this does not mean it is limited to a merely cognitive change. During the eucharist, the Spirit fills our hearts and minds with a vision of the coming kingdom, a vision that promotes in us longing and wonder. And it is (in part) through this imaginative renewing of our minds that the Spirit transforms us. Regarding the second aspect, the Spirit's mediation of the presence of Christ to us is primarily ontic, although this does not mean that any change effected in us is magical, involuntary, or automatic, intrinsically separated from our own creaturely actions. During the eucharist, we genuinely commune with Christ who is present to us through the Spirit. This presence is the divine empowering of the transformation we experience, as the Spirit writes the laws of the coming kingdom on our hearts and moves us to follow Christ's kingly decrees. "This is the age … when by the power of the Holy Spirit, who inhabits the Church … all who believe in Jesus Christ

---

[44] See the similar discussion in Liston, *The Anointed Church*, 137–8.

may taste the powers of the age to come through sacramental incorporation into the new creation."[45] Regarding the final aspect, the Spirit's work in our "practices" is primarily telic, although that does not mean that it is only through our actions that transformation occurs. Practice, alone, does not make perfect. All three aspects—imagination, presence, and practice—are interrelated and intertwined. During the eucharist, we are "practicing" for the future kingdom we will inhabit, while simultaneously recognizing that the future is (at least in part) already experienced as a present reality. While human "practice" alone is completely ineffectual at implementing genuine transformation, the presence of Christ through his Spirit in the eucharist bestows our finite human actions with genuine transformational efficacy.

---

[45] Thomas F. Torrance, "Eschatology and the Eucharist," in *Intercommunion* (ed. D. M. Baillie and J. Marsh; London: SCM, 1952), 308–9.

12
Conclusion

TAT is an approach to dogmatics that is at once traditional and contemporary. Working within the Great Tradition and attuned to contemporary contexts, TAT seeks to speak out of the received revelation of God and into the various contexts we live in today. There is no attempt in a TAT to write new theology, if new means novel or invented. TAT is a faithful servant of the Catholic Church and seeks to make a significant contribution to equipping the saints for service. While not novel, TAT is a way of seeing the world in theological terms that have been overlooked or passed over too quickly. The year 2025 is the 1,700th anniversary of the Council of Nicaea (AD 325). As the present work highlights, a commitment to pro-Nicene theology does not equate to a staid and tired theology, but rather, it focuses on theological thinking that is deep and profound rather than broad and shallow. TAT is committed to this deep and profound principle of the conciliar tradition, and it is at the forefront of what a faithful rendition of pro-Nicene theology looks like in the twenty-first century.

In Part I, the present work sought to provide methodological and conceptual clarity on what TAT is and how it is conducted. After defining TAT as clearly as possible as an attempt to do theology that looks through the Spirit rather than at the Spirit or around the Spirit, several methodological commitments were identified. These methodological commitments included a set of ten theses and a model, namely a Wolterstorffian account. According to this model, we can look from the vantage point of control beliefs at various data beliefs through the lens of the Spirit. In other words, the Spirit can provide a connective mechanism between different theological *loci*. The method is rigorous and comprehensive, and various illustrations were provided, notably from ecclesiology. Because several scholars have found issues with TAT, an attempt was made to respond charitably to such criticisms and further explain what is and is not being claimed in a TAT. It is hoped that our critics will find more light than heat in these replies and that it will alleviate some of their concerns. Indeed, none of the current critiques has proved fatal or damaging. In most instances, it is a case of mistaken identity. Another feature of Part I was the attempt to highlight the practicality of TAT, showing how it can be used in various ways for numerous ends. TAT is especially conducive to qualitative work, and it is hoped that others will take up the challenge to use TAT in theologically rich, qualitative projects. In order to clearly illustrate these methodological principles, it was shown how fecund TAT is for biblical and theological study focusing on Christology. When TAT is applied to the Gospels, we see texts and theological features of Christology that we have not seen before, which draws us into a deeper appreciation of Christ and his central role in redemptive history (and beyond).

Part II of the present work provides dogmatic sketches of TAT in practice, visiting essential doctrines to see what yield this offers. While concise, each chapter lays out a theological vista for others to see, not to provide a gallery to be admired but (to change metaphors) to provide a seed to grow and mature. The doctrine of the Trinity was canvassed in Chapter 6, presenting a dynamic trinitarianism with a fully intersubjective account of the divine Persons. The Spirit, it was shown, is essential to the fully *perichoretic* being of God and central to understanding the divine missions. The opening words of the Lord's Prayer were then used to show the worshipful practicality of TAT.

The *locus* of community is the church, and in Chapter 7, ecclesiology was the focus of a TAT account. When seen through the Spirit, the church is the sequel to the incarnation, and faith communities are the primary place for trinitarian participation. A meditation on worship was the only fitting way to conclude.

Chapter 8 examined how human salvation is achieved through the motif of *theosis* and how the Spirit is involved with Christ in our salvation. Incarnation and atonement are part of the one cloth, and the Spirit's work is critical to a deeper appreciation of the work of the triune God in the economy of salvation. A theological meditation on evangelism, which Lewis spoke of as a concern for our neighbor's glory, concluded that discussion.

Given the commitment to the centrality of Christ and the fact that he is the *imago Dei*, Chapter 9 on anthropology made the case for seeing all humans as *imago Christi* before outlining what TAT has to contribute to our sanctification. An application to the costly business of forming our identity according to God and his will for us concluded the discussion.

Missiology was the concern of Chapter 10 as this doctrine was viewed through the lens of pneumatology. Recognizing the significant attention already given to the intersection of pneumatology and missiology, it was also highlighted there how the rigorous approach of TAT avoids the bifurcation of ecclesiology and mission and, in its place, offers a richer understanding of how the Trinity's missional outworking can be ecclesially enacted and indwelled in a way that is broad, sustainable, and far-reaching.

Finally, Chapter 11 explored eschatology as the Spirit transforming and perfecting human creatures for God's glory. The extent of the Spirit's work was seen to be broader than simply humanity, and to encompass the whole of creation and time itself. The reign of Christ is not limited to individuals, the church, or even the cosmos; it is all-encompassing, and Christ already works in the present, drawing us and all of creation toward the final kingdom come. What do we do in this time between the times? A final meditation on the Eucharist provides a sacramental summary of the work whereby we anticipate the *eschaton* by worshipping Christ the *eschatos*.

Despite the broad-ranging analysis of this volume, there is much more to be done. Good theology is generative of more good theology, and no work will have the last word because there is no end to the praise that creatures can give to the eternal God of grace and glory. A great hope of the current work is that others will catch a vision for TAT and add their keen insights to the growing chorus of voices promoting a Spiritually rich, Christ-centered theology that honors God the Father. In the fields of ontology, epistemology, hermeneutics, and theological method, TAT can offer still more fruitful contributions as others use TAT and bring their insights to bear upon these areas of study. Recent works have retrieved a good effect on prosopological exegesis; TAT could contribute much to that discourse. The renewed recognition that in Scripture, we hear the voices of the three persons of the Trinity is a related area that TAT could be helpful in further explicating. The notion of a retroactive hermeneutic noted in the fifth methodological criteria in Chapter 3 provides fertile ground for development and advancement by others. Finally, the sorts of interdisciplinary work that many today are pursuing promises a lot for theological studies, and again, TAT could be a meaningful vehicle to locate some of that research.

Each of the theological doctrines sketched in this work could be amplified, developed, and extended in helpful ways, and it is hoped that some readers will take up what we have offered and do that developmental work. We know of many researchers who are already using TAT to good effect, and we look forward to the fruits of their labors. Many Gospel texts require a TAT reading to bring out further insights and meaning, such as those already conducted on the *Messianic kairoi*. And what of the wider New Testament books? There is no end to work that can be done there. The ontological dynamics of the incarnation are another area ripe for study from the perspective of TAT. Of course, doctrines not covered in this study are also suitable topics for further research, including but not limited to hamartiology, angelology, providence, theodicy, creation, election, and so forth.

As an introduction, the present work is intended to whet the appetite, tempt into further work, and foster future research. It would have fulfilled its purpose if this work did even some of this. As we work with the Holy Spirit for the praise of Christ and the glory of God the Father, we remember God's promise in Ezek 36:26–28:

> And I will give you a new heart, and a new spirit I will put within you. And I will remove the heart of stone from your flesh and give you a heart of flesh. And I will put my Spirit within you, and cause you to walk in my statutes and be careful to obey my rules. You shall dwell in the land that I gave to your fathers, and you shall be my people, and I will be your God.

Suggested Further Reading

Bryant, Herschel O. *Spirit Christology in the Christian Tradition: From the Patristic Period to the Rise of Pentecostalism in the Twentieth Century.* Cleveland, OH: CPT Press, 2014.

Dabney, D. Lyle. "Starting with the Spirit: Why the Last Should Now Be First." Pages 3–27 in *Starting with the Spirit.* Edited by Stephen Pickard and Gordon Preece. Hindmarsh: Australian Theological Forum, 2001.

Del Colle, Ralph. *Christ and the Spirit: Spirit-Christology in Trinitarian Perspective.* Oxford: Oxford University Press, 1994.

Habets, Myk. *The Anointed Son: A Trinitarian Spirit Christology.* Eugene, OR: Pickwick Publications, 2010.

Habets, Myk, ed. *Third Article Theology: A Pneumatological Dogmatics.* Minneapolis, MN: Fortress Press, 2016.

Hawthorne, Gerald F. *The Presence and the Power: The Significance of the Holy Spirit in the Life and Ministry of Jesus.* Eugene, OR: Wipf and Stock, 2003.

Keener, Craig S. *The Spirit in the Gospels and Acts: Divine Purity and Power.* Peabody, MA: Hendrickson, 1997.

Liston, Gregory J. *The Anointed Church: Toward a Third Article Ecclesiology.* Minneapolis, MN: Fortress Press, 2015.

Liston, Gregory J. *Kingdom Come: An Eschatological Third Article Ecclesiology.* London: T&T Clark, 2022.

McDonnell, Killian. "The Determinative Doctrine of the Holy Spirit." *Theology Today* 39 (1982): 142–61.

O'Donnell, John J. "In Him and Over Him: The Holy Spirit in the Life of Jesus." *Gregorianum* 70 (1989): 25–45.

Pinnock, Clark H. *Flame of Love: A Theology of the Holy Spirit.* Downers Grove, IL: IVP Academic, 1996.

Sánchez M., Leopoldo A. *Receiver, Bearer, and Giver of God's Spirit: Jesus' Life in the Spirit as a Lens for Theology and Life.* Eugene, OR: Pickwick Publications, 2015.

Sánchez M., Leopoldo A. *Sculptor Spirit: Models of Sanctification from Spirit Christology.* Downers Grove, IL: IVP Academic, 2019.

Sánchez M., Leopoldo A. *T&T Clark Introduction to Spirit Christology.* London: T&T Clark, 2021.

Smail, Thomas A. *Reflected Glory: The Spirit in Christ and Christians.* London: Hodder and Stoughton, 1975.

van der Kooi, Cornelis. *This Incredibly Benevolent Force: The Holy Spirit in Reformed Theology and Spirituality.* Grand Rapids, MI: Eerdmans, 2018.

Bibliography

Allison, Gregg R., and Andreas J. Köstenberger. *The Holy Spirit*. Nashville, TN: B&H Academic, 2020.

Anatolios, Khaled. *Deification through the Cross: An Eastern Christian Theology of Salvation*. Grand Rapids, MI: Eerdmans, 2020.

Athanasius. *On the Incarnation*. Translated by John Behr. Yonkers, NY: St Vladimir's Seminary Press, 2011.

Athanasius. *Works on the Spirit: Athansius's Letters to Serapion on the Holy Spirit, and Didymus's on the Holy Spirit*. Edited and translated by Mark DelCogliano, Andrew Radde-Gallwitz, and Lewis Ayres. Yonkers, NY: St Vladimir's Seminary Press, 2011.

Badcock, Gary D. *The House Where God Lives: Renewing the Doctrine of the Church for Today*. Grand Rapids, MI: Eerdmans, 2009.

Balthasar, Hans Urs von. *The Theology of Karl Barth*. Translated by John Drury. New York: Holt, Rinehart and Winston, 1971.

Barth, Karl. *Church Dogmatics*. Translated by G. W. Bromiley and T. F. Torrance. Peabody, MA: Hendrickson, 2010.

Barth, Karl. "Concluding Unscientific Postscript on Schleiermacher." Pages 261–79 in *The Theology of Schleiermacher*. Edited by D. Ritschl. Grand Rapids, MI: Eerdmans, 1982.

Basil, *De Spiritu Sanctu*. Edinburgh: T&T Clark, 1989.

Bauckham, Richard. "Jürgen Moltmann's *The Trinity and the Kingdom of God* and the Question of Pluralism." Pages 155–64 in *The Trinity in a Pluralistic Age*. Edited by Kevin J. Vanhoozer. Grand Rapids, MI: Eerdmans, 1997.

Bauckham, Richard. *God Crucified: Monotheism and Christology in the New Testament*. Carlisle: Paternoster, 1998.

Begbie, Jeremy S. *Theology, Music and Time*. Cambridge: Cambridge University Press, 2000.

Belsky, Jay, Avshalom Caspi, Terrie E. Moffit, and Richie Poulton. *The Origins of You: How Childhood Shapes Later Life*. Cambridge, MA: Harvard University Press, 2020.

Bender, Kimlyn J. *Karl Barth's Christological Ecclesiology*. Aldershot: Ashgate, 2005.

Bhaskar, Roy. *A Realist Theory of Science*, 2nd ed. London: Routledge, 2008.

Billings, J. Todd. *Union with Christ: Reframing Theology and Ministry for the Church*. Grand Rapids, MI: Baker Academic, 2011.

Bloesch, Donald G. *The Holy Spirit*. Christian Foundations. Downers Grove, IL: Intervarsity Press, 2000.

Blomberg, Craig L. *1 Corinthians*. Grand Rapids, MI: Zondervan Academic, 2009.

Bobrinskoy, Boris. "Holy Spirit." Pages 470–3 in *Dictionary of the Ecumenical Movement*. Edited by Nicholas Lossky, José Miguez Bonino, John S. Pobee, Tom F. Stransky, Geoffry Wainwright, and Pauline Webb. Grand Rapids, MI: Eerdmans, 1991.

Bobrinskoy, Boris. *The Mystery of the Trinity: Trinitarian Experience and Vision in the Biblical and Patristic Tradition*. Crestwood, NY: St Vladimir's Seminary Press, 1999.

Bracken, Joseph. "Trinitarian Spirit Christology: In Need of a New Metaphysics?" *Theological Studies* 72 (2011): 750–67.

Briggman, Anthony. *Irenaeus of Lyons and the Theology of the Holy Spirit*. Oxford: Oxford University Press, 2012.

Bryant, Herschel O. *Spirit Christology in the Christian Tradition: From the Patristic Period to the Rise of Pentecostalism in the Twentieth Century*. Cleveland, OH: CPT Press, 2014.

Buxton, Graham. *Dancing in the Dark: The Privilege of Participating in God's Ministry in the World*, rev. ed. Eugene, OR: Cascade Books, 2016.

Calvin, John. *Institutes of the Christian Religion* (1559), Library of Christian Classics XX. Edited by John T. McNeill. Translated by Ford L. Battles. Philadelphia: Westminster Press, 1960.

Calvin, John. *Calvin's Commentaries*, 22 vols. Translated by John Pringle. Grand Rapids, MI: Baker Books, 2009.

Canlis, Julie. "Trinitarian Prayer: Praying from Slave-Narratives to Son-Narratives." Pages 178–91 in *Essays on the Trinity*. Edited by Lincoln Harvey. Eugene, OR: Cascade, 2018.

Cantalamessa, Raniero. *The Holy Spirit in the Life of Jesus*. Collegeville, PA: Liturgical Press, 1994.

Cantalamessa, Raniero. "The Incarnation and the Mystery of the Anointing: Christology and Pneumatology in the Early Centuries of the Church." Pages 175–92 in *Third Article Theology: A Pneumatological Dogmatics*. Edited by Myk Habets. Minneapolis, MN: Fortress Press, 2016.

Ciraulo, Jonathan Martin. "Sacraments and Personhood: John Zizioulas' Impasse and a Way Forward." *The Heythrop Journal* 53 (2012): 993–1004.

Clark, Jason Swan. "Just Go to Church." Paper presented at the Society of Vineyard Scholars Conference. London, 2019.

Claunch, Kyle D. "The Son and the Spirit: The Promise of Spirit Christology in Traditional Trinitarian and Christological Perspective." PhD diss., The Southern Baptist Theological Seminary, Louisville, KY, 2017.

Coakley, Sarah. *God, Sexuality, and the Self*. Cambridge: Cambridge University Press, 2013.

Coffey, David. *Deus Trinitas: The Doctrine of the Triune God*. New York: Oxford University Press, 1999.

Coffey, David. "The Method of Third Article Theology." Pages 21–36 in *Third Article Theology: A Pneumatological Dogmatics*. Edited by Myk Habets. Minneapolis, MN: Fortress Press, 2016.

Coffey, David. "Spirit Christology and the Trinity." Pages 315–38 in *Advents of the Spirit: An Introduction to the Current Study of Pneumatology*. Edited by Bradford E. Hinze and D. Lyle Dabney. Milwaukee, WI: Marquette University Press, 2005.

Congar, Yves. *The Word and the Spirit*. Translated by David Smith. San Francisco: Harper & Row, 1986.

Congar, Yves. *I Believe in the Holy Spirit*, 3 vols. New York: Crossroad, 1997.

Cortez, Marc. *Christological Anthropology in Historical Perspective: Ancient and Contemporary Approaches to Theological Anthropology*. Grand Rapids, MI: Zondervan, 2016.

Cortez, Marc. "Idols, Images, and a Spirit-ed Anthropology: A Pneumatological Account of the *Imago Dei*." Pages 267–82 in *Third Article Theology: A Pneumatological Dogmatics*. Edited by Myk Habets. Minneapolis, MN: Fortress Press, 2016.

Cortez, Marc. *Resourcing Theological Anthropology: A Constructive Account of Humanity in the Light of Christ*. Grand Rapids, MI: Zondervan, 2017.

Cortez, Marc. *Theological Anthropology: A Guide for the Perplexed*. London: T&T Clark, 2010.

Crisp, Oliver D. *Revisioning Christology: Theology in the Reformed Tradition*. Farnham: Ashgate, 2011.

Crowe, Brandon D. *The Last Adam: A Theology of the Obedient Life of Jesus in the Gospels*. Grand Rapids, MI: Baker Academic, 2017.

Dabney, D. Lyle. "Saul's Armour: The Problem and Promise of Pentecostal Theology." *Pneuma* 23 (2001): 115–46.

Dabney, D. Lyle. "Naming the Spirit: Towards a Pneumatology of the Cross." Pages 28–58 in *Starting with the Spirit*. Edited by Stephen Pickard and Gordon Preece. Hindmarsh: Australian Theological Forum, 2001.

Dabney, D. Lyle. "Starting with the Spirit: Why the Last Should Now Be First." Pages 3–27 in *Starting with the Spirit*. Edited by Stephen Pickard and Gordon Preece. Hindmarsh: Australian Theological Forum, 2001.

Daley, Brian E. *God Visible: Patristic Christology Revisited*. Oxford: Oxford University Press, 2018.

Danermark, Berth, Mats Ekström, Liselotte Jakobsen, and Jan Ch. Karlsson. *Explaining Society: Critical Realism in the Social Sciences*. London: Routledge, 2002.
Del Colle, Ralph. *Christ and the Spirit: Spirit-Christology in Trinitarian Perspective*. Oxford: Oxford University Press, 1994.
Del Colle, Ralph. "A Response to Jürgen Moltmann and David Coffey." Pages 339–46 in *Advents of the Spirit: An Introduction to the Current Study of Pneumatology*. Edited by Bradford E. Hinze and D. Lyle Dabney. Milwaukee, WI: Marquette University Press, 2005.
DeSilva, David A. *Transformation: The Heart of Paul's Gospel*. Bellingham, WA: Lexham Press, 2014.
DeWeese, Garrett J. "One Person, Two Natures: Two Metaphysical Models of the Incarnation." Pages 114–53 in *Jesus in Trinitarian Perspective: An Introductory Christology*. Edited by Fred Sanders and Klaus D. Issler. Nashville, TN: B&H Academic, 2007.
Duby, Steven J. *Jesus and the God of Classical Theism: Biblical Christianity in Light of the Doctrine of God*. Grand Rapids, MI: Baker Academic, 2022.
Durst, Rodrick K. *Reordering the Trinity: Six Movements of God in the New Testament*. Grand Rapids, MI: Kregel Academic, 2015.
Emery, Gilles. *The Trinitarian Theology of St. Thomas Aquinas*. Translated by Francesca A. Murphy. Oxford: Oxford University Press, 2007.
Erickson, Millard J. "Christology from Above and Christology from Below: A Study of Contrasting Methodologies." Pages 43–55 in *Perspectives on Evangelical Theology*. Edited by Kenneth S. Kantzer and Stanley N. Gundry. Grand Rapids, MI: Baker Books, 1979.
Erickson, Millard. *Christian Theology*, 3rd ed. Grand Rapids, MI: Baker Academic, 2013.
Fee, Gordon. *Pauline Christology*. Peabody, MA: Hendrickson, 2007.
Fiddes, Paul S. *Participating in God: A Pastoral Doctrine of the Trinity*. London: Darton Longman Todd, 2000.
Florovsky, Georges V. *Collected Works*, 14 vols. Belmont, MA: Nordland, 1972–89.
Foster, Richard. "Foreword." In *The Spirit of the Disciplines*. London: Hodder and Stoughton, 1988.
Fowler, James. "Practical Theology and the Shaping of Christian Lives." Pages 148–66 in *Practical Theology*. Edited by Don S. Browning. Philadelphia: Harper and Row, 1983.
Franklin, Patrick S. "The God Who Sends Is the God Who Loves: Mission as Participating in the Ecstatic Love of the Triune God." *Didaskalia* 28 (2017): 75–95.

Frost, Michael, and Alan Hirsch. *The Shaping of Things to Come: Innovation and Mission for the 21st-Century Church*. Peabody, MA: Hendrickson, 2003.

George, Roji T., ed. *The Holy Spirit and Christian Mission in a Pluralistic Context*. Bangalore: SAIACS Press, 2017.

Green, Joel. "Kaleidoscopic View." Pages 157–85 in *The Nature of the Atonement: Four Views*. Edited by James Beilby and Paul R. Eddy. Downers Grove, IL: IVP Academic, 2006.

Greggs, Tom. *The Breadth of Salvation: Rediscovering the Fullness of God's Saving Work*. Grand Rapids, MI: Baker Academic, 2020.

Grenz, Stanley J. *Theology for the Community of God*. Grand Rapids, MI: Eerdmans, 1994.

Grenz, Stanley J. *Rediscovering the Triune God: The Trinity in Contemporary Theology*. Minneapolis, MN: Fortress Press, 2004.

Grenz, Stanley J. *The Named God and the Question of Being: A Trinitarian Theo-Ontology*. Louisville, KY: Westminster John Knox Press, 2005.

Grosso, Andrew. "Spirit Christology and the Shape of the Theological Enterprise." Pages 206–22 in *A Man of the Church: Honoring the Theology, Life, and Witness of Ralph Del Colle*. Edited by Michel René Barnes. Eugene, OR: Pickwick Publications, 2012.

Guder, Darrell L. *Be My Witnesses*. Grand Rapids, MI: Eerdmans, 1985.

Guidero, Kirsten L. "Filled with 'The Fullness of the Gifts of God': Towards a Pneumatic Theosis." PhD Diss., Marquette University, Wisconsin, 2020.

Guidero, Kirsten L. " 'In the Unity of the Spirit': A Third Article Theology of Receptive Ecumenism." Pages 463–78 in *Third Article Theology: A Pneumatological Dogmatics*. Edited by Myk Habets. Minneapolis, MN: Fortress Press, 2016.

Gunton, Colin E. *Yesterday and Today: A Study of Continuities in Christology*. London: Darton, Longman & Todd, 1983.

Gunton, Colin. "The Church on Earth: The Roots of Community." Pages 48–80 in *On Being the Church*. Edited by C. Gunton and D. Hardy. Edinburgh: T&T Clark, 1989.

Gunton, Colin E. *Christ and Creation*. Grand Rapids, MI: Eerdmans, 1992.

Gunton, Colin. "John Owen and John Zizioulas on the Church." Pages 187–205 in *Theology through the Theologians: Selected Essays (1972–1995)*. London: T&T Clark, 1996.

Gunton, Colin. "Two Dogmas Revisited: Edward Irving's Christology." Pages 151–68 in *Theology through the Theologians: Selected Essays (1972–1995)*. London: T&T Clark, 1996.

Gunton, Colin. *The Promise of Trinitarian Theology*, 2nd ed. Edinburgh: T&T Clark, 1997.

Gunton, Colin. "Salvation." Pages 143–58 in *The Cambridge Companion to Karl Barth*. Edited by John Webster. Cambridge: Cambridge University Press, 2000.

Gunton, Colin. "Baptism: Baptism and the Christian Community." Pages 201–15 in *Father, Son and Holy Spirit: Toward a Trinitarian Theology*. London: T&T Clark, 2003.

Habets, Myk. "Spirit Christology: Seeing in Stereo." *Journal of Pentecostal Theology* 11 (2003): 199–235.

Habets, Myk. "Developing a Retroactive Hermeneutic: Johannine Theology and Doctrinal Development." *American Theological Inquiry* 1 (2008): 77–89.

Habets, Myk. "'The Dogma Is the Drama': Dramatic Developments in Biblical Theology." *Stimulus* 16 (2008): 2–5.

Habets, Myk. *Theosis in the Theology of Thomas F. Torrance*. Farnham: Ashgate, 2009.

Habets, Myk. *The Anointed Son: A Trinitarian Spirit Christology*. Eugene, OR: Pickwick Publications, 2010.

Habets, Myk. "*Filioque? Nein*: A Proposal for Coherent Coinherence." Pages 161–202 in *Trinitarian Theology after Barth*. Edited by Myk Habets and Phillip Tolliday. Eugene, OR: Pickwick Publications, 2011.

Habets, Myk. "Getting Beyond the *Filioque* with Third Article Theology." Pages 211–30 in *Ecumenical Perspectives on the Filioque for the Twenty-First Century*. Edited by Myk Habets. London: Bloomsbury T&T Clark, 2014.

Habets, Myk. "The Surprising Third Article Theology of Jonathan Edwards." Pages 195–212 in *The Ecumenical Edwards: Jonathan Edwards and the Theologians*. Edited by Kyle Strobel. Farnham: Ashgate, 2014.

Habets, Myk. "The Fallen Humanity of Christ: A Pneumatological Clarification of the Theology of Thomas F. Torrance." *Participatio* 5 (2015): 18–44.

Habets, Myk. "Prolegomenon: On Starting with the Spirit." Pages 1–20 in *Third Article Theology: A Pneumatological Dogmatics*. Edited by Myk Habets. Minneapolis, MN: Fortress Press, 2016.

Habets, Myk. "Spirit Christology: The Future of Christology?" Pages 207–31 in *Third Article Theology: A Pneumatological Dogmatics*. Edited by Myk Habets. Minneapolis, MN: Fortress Press, 2016.

Habets, Myk, ed. *Third Article Theology: A Pneumatological Dogmatics*. Minneapolis, MN: Fortress Press, 2016.

Habets, Myk. "Review Essay, Matthew Levering, *Engaging the Doctrine of the Holy Spirit: Love and Gift in the Trinity and the Church* (Grand Rapids: Baker Academic, 2016)." *Modern Theology* 34 (2017): 677–9.

Habets, Myk. (With Leopoldo A. Sánchez, M.). "Introduction: Spirit Christology and the Theological Interpretation of Scripture." *Journal of Theological Interpretation* 12 (2018): 1–2.

Habets, Myk. *The Progressive Mystery: Tracing the Elusive Spirit in Scripture and Tradition*. Bellingham, WA: Lexham Press, 2019.

Habets, Myk. "Spirit Christology and the Power of Jesus." NP, in *T&T Clark Handbook of Christology*. Edited by Chris Tilling and Darren Sumner. London: Bloomsbury T&T Clark, forthcoming.

Haight, Roger. "The Case for Spirit Christology." *Theological Studies* 53 (1992): 257–87.

Hauerwas, Stanley. *The Peaceable Kingdom*. Notre Dame, IN: SCM Press, 1983.

Hawthorne, Gerald F. *The Presence and the Power: The Significance of the Holy Spirit in the Life and Ministry of Jesus*. Eugene, OR: Wipf and Stock, 2003.

Hildebrandt, Wilf. *On Old Testament Theology of the Spirit of God*. Peabody, MA: Hendrickson, 1995.

Hill, Wesley. *Paul and the Trinity: Persons, Relations, and the Pauline Letters*. Grand Rapids, MI: Eerdmans, 2015.

Hinze, Bradford E., and D. Lyle Dabney, eds. *Advents of the Spirit: An Introduction to the Current Study of Pneumatology*. Milwaukee, WI: Marquette University Press, 2001.

Hirsch, Alan. *The Forgotten Ways*. Grand Rapids, MI: Brazos Press, 2006.

Holmes, Christopher R. J. *The Holy Spirit*. Grand Rapids, MI: Zondervan, 2015.

Holmes, Stephen R. *The Quest for the Trinity: The Doctrine of God in Scripture, History and Modernity*. Downers Grove, IL: IVP Academic, 2012.

Holwerda, David E. "Suffering Witnesses—to What End?: A Sermon on Revelation 11:1-14." *Calvin Theological Journal* 41 (2006): 127–32.

Hunsinger, George. "Baptism and the Soteriology of Forgiveness." *International Journal of Systematic Theology* 2 (2000): 247–69.

Hunsinger, George. *The Eucharist and Ecumenism*. Cambridge: Cambridge University Press, 2008.

Hunsinger, George. *How to Read Karl Barth: The Shape of His Theology*. New York: Oxford University Press, 1991.

Hunt, Anne. "The Trinity and the Church: Explorations in Ecclesiology from a Trinitarian Perspective." *Irish Theological Quarterly* 70(3): 215–35.

Hurtado, Larry W. *God in New Testament Theology*. Library of Biblical Theology. Nashville, TN: Abingdon, 2010.

Irenaeus. *On the Apostolic Preaching*. St. Vladimir's Popular Patristics Series No. 17. Translated by John Behr. Crestwood, KY: St Vladimir's Seminary Press, 1997.

Issler, Klaus. "Jesus' Example: Prototype of the Dependent, Spirit-Filled Life." Pages 189–225 in *Jesus in Trinitarian Perspective: An Introductory Christology*. Edited by Fred Sanders and Klaus D. Issler. Nashville, TN: B&H Academic, 2007.

Issler, Klaus. *Living into the Life of Jesus: The Formation of Christian Character*. Downers Grove, IL: InterVarsity, 2012.

Jamieson, R. B., and Tyler R. Wittman. *Biblical Reasoning: Christological and Trinitarian Rules for Exegesis*. Grand Rapids, MI: Baker, 2022.

Johnson, Adam J. *Atonement: Guide for the Perplexed*. London: Bloomsbury T&T Clark, 2015.

Johnson, Keith E. "The Work of the Holy Spirit in the Ministry of Jesus Christ: A Trinitarian Perspective." Paper presented at the annual meeting of the Evangelical Theological Society, San Diego, CA, November 20, 2014.

Jones, Paul H. *Christ's Eucharistic Presence: A History of the Doctrine*. New York: Peter Lang, 1994.

Kapic, Kelly M. "The Spirit as Gift: Explorations in John Owen's Pneumatology." Pages 113–40 in *The Ashgate Research Companion to John Owen's Theology*. Edited by K. M. Kapic and M. Jones. Surrey: Ashgate, 2012.

Kärkkäinen, Veli-Matti. *An Introduction to Ecclesiology: Ecumenical, Historical and Global Perspectives*. Downers Grove, IL: IVP Academic, 2002.

Kärkkäinen, Veli-Matti. *Toward a Pneumatological Theology: Pentecostal and Ecumenical Perspectives on Ecclesiology, Soteriology, and Theology of Mission*. Lanham, MD: University Press of America, 2002.

Keener, Craig S. *The Spirit in the Gospels and Acts: Divine Purity and Power*. Peabody, MA: Hendrickson, 1997.

Kieser, Ty. "The Holy Spirit and the Humanity of Christ in John Owen: A Re-examination." *International Journal of Systematic Theology* 25 (2023): 93–113.

Kilby, Karen. "Perichoresis and Projection: Problems with Social Doctrines of the Trinity." *New Blackfriars* 81 (2000): 432–45.

Kim, Kirsteen. *Mission in the Spirit: The Holy Spirit in Indian Christian Theologies*. Delhi: ISPCK, 2003.

Kim, Kirsteen. "The Shift from *Missio Dei* to *Missio Spiritus* in Recent Mission Thinking: The Indian Contribution." Pages 152–64 in *The Holy Spirit and Christian Mission in a Pluralistic Context*. Edited by Roji T. George. Bangalore: SAIACS Press, 2017.

Kim, Kirsteen. "Foreword." Pages xiii–xiv in *Third Article Theology: A Pneumatological Dynamics*. Edited by Myk Habets. Minneapolis, MN: Fortress Press, 2016.

Langdon, Adrian. *God the Eternal Contemporary: Trinity, Eternity and Time in Karl Barth*. Eugene, OR: Wipf & Stock, 2012.

Leithart, Peter J. "The Way Things Really Ought to Be: Eucharist, Eschatology, and Culture." *The Westminster Theological Journal* 59 (1997): 159–76.

Levison, Jack. *A Boundless God: The Spirit according to the Old Testament*. Grand Rapids, MI: Baker Academic, 2020.

Levison, Jack. *An Unconventional God: The Spirit according to Jesus*. Grand Rapids, MI: Baker Academic, 2021.
Lewis, Clive S. *Reflections on the Psalms*. Collins: Fount Paperbacks, 1961.
Lewis, Clive S. *A Grief Observed*. London: Faber and Faber, 1966.
Lewis, Clive S. "Meditation in a Toolshed." Pages 52–5 in *Compelling Reason: Essays on Ethics and Theology*. Edited by W. Hooper. London: Fount, 1998.
Lewis, Clive S. *Mere Christianity*. London: Collins, 2012.
Lewis, Clive S. *Faith, Christianity, and the Church*. C. S. Lewis Essay Collection. Edited by Lesley Walmsley. London: HarperCollins, 2020.
Liston, Gregory J. *The Anointed Church: Toward a Third Article Ecclesiology*. Minneapolis, MN: Fortress Press, 2015.
Liston, Gregory J. "A 'Chalcedonian' Spirit Christology." *Irish Theological Quarterly* 81 (2016): 74–93.
Liston, Gregory J. "The Church's Journey through Time: Toward a Spirit Eschatology." *Pneuma* 41 (2019): 43–60.
Liston, Gregory J. "Eschatology and Munus Triplex: The Threefold Anointing of the Spirit in Time." *Journal of Reformed Theology* 14 (2020): 323–43.
Liston, Gregory J. *Kingdom Come: An Eschatological Third Article Ecclesiology*. London: T&T Clark, 2022.
Liston, Gregory J. "Where the Love of Christ Is Found: Toward a Third Article Ecclesiology." Pages 321–46 in *Third Article Theology: A Pneumatological Dogmatics*. Edited by Myk Habets. Minneapolis, MN: Fortress Press, 2016.
Lord, Andrew. *Spirit-Shaped Mission: A Holistic Charismatic Missiology*. Milton Keynes: Paternoster, 2005.
Macchia, Frank D. *Baptized in the Spirit: A Global Pentecostal Theology*. Grand Rapids, MI: Zondervan, 2006.
Macchia, Frank D. *Jesus the Spirit Baptizer: Christology in the Light of Pentecost*. Grand Rapids, MI: Eerdmans, 2018.
Macchia, Frank D. *The Spirit-Baptized Church: A Dogmatic Inquiry*. London: T&T Clark, 2020.
MacDougall, Scott. *More than Communion: Imagining an Eschatological Ecclesiology*. London: T&T Clark, 2015.
Maclean, Stanley S. *Resurrection, Apocalypse, and the Kingdom of Christ: The Eschatology of Thomas F. Torrance*. Eugene, OR: Pickwick Publications, 2012.
Macy, Gary. *The Banquet's Wisdom: A Short History of the Theologies of the Lord's Supper*. New York: Paulist, 1992.
Marshall, I. Howard. *Last Supper and Lord's Supper*. Vancouver: Regent College Publishing, 1980.

McCall, Thomas H. *Which Trinity? Whose Monotheism? Philosophical and Systematic Theologians on the Metaphysics of Trinitarian Theology*. Grand Rapids, MI: Eerdmans, 2010.

McDonnell, Killian. "The Determinative Doctrine of the Holy Spirit." *Theology Today* 39 (1982): 142–61.

McDonnell, Killian. "A Trinitarian Theology of the Holy Spirit." *Theological Studies* 46 (1985): 191–227.

McDonnell, Killian. "A Response to D. Lyle Dabney." Pages 262–4 in *Advents of the Spirit: An Introduction to the Current Study of Pneumatology*. Edited by Bradford E. Hinze and D. Lyle Dabney. Milwaukee, WI: Marquette University Press, 2005.

McFarland, Ian A. "Spirit and Incarnation: Toward a Pneumatic Chalcedonianism." *International Journal of Systematic Theology* 16 (2014): 143–58.

McFarland, Ian A. "The Saving God." Pages 61–74 in *Sanctified by Grace: A Theology of the Christian Life*. Edited by Kent Eilers and Kyle C. Strobel. London: Bloomsbury T&T Clark, 2014.

McGowan, Andrew T. B. *The Divine Spiration of Scripture: Challenging Evangelical Perspectives*. Nottingham: Apollos, 2007.

McGrath, Alister E. *Christian Theology*, 2nd ed. Malden, MA: Blackwell, 1994.

McGrath, Alister E. *Reality: A Scientific Theology*, vol 2. Grand Rapids, MI: Eerdmans, 2002.

McMaken, W. Travis. *The Sign of the Gospel: Toward an Evangelical Doctrine of Infant Baptism after Karl Barth*. Minneapolis, MN: Fortress Press, 2013.

McNall, Joshua M. *The Mosaic of Atonement: An Integrated Approach to Christ's Work*. Grand Rapids, MI: Zondervan Academic, 2019.

Moltmann, Jürgen. *The Spirit of Life: A Universal Affirmation*. Translated by Margaret Kohl. Minneapolis, MN: Fortress Press, 1992.

Moore, Russell D., I. John Hesselink, David P. Scaer, and Thomas A. Baima. *Understanding Four Views on the Lord's Supper*. Grand Rapids, MI: Zondervan, 2007.

Mühlen, Heribert. *Una Mystica Persona. Die Kirche als das Mysterium der heilsgeschichtlichen Identität des Heiligen Geistes in Christus und den Christen: Eine Person in vielen Personen*, 2nd ed. Paderborn: Ferdinand Schöningh, 1967.

Mühlen, Heribert. "The Person of the Holy Spirit." Pages 11–33 in *The Holy Spirit and Power*. Edited by Kilian McDonnell. Garden City, NY: Doubleday, 1975.

Neuhaus, Richard John. "Wolfhart Pannenberg: Profile of a Theologian." Pages 9–50 in *Theology and the Kingdom of God*. Edited by Richard John Neuhaus. Philadelphia: Westminster, 1969.

Newbigin, Lesslie. *One Body, One Gospel, One World: The Christian Mission Today*. London: Wm. Carling & Co., 1958.
O'Byrne, Declan. *Spirit Christology and Trinity in the Theology of David Coffey*. Bern: Peter Lang, 2010.
O'Collins, Gerald, and Michael Keenan Jones. *Jesus Our Priest: A Christian Approach to the Priesthood of Christ*. Oxford: Oxford University Press, 2010.
O'Donnell, John J. "In Him and Over Him: The Holy Spirit in the Life of Jesus." *Gregorianum* 70 (1989): 25–45.
Pannenberg, Wolfhart. *Jesus—God and Man*. Translated by L. L. Wilkins and D. A. Priebe. London: SCM, 1968.
Payne, Don J. *Already Sanctified: A Theology of the Christian Life in Light of God's Completed Work*. Grand Rapids, MI: Baker Academic, 2020.
Pelikan, Jaroslav. *Creedo: Historical and Theological Guide to Creeds and Confessions of Faith in the Christian Tradition*. New Haven: Yale University Press, 2003.
Pelikan, Jaroslav, and Valerie Hotchkiss, eds. *Creeds and Confessions of Faith in the Christian Tradition: Early, Eastern and Medieval*. New Haven, CT: Yale University Press, 2003.
Peppiatt, Lucy. "Spirit Christology and Mission." PhD thesis, University of Otago, Dunedin, New Zealand, 2010.
Peppiatt, Lucy. "New Directions in Spirit Christology: A Foundation for a Charismatic Theology." *Theology* 117 (2014): 3–10.
Persaud, Winston D. "The Theology of the Cross as Christian Witness: A Theological Essay." *Currents in Theology and Mission* 41 (2014): 11–16.
Peterson, Cheryl M. "Who Is the Church?" *Dialog* 51 (2012): 24–30.
Peterson, Cheryl M. *Who Is the Church? An Ecclesiology for the Twenty-First Century*. Minneapolis, MN: Fortress Press, 2013.
Peterson, Eugene. *Practise Resurrection*. London: Hodder & Stoughton, 2010.
Pinnock, Clark H. *Flame of Love: A Theology of the Holy Spirit*. Downers Grove, IL: IVP Academic, 1996.
Polanyi, Michael. *Personal Knowledge: Towards a Post-Critical Philosophy*. London: Routledge & Kegan Paul, 1969.
Polkinghorne, John. *The Faith of a Physicist*. Minneapolis, MN: Fortress Press, 1996.
Pugh, Ben. *SCM Study Guide to Theology in the Contemporary World*. London: SCM Press, 2017.
Purves, Andrew. "The Advent of Ministry: Torrance on Eschatology, the Church, and Ministry." Pages 95–127 in *Evangelical Calvinism: Volume 2. Dogmatics and Devotion*. Edited by Myk Habets and Bobby Grow. Eugene, OR: Pickwick, 2017.

Rahner, Karl. *Theological Investigations*, vol. 13, *Theology, Anthropology, Christology*. Translated by D. Bourke. London: Darton, Longman & Todd, 1974.

Rahner, Karl. *The Trinity*. Translated by Joseph Donceel. Tunbridge Wells: Burns & Oates, 1997.

Rosato, Philip J. "Called by God, in the Holy Spirit: Pneumatological Insights into Ecumenism." *Ecumenical Review* 30 (1978): 110–26.

Rosato, Philip J. "The Mission of the Spirit within and beyond the Church." *Ecumenical Review* 41 (1989): 388–97.

Rothman, Joshua. "Are You the Same Person You Used to Be?" *The New Yorker* (October 3, 2022): https://www.newyorker.com/magazine/2022/10/10/are-you-the-same-person-you-used-to-be-life-is-hard-the-origins-of-you; accessed March 13, 2023.

Sánchez M., Leopoldo A. *Receiver, Bearer, and Giver of God's Spirit: Jesus' Life in the Spirit as a Lens for Theology and Life*. Eugene, OR: Pickwick Publications, 2015.

Sánchez M., Leopoldo A. "Sculpting Christ in Us: Public Faces of the Spirit in God's World." Pages 297–320 in *Third Article Theology: A Pneumatological Dogmatics*. Edited by Myk Habets. Minneapolis, MN: Fortress Press, 2016.

Sánchez, M., Leopoldo A. (With Myk Habets). "Introduction: Spirit Christology and the Theological Interpretation of Scripture." *Journal of Theological Interpretation* 12 (2018): 1–2.

Sánchez M., Leopoldo A. *Sculptor Spirit: Models of Sanctification from Spirit Christology*. Downers Grove, IL: IVP Academic, 2019.

Sánchez M., Leopoldo A. *T&T Clark Introduction to Spirit Christology*. London: T&T Clark, 2021.

Sanders, Fred. *Fountain of Salvation: Trinity and Soteriology*. Grand Rapids, MI: Eerdmans, 2021.

Sarot, Marcel. "Trinity and Church: Trinitarian Perspectives on the Identity of the Christian Community." *International Journal of Systematic Theology* 12(1): 33–45.

Scheeben, Matthias J. *The Mysteries of Christianity*. Translated by Cyril Vollert from the 1941 original. New York: Herder and Herder, 2006.

Schleiermacher, Friedrich. *The Christian Faith*. London: T&T Clark, 1999.

Seitz, Christopher R. *The Elder Testament: Canon, Theology, Trinity*. Waco, TX: Baylor University Press, 2018.

Sirks, G. J. "The Cinderella of Theology: The Doctrine of the Holy Spirit." *Harvard Theological Review* 50 (1957): 77–89.

Smail, Thomas A. *Reflected Glory: The Spirit in Christ and Christians*. London: Hodder and Stoughton, 1975.

Smith, Christian. *What Is a Person? Rethinking Humanity, Social Life, and the Moral Good from the Person Up*. Chicago: University of Chicago Press, 2010.
Smith, James K. A. *The Nicene Option: An Incarnational Phenomenology*. Waco, TX: Baylor University Press, 2021.
Smith, James K. A. *Thinking in Tongues: Pentecostal Contributions to Christian Philosophy*. Grand Rapids, MI: Eerdmans, 2010.
Smith, James K. A. *Desiring the Kingdom: Worship, Worldview, and Cultural Formation*. Grand Rapids, MI: Baker Academic, 2009.
Smith, Steven G. *The Concept of the Spiritual: An Essay in First Philosophy*. Philadelphia: Temple University Press, 1988.
Snavely, Andréa. *Life in the Spirit: A Post-Constantinian and Trinitarian Account of the Christian Life*. Eugene, OR: Pickwick, 2015.
Soulen, R. Kendall. *The Divine Name(s) and the Holy Trinity: Distinguishing the Voices*. Louisville, KY: Westminster John Knox, 2011.
Spence, Alan. "The Significance of John Owen for Modern Christology." Pages 171–84 in *The Ashgate Research Companion to John Owen's Theology*. Edited by Kelly M. Kapic and Mark Jones. Surrey: Ashgate, 2012.
Stăniloae, Dumitru. *Orthodox Dogmatic Theology*, vol. 1. *Revelation and Knowledge of the Triune God: The Experience of God*. Translated and edited by Ioana Ionita and Robert Barringer. Brookline, MA: Holy Cross Orthodox Press, 1994.
Studebaker, Steven M. *From Pentecost to the Triune God: A Pentecostal Trinitarian Theology*. Grand Rapids, MI: Eerdmans, 2012.
Studebaker, Steven M. *The Trinitarian Vision of Jonathan Edwards and David Coffey*. New York: Cambria, 2011.
Sutherland, Martin. "Pine Trees and Paradigms: Rethinking Mission in the West." Pages 131–48 in *Mission without Christendom: Exploring the Site*. Edited by Martin Sutherland. Auckland: Carey Baptist College, 2000.
Swinton, John, and Harriet Mowat. *Practical Theology and Qualitative Research*. London: SCM, 2006.
Tan, Carolyn E. L. *The Spirit at the Cross: Exploring a Cruciform Pneumatology: An Investigation into the Holy Spirit's Role at the Cross*. Eugene, OR: Wipf and Stock, 2019.
Tanner, Kathryn. *Christ the Key*. Cambridge: Cambridge University Press, 2010.
Tanner, Kathryn. "Beyond the East/West Divide." Pages 198–210 in *Ecumenical Perspectives on the Filioque for the Twenty-First Century*. Edited by Myk Habets. London: Bloomsbury/T&T Clark, 2014.
Tanner, Kathryn. *Jesus, Humanity and the Trinity: A Brief Systematic Theology*. Minneapolis, MN: Fortress Press, 2001.
Taylor, Charles. *Modern Social Imaginaries*. Durham, NC: Duke University Press, 2004.

Taylor, John V. *The Go-Between God*. London: SCM, 1972.

Teer, Torey J. S. "Inseparable Operations, Trinitarian Missions, and the Necessity of a Christological Pneumatology." *Journal of Theological Studies* 72 (2021): 337–61.

Teer, Torey J. S. "The Perfector of All Divine Acts: The Holy Spirit and the Providence of God." *Bibliotheca Sacra* 177 (2020): 402–21.

Thompson, Marianne Meye. *The Promise of the Father: Jesus and God in the New Testament*. Louisville, KY: Westminster/John Knox, 2000.

Thompson, Matthew K. *Kingdom Come: Revisioning Pentecostal Ecclesiology*. Dorset: Deo Publishing, 2010.

Torrance, Alexis. *Human Perfection in Byzantine Theology: Attaining the Fullness of Christ*. Oxford: Oxford University Press, 2020.

Torrance, James B. *Worship, Community and the Triune God of Grace*. Downers Grove, IL: IVP Academic, 1996.

Torrance, Thomas F. "Eschatology and the Eucharist." Pages 303–50 in *Intercommunion*. Edited by D. M. Baillie and J. Marsh. London: SCM, 1952.

Torrance, Thomas F. "The Modern Eschatological Debate." *Evangelical Quarterly* 25 (1953): 45–54, 94–106, 67–78, 224–32.

Torrance, Thomas F. "Atonement and the Oneness of the Church." *Scottish Journal of Theology* 7 (1954): 245–69.

Torrance, Thomas F. *Theology in Reconstruction*. Grand Rapids, MI: Eerdmans, 1965.

Torrance, Thomas F. *Space, Time and Resurrection*. Edinburgh: T&T Clark, 1976.

Torrance, Thomas F. *Reality and Scientific Theology*. Edinburgh: Scottish Academic Press, 1985.

Torrance, Thomas F. "The Soul and Person in Theological Perspective." Pages 103–18 in *Religion, Reason, and the Self: Essays in Honour of Hywel D. Lewis*. Edited by S. R. Sutherland and T. A. Roberts. Cardiff: University of Wales Press, 1989.

Torrance, Thomas F. *Royal Priesthood: A Theology of Ordained Ministry*. Edinburgh: T&T Clark, 1993.

Torrance, Thomas F. *Incarnation: The Person and Life of Christ*. Edited by Robert T. Walker. Downers Grove, IL: IVP Academic, 2008.

Torrance, Thomas F. *The Christian Doctrine of God: One Being Three Persons*. Cornerstones Edition. London: Bloomsbury T&T Clark, 2016.

Torrance, Thomas F. *The Trinitarian Faith: The Evangelical Theology of the Ancient Catholic Church*. Cornerstones Series. London: Bloomsbury T&T Clark, 2016.

Treier, Daniel J. *Introducing Theological Interpretation of Scripture: Recovering a Christian Practice*. Grand Rapids, MI: Baker Academic, 2008.

Tyra, Gary. *The Holy Spirit in Mission: Prophetic Speech and Action in Christian Witness*. Downers Grove, IL: Intervarsity Press, 2011.

Vahanian, Gabriel "Introduction." Pages 7–22 in Karl Barth, *The Faith of the Church: A Commentary on the Apostle's Creed*. London: Fontana, 1960.

van der Kooi, Cornelis. "On the Identity of Jesus Christ: Spirit Christology and Logos Christology in Converse." Pages 193–206 in *Third Article Theology: A Pneumatological Dogmatics*. Edited by Myk Habets. Minneapolis, MN: Fortress Press, 2016.

van der Kooi, Cornelis. *This Incredibly Benevolent Force: The Holy Spirit in Reformed Theology and Spirituality*. Grand Rapids, MI: Eerdmans, 2018.

van der Kooi, Cornelis, and Gijsbert van den Brink. *Christian Dogmatics: An Introduction*. Grand Rapids, MI: Eerdmans, 2017.

Vidu, Adonis. *The Same God Who Works All Things: Inseparable Operations in Trinitarian Theology*. Grand Rapids, MI: Eerdmans, 2021.

Volf, Miroslav. *After Our Likeness: The Church as the Image of the Trinity*. Grand Rapids, MI: Eerdmans, 1998.

Vondey, Wolfgang. *Heribert Mühlen: His Theology and Praxis*. Dallas, TX: University Press of America, 2004.

Vondey, Wolfgang. "The Holy Spirit and Time in Contemporary Catholic and Protestant Theology." *Scottish Journal of Theology* 58 (2005): 393–409.

Wainwright, Arthur W. *The Trinity in the New Testament*. London: SPCK, 1962, 1969.

Wainwright, Geoffrey. *Eucharist and Eschatology*. London: Epworth Press, 1971.

Ware, Bruce A. *The Man Christ Jesus: Theological Reflections on the Humanity of Christ*. Wheaton, IL: Crossway, 2013.

Watson, Francis. "The Triune Divine Identity: Reflections on Pauline God-Language, in Disagreement with J. D. G. Dunn." *Journal for the Study of the New Testament* 80 (2000): 91–111.

Webster, John. "In the Society of God: Some Principles of Ecclesiology." Pages 200–22 in *Perspectives on Ecclesiology and Ethnography*. Edited by Pete Ward. Grand Rapids, MI: Eerdmans, 2012.

Weinandy, Thomas G. *The Father's Spirit of Sonship: Reconceiving the Trinity*. Edinburgh: T&T Clark, 1995.

Weinandy, Thomas G. *Jesus Becoming Jesus: A Theological Interpretation of the Synoptic Gospels*. Washington, DC: Catholic University of America Press, 2018.

Weinandy, Thomas G. "The Trinity and the Father's Spirit of Sonship: Further Considerations on Reconceiving the Trinity." Pages 455–78 in *Engaging Catholic Doctrine: Essays in Honor of Matthew Levering*. Edited by

Robert Brown, Scott W. Hahn, and James R. A. Merrick. Steubenville, OH: Emmaus Academic, 2023.

Welker, Michael. *God the Spirit*. Translated by J. F. Hoffmeyer. Minneapolis, MN: Fortress Press, 1994.

Wellum, Stephen J. *God the Son Incarnate: The Doctrine of Christ*. Wheaton, IL: Crossway, 2016.

Wessel, Walter W. "Mark." In *Expositor's Bible Commentary*, vol. 8. Edited by Frank E. Gaebelein. Grand Rapids, MI: Zondervan, 1984.

Witt, Willian G., and Joel Scandrett. *Mapping Atonement: The Doctrine of Reconciliation in Christian History and Theology*. Grand Rapids, MI: Baker Academic, 2022.

Wolterstorff, Nicholas. *Reason within the Bounds of Religion*. Grand Rapids, MI: Eerdmans, 1976.

Yarhouse, Mark A. *Homosexuality and the Christian*. Minneapolis, MN: Bethany House, 2010.

Yong, Amos. *In the Days of Caesar: Pentecostalism and Political Theology*. Grand Rapids, MI: Eerdmans, 2010.

Yong, Amos. *The Missiological Spirit: Christian Mission Theology in the Third Millenium Global Context*. Eugene, OR: Cascade Books, 2014.

Yong, Amos. *Mission after Pentecost: The Witness of the Spirit from Genesis to Revelation*. Grand Rapids, MI: Baker Academic, 2019.

Yong, Amos. *Renewing Christian Theology: Systematics for a Global Christianity*. Waco, TX: Baylor University Press, 2014.

Yong, Amos. "Introduction: Pentecostalism and a Theology of the Third Article." Pages xiii–xx in *Toward a Pneumatological Theology: Pentecostal and Ecumenical Perspectives on Ecclesiology, Soteriology, and Theology of Mission*. Edited by Amos Yong. Lanham, MD: University Press of America, 2002.

Zizioulas, John. *Communion and Otherness: Further Studies in Personhood and the Church*. London: T&T Clark, 2006.

Author Index

Alfaro, Sammy 71, 80
Allison, Greg 66, 68-71, 75-6, 161, 217
Aquinas, Thomas 75, 101, 106-7, 220
Augustine 26, 140
Ayres, Lewis 217

Badcock, Gary D. 117, 217
Baima, Thomas A. 205, 226
Balthasar, Hans Urs von 192, 217
Barringer, Robert 110, 229
Barth, Karl 12-13, 48, 62-4, 85, 116-17, 120, 122-3, 192-4, 196-7, 217, 221-4, 226, 230
Basil of Caesarea 53, 162
Bauckham, Richard 100, 131-2, 217
Begbie, Jeremy S. 172, 217
Bender, Kimlyn J. 62-3, 217
Belsky, Jay 161, 217
Bhaskar, Roy 91, 217
Billings, J. Todd 162, 217
Bloesch, Donald G. 66-8, 218
Blomberg, Craig L. 203, 218
Bobrinskoy, Boris 5, 47, 96, 218
Bonino, José Miguez 5, 218
Bracken, Joseph 85, 218
Briggman, Anthony 7, 218
Brown, Robert 106, 231
Brümmer, Vincent 133
Bryant, Herschel O. 31, 34, 215, 218
Buxton, Graham 86, 218

Calvin, John 38, 71, 128, 158, 182-3, 218, 223
Canlis, Julie 112-13, 218

Cantalamessa, Raniero 32, 39, 42-3, 77, 89, 218
Caspi, Avshalom 161, 217
Claunch, Kyle D. 70, 72, 74, 76, 81, 218
Coakley, Sarah 13, 75, 110, 219
Coffey, David 11, 15, 32, 48, 56, 59-60, 71, 76, 80, 126, 132, 219-20, 226, 229
Congar, Yves 11, 25, 219
Cortez, Marc 152, 154, 219
Crisp, Oliver D. 66, 68, 70, 72-4, 86-7, 219
Crowe, Brandon D. 37-9, 219
Cyril of Alexandria 37

Dabney, D. Lyle 4, 6, 9, 11, 14, 17-18, 45-7, 49-52, 54-6, 75, 116, 126, 132, 215, 219-20, 223, 225-6
Daley, Brian E. 33, 219
Danermark, Berth 90-1, 219
Del Colle, Ralph 11, 31-2, 34-5, 46, 56, 70, 80, 132, 215, 220-1
deSilva, David 160, 162-3, 166
DeWeese, Garrett J. 68-72, 220
Didymus the Blind 99-100, 217
Donceel, Joseph 59, 227
Duby, Steven J. 26, 30, 220
Durst, Rodrick K. 76, 220

Eddy, Paul R. 144, 221
Ekström, Mats 90, 219
Emery, Gilles 101, 220
Erickson, Millard J. 16, 69, 78, 121, 220

Fiddes, Paul S. 131, 220
Fitch, David 178

Florovsky, Georges V. 84–5, 220
Foster, Richard 207, 220
Fowler, James 90, 220
Franklin, Patrick S. 178, 220
Frost, Michael 177–8, 220

George, Roji T. 170, 220, 224
Gijsbert van den 67, 230
Green, Joel 144, 221
Greggs, Tom 143, 153, 221
Grenz, Stanley J. 9, 110, 121, 186, 221
Grosso, Andrew 46, 49, 52, 61, 221
Guder, Darrell L. 178, 221
Guidero, Kirsten L. 85, 221
Gunton, Colin 7, 9–10, 39, 50, 78, 116, 119–20, 122, 125, 192, 221

Habets, Myk 5, 7, 9, 11–14, 26–9, 31–3, 35, 37–43, 45–6, 48–50, 53, 55–6, 67, 69, 71–81, 83, 85, 87, 100, 105, 107, 111, 123, 126, 133, 145, 155, 157, 163, 184, 189, 193, 208, 215, 218–19, 221–2, 224–5, 227–30
Haight, Roger 31, 49, 67, 222
Hauerwas, Stanley 186, 223
Hawthorne, Gerald F. 68–74, 215, 223
Hesselink, John 205, 226
Hildebrandt, Wilf 27, 223
Hildegard of Bingen 149
Hill, Wesley 100, 223
Hirsch, Alan 177–8, 220, 223
Holmes, Christopher R. J. 66, 76–7, 223
Holmes, Stephen R. 10, 223
Holwerda, David E. 182, 223
Hotchkiss, Valerie 3, 6–7, 115, 191, 193, 227
Hunsinger, George 19, 62–3, 116, 120, 122, 223
Hunt, Anne 132, 223
Hurtado, Larry W. 97–8, 100, 110, 113, 223

Irenaeus of Lyon 7, 38, 157, 162, 218, 223
Irving, Edward 7, 221
Issler, Kluas 68–74, 220, 223

Jakobsen, Liselotte 90, 219
Johnson, Adam J. 137, 143–4, 223
Johnson, Keith E. 74, 223
Jonathan Martin C. 121, 218
Jones, Michael K. 129, 226
Jones, Paul H. 205, 229

Kapic, Kelly M. 7, 224, 229
Kärkkäinen, Veli-Matti 12, 18, 20, 53, 56, 75, 80, 117, 119, 224
Karlsson, Jan Ch. 90, 219
Kegan, Paul 16, 227
Khaled, Anatolios 101, 108, 137, 217
Kieser, Ty 72, 224
Kilby, Karen 125, 224
Kim, Kirsteen 5, 75, 170, 224
Köstenberger, Andreas J. 66, 68–71, 75–6, 217

Lampe, Geoffrey 31, 80
Langdon, Adrian 192, 224
Leithart, Peter J. 205–8, 224
Levison, Jack 26–7, 30, 36–7, 224
Lewis, Clive S. 16, 85, 133–4, 148–51, 157, 208, 212, 217, 224–5, 230
Liston, Gregory J. 11, 33–5, 42, 46, 48–50, 56–7, 73–6, 81, 118, 121–2, 126, 131, 180, 183–6, 189–91, 193, 209, 215, 225
Luther, Martin 145

Macchia, Frank D. 12, 173, 193, 225
MacDougall, Scott 205, 225
Maclean, Stanley S. 192–3, 225
Macy, Gary 205, 225
Marshall, I. Howard 203, 225
McCall, Thomas H. 110, 225
McDonnell, Killian 16–17, 47, 215, 225–6
McFarland, Ian A. 74, 160, 226

McGowan, Andrew T. B. 51, 226
McGrath, Alister E. 10, 90, 226
McMaken, W. Travis 122, 226
McNall, Joshua M. 144, 226
Moffit, Terrie E. 161, 217
Moltmann, Jürgen 40, 71, 76, 124, 131–2, 173, 197, 217, 220, 226
Moore, Russell D. 205, 226
Mowat, Harriet 90, 229
Mühlen, Heribert 11, 16–17, 42, 47, 61, 226, 231

Nazianzen, Gregory 95–6, 99–100, 159
Neuhaus, Richard John 205, 226
Newbigin, Lesslie 169, 184–5, 226

Owen, John 7, 72–3, 75, 86, 221, 224, 229
O'Byrne, Declan 60, 226
O'Donnell, John 40, 215, 226

Pannenberg, Wolfhart 78, 197, 205, 226
Payne, Don J. 158–60, 162, 227
Pelikan, Jaroslav 3, 6–7, 84–5, 115, 191, 193, 227
Peppiatt, Lucy 71, 73, 169–70, 227
Persaud, Winston D. 182, 227
Peterson, Cheryl M. 115, 227
Peterson, Eugene 118, 181, 227
Pinnock, Clark H. 4, 13, 15, 25, 42, 46–7, 56, 75, 174, 215, 227
Polanyi, Michael 16, 61, 227
Polkinghorne, John 49, 60, 227
Poulton, Richie 161, 217
Pugh, Ben 75, 227
Purves, Andrew 193, 227

Radde-Gallwitz, Andrew 217
Rahner, Karl 59–60, 63, 78–9, 227
Rosato, Philip J. 19, 50, 68, 200, 227
Rothman, Joshua 161, 227

Sánchez M., Leopoldo A. 13, 31–3, 35, 43, 54, 56, 70–1, 81, 84, 87, 170, 193, 207, 215, 222, 228
Sanders, Fred 68, 135, 137–43, 220, 223, 228
Sarot, Marcel 133, 228
Scaer, David P. 205, 226
Scandrett, Joel 144, 231
Scheeben, Matthias J. 98, 101–5, 136, 138–42, 228
Schleiermacher, Friedrich 13, 48, 119, 217, 228
Seitz, Christopher R. 100, 228
Sirks, G. J. 10, 228
Smail, Thomas A. 144–5, 147–8, 152–3, 216, 228
Smith, Christian 153, 228
Smith, James K. A. 12, 204, 228
Smith, Steven G. 17, 228
Snavely, Andréa 67, 79–81, 228
Soulen, R. Kendall 111, 229
Spence, Alan 7, 229
St. Symeon 142
Stăniloae, Dumitru 110, 229
Strauss, Mark L. 110
Studebaker, Steven M. 15, 56, 66, 74–5, 195, 229
Sutherland, Martin 8, 157, 229–30
Swinton, John 90, 229

Tan, Carolyn E. L. 145, 229
Tanner, Kathryn 76, 107–10, 124–6, 129, 229
Taylor, Charles 204, 229
Taylor, John V. 148, 229
Teer, Torey J. S. 26, 229
Thompson, Marianne Meye 111, 229
Thompson, Matthew K. 195, 229
Torrance, Thomas F. 49, 62, 87, 90, 95–6, 99–100, 110, 132, 137–8, 142, 154, 157, 159, 180–1, 192–8, 202–3, 210, 217, 222, 225, 227, 229–30

Treier, Daniel J. 60, 230
Tyra, Gary 169, 230

Vahanian, Gabriel 85, 230
van der Kooi, Cornelis 67, 70, 197, 199, 216, 230
Vanhoozer, Kevin J. 50, 131, 217
Vidu, Adonis 26, 96, 98, 231
Volf, Miroslav 124–5, 131–2, 231
Vondey, Wolfgang 11, 17, 61, 192, 231

Wainwright, Arthur W. 100, 231
Wainwright, Geoffrey 5, 206, 218, 231
Ware, Bruce A. 69, 72–4, 231
Watson, Francis 100, 231
Webster, John 125, 192, 221, 231

Weinandy, Thomas G. 11, 64, 76–7, 101, 105–19, 112, 123, 126, 156, 183, 231
Welker, Michael 17, 68, 231
Wellum, Stephen J. 66, 68–72, 779, 231
Wessel, Walter W. 38, 231
Witt, Willian G. 144, 231
Wittman, Tyler R. 100, 223
Wolterstorff, Nicholas 21, 56, 58–61, 116, 191, 231

Yarhouse, Mark A. 164–6, 232
Yong, Amos 8, 10, 12, 56, 75, 80, 169, 174, 191, 194, 232

Zizioulas, John 7, 121, 124, 132, 192, 197, 218, 221, 232

Subject Index

Abba 40, 110–13, 128, 139, 145–6
Adam 37–8, 42, 137, 155
adoptionism, adoptionist 66–7, 68, 79, 139–40
analogical, analogous 57–8, 62–4, 116, 123, 125–7, 133, 181
anhypostasia, anhypostatic 63, 87, 120, 155
anoint 28–9, 34–5, 40, 43, 50–1, 88–9, 99, 142, 160, 169, 181, 187, 193
anthropology, anthropological 9, 22, 79, 85, 87, 89, 92, 136–7, 143–4, 152–9, 163–5, 189, 212
architectonic, archaeologically 24, 66, 135, 137
arrabōn 149, 209
ascended, ascension 41–2, 147, 153, 159
ascending Christology 33, 78
Athanasian, Athanasius 71, 97–9
atone, atonement 136–7, 142–4, 159, 212

banquet 203, 205, 225
baptism, baptistic, baptismal 12, 30, 36–7, 40, 43, 73, 86, 88, 111, 119–22, 129, 137, 145–7, 149, 161, 203
begets, begotten 6, 11, 98, 102, 104–9, 112, 123, 126, 128
beloved 40, 113, 145
blasphemous, blasphemy 30, 112, 149
blood 147, 203
bodily, body 42–3, 47, 80, 86, 88, 117, 119–20, 128–9, 133, 147–8, 155–6, 178, 180–1, 187
breath 15, 127, 129, 138, 162, 184–5

bride 119, 142, 204

Calvinisticum 70–1, 88
canon 28, 33, 50, 86
Chalcedon, Chalcedonian 31–3, 62–3, 71, 73–7, 84, 87, 116, 120, 137–8, 193
charismatic 50, 145, 169, 170–1, 173–6
children of God 112, 139, 157, 163, 167
Christendom 19, 54, 115
Christlike, Christification, Christoform 42, 53, 89, 89, 118, 156–7, 163, 166
Christocentric 12, 51
commune, communion 85–6, 103–4, 106, 111–13, 117, 124, 142, 148, 153, 159, 180, 183, 191, 203, 205–9
conformation, conformity 85, 89, 146, 151, 155, 158, 162, 164
consummation 25, 27, 29, 148, 151, 194
conversion, converts 15, 77, 89, 135, 137
coronation 41–2, 145, 151
corruption 139, 199
covenant 111, 157
creator 123, 125, 154, 207
creature, creaturely 9, 53, 63, 73, 89, 98, 99, 113, 123, 125, 138–40, 143, 147, 148, 155, 207, 209, 213
creed, creedal 6–7, 54, 61, 84–6, 191
crucicentric, crucifixion, cruciform 42, 51, 118, 145, 191

Davidic, David 11, 29, 29, 37, 56, 80, 160
deification, deified 114, 136–8, 140, 156
demonic, demons 39, 149, 172

Subject Index

denominational, denominations 10, 13, 19–20, 43, 83, 85, 119
dialogical (epistemology) 56, 58, 61
disciples, discipleship 4, 8, 16, 38, 40, 43, 55, 75, 79, 81, 87, 97, 110–11, 145–7, 150, 156–8, 172, 182
Docetism, Docetic 117, 120
donum 107, 138

Eastern, East (church) 13, 96, 104–7, 121
economic, economy 21–2, 26, 42–3, 52, 59, 63, 73–4, 77, 79, 87, 91, 96–7, 99–100, 113, 123, 126–7, 139, 212
ecumenical, ecumenism 10, 18–19, 43, 54–6, 83–6, 97, 109, 18–19
empowered, endowed, enlivened 8, 15, 29, 29, 34, 57, 88, 107, 151, 155, 157, 161, 163, 174, 181, 182, 188, 195, 207, 209
enhypostasia, enhypostatic 39, 63, 87, 120
epistemological, epistemology 4, 8, 9, 12, 17, 48, 49, 56, 58–60, 80, 90–1, 96, 178, 213
eschatological, eschatology, eschaton 22, 41, 46, 52, 58, 61, 85, 92, 119, 151, 171–2, 179–80, 188–96, 198, 204–7, 209, 213
essence 53, 73, 76, 106, 109, 111, 141, 163, 178, 208
Eucharist 151, 202–10, 213
evangelical, evangelism, evangelistic 43, 67, 96, 150–1, 172, 187, 212
evil 18, 37, 39–40, 146, 172, 198
exaltation 29, 41, 73, 145, 159

faith, faithful 14, 21, 24–5, 34–5, 39, 54–5, 79, 83–6, 89–91, 98, 112, 118, 121–2, 137, 144, 158, 162, 166, 203, 211–12
fallen 6, 8, 87–9, 113, 119, 143, 154–5, 190, 194–7, 203
fatherhood 106, 108, 133
fellowship 131, 142, 147, 162, 171, 203

filled 41, 71, 95, 125, 156, 163, 199–200
flesh 42, 87–9, 160, 194, 203, 214
freedom 36, 186–8, 199–201

Garden
  of Eden 163
  of Gethsemane 40, 145–6
global Christianity 19, 51
glorification, glory 88–9, 113, 132, 135, 137, 145, 147, 150–1, 154–8, 160, 195, 199, 212–14
Godhead 8, 16, 27, 52, 59, 98, 100–1, 103–5, 107, 127, 154, 160
Good News 142, 149–50, 166
gospel 25–26, 30, 35–40, 39, 51, 51, 79–81, 86, 88, 96, 99, 110–13, 145–7, 150, 163, 178, 212, 214
grace 6–7, 21, 36, 42, 83, 86, 113, 129, 138–41, 147, 150–1, 158, 176, 213
Grundaxiom, grundaxiom 59–60, 63

heal, healing 29, 39, 74, 171, 186, 197, 199, 201
hearts 128, 157, 175, 200, 206, 209
heaven, heavenly 6, 37, 43, 71, 141, 152, 164, 171–2, 196, 203
heresies, heresy 31, 67, 120, 158
hermeneutic 50, 213
historical 6, 19, 48, 78, 118–19
holiness 53, 176, 195, 198
homoousion, homoousios 33, 71, 99–100
hope 11, 18–20, 29, 36, 86, 89, 142, 146, 149, 151, 164, 167, 205, 213
human beings 135, 154, 160–2, 200
humanity (of Christ) 22, 33, 39, 41, 50, 78–9, 87–8, 123, 127–8, 138, 152, 154–5, 158, 169, 196, 198
humanity (of church) 117, 153, 166–7, 186, 200, 203
humility 29, 86
hypostases, hypostatic 63, 87, 95, 103, 124, 126–8, 138, 183, 193–4

imago Christi 212, 154–6
imago Dei 137, 152, 154–5, 212
immanence 15, 79, 173
immortal, immortality 139, 148–9, 166
incarnandus, incarnate, incarnation 15, 22, 25, 30, 33–4, 38, 42, 46, 57, 64, 68–73, 77, 78, 87–9, 96, 100, 114, 118, 125, 127–8, 136, 138, 139, 142–3, 155–7, 159, 161, 180, 192–3, 212, 214
individualism, individualistic 178, 206
indwell 38, 88, 117, 124, 126, 130–1, 143, 160
infancy 8, 37, 157, 164
infused (with the Spirit) 14, 20, 148
institution 185–6, 188
Israel 15, 28–30, 36–7

Jewish 36, 88, 111, 26–7
journey 5, 53, 55, 161, 172, 186, 189–91
judge 29, 144, 199
judgment 200, 209
justice 29, 144, 171, 185–7, 198–202
justification, justified 7, 9, 20, 65, 89, 91–2, 118, 135, 144, 152, 158, 160, 191, 199

kairoi 24, 35, 41, 86, 99, 145, 214
king, kingship 28–9, 34, 37, 53, 185, 200–2, 204–9, 197–8

liberal, liberty 31, 121, 159, 199–201
liberation 13, 38, 167
Light 26, 50, 96
likeness 124, 156, 160, 162
Logos 21–2, 27, 31–3, 35, 49, 63–4, 68, 70, 73, 80, 87, 117, 155, 190, 192–6
love 39, 76, 77, 89, 96, 102, 106–9, 112, 127, 130, 138–41, 148, 150–1, 160, 171, 183–4, 186–7, 198, 200–2
Lutheran, Lutherans 13, 31, 54, 87, 121

manifest, manifestation 29, 52, 98, 103, 105, 132, 137

martyrdom, martyrs 30, 182
Mary 25, 30, 36–7, 64, 87, 147
maturation, maturity 88, 155, 157, 161, 164
meditation 22, 212–13
Messiah, messianic 24, 26, 29, 33–42, 38, 39, 51, 81, 86, 87, 89, 99, 145–6, 160, 214
ministerially, ministry 15, 26, 28–9, 35–43, 74, 86, 88, 146–7, 151, 158–9, 176, 201, 205
missiological, missiology 22, 92, 168–71, 173–4, 176–87, 213
missionary 19, 169, 175–7, 183, 188
mystery 24, 96, 98, 148, 165
mystical 121, 126, 128–9, 183

narrative, story 9, 30, 37, 51–2, 77, 81, 86, 110, 112, 118, 142, 145, 149, 153, 155, 163–4, 172, 178, 181–2
Nazareth 33, 35, 43, 72, 87
neighbor, neighborhoods 136, 150–1, 169, 212
Nicaea, Nicene, Niceno 6–7, 12, 32–3, 77, 84, 159, 211

obedience, obey 37–9, 88–9, 155, 157, 159, 162, 214
ontic, ontological, ontology 8, 17, 33, 48, 58, 79, 85–8, 91, 97, 106, 109, 112–13, 116, 119, 127, 196–7, 206, 209, 213–14
opera trinitatis ad extra indivisa sunt 89, 98
operations 22, 26–7, 69, 73–4, 87, 97–100, 148, 174
oppression 40, 185–6, 199, 201
ordo cognoscendi, ordo essendi 47, 77
Orthodox 13, 71, 84–5, 110, 121, 136, 142

Paraclete, *paraclētos* 42, 151
participation (in Christ's offices) 43, 51, 90, 158

participation (in the coming Kingdom) 199, 204
participation (of church in Christ, Trinity) 7–8, 22, 129, 131–3, 138, 141–2, 147, 152, 199, 212
participatory 126, 129–30
passion 38, 40–1, 73, 79, 142–7, 151
pastoral 13, 20, 86, 146
Paul (apostle) 42, 86, 112, 128, 146, 150, 159, 162–3, 166, 200
Pentecost 29, 38, 41–2, 74–5, 80–1, 145, 151
Pentecostal, Pentecostalism 12, 31, 56, 74, 79–80, 84, 156, 169, 171, 173–4
perfector 24, 27, 34, 52
perichoresis, perichoretic 106, 108–9, 124, 127, 132, 212
personal 22, 51, 54, 73, 87, 89, 102–5, 107, 124–5, 127, 152, 162–3, 165, 174
person 11, 47, 68, 102–4, 153, 157, 161, 194, 220, 226–8, 230
personed 104, 127–31
personhood 157, 164–5
physical 121, 155–6, 180, 199
poor, poverty 40, 43, 146, 159, 185, 199–200
possession 39, 42, 88, 102–4, 149
postmodern, postmodernism 18, 48, 53, 58
pour, outpouring 42, 147, 156
power, powerful 6–7, 14–15, 20, 27, 29, 35, 38–41, 43, 69, 74, 87–9, 108, 128, 148, 160, 162, 164, 166, 171, 198–9, 209
practice 11, 20, 40, 49, 54–5, 79, 116, 121, 202–3, 207–10, 212
praise 30, 37, 150–1, 171, 213–14
pray 30, 40, 89, 97, 110–13, 132–3, 145–6, 173, 176, 183, 208, 212
preach 40, 150
pregnancy, pregnant 30, 37
presence (of Christ in the church through the Spirit) 50, 80, 117, 143, 156, 181, 196, 199–201
presence (of Christ in the practices of the Church (e.g. Eucharist)) 205–6, 209–10
presence (of Spirit transformation of individuals to be like Christ) 20, 97, 141, 149, 156–7, 160, 162
presence (of the kingdom) 191, 193, 201–2, 205–6
priest, priesthood 34, 37, 88–9, 129, 206
procession 76, 97, 103, 107, 139–40
proclaim, proclamation 9, 18, 40, 198–9
prolegomena, proleptic 24, 85, 180, 185
prophecy 29, 36, 39, 148, 171
prophet 15, 29, 28–9, 34–5, 37, 88, 206
prophetic 37, 156, 169, 196–7
Protestant, Protestantism 7, 12–13, 56, 84, 87, 119, 203
purity 158, 176

radiance 88, 154–5
realism, realist 21, 83, 90–1
receive, receiver 28, 98, 130, 146–7, 150, 159, 207
Reformation, Reformed, Reformers 7, 12–13, 87, 143, 206
reign 133, 147, 197, 201–2, 206, 213
relational, relationality 12, 17–18, 48, 53, 85, 97, 101, 109, 112–13, 118, 124, 127, 130, 142
resurrection 15, 41, 51–2, 80–1, 129, 145, 147–8, 155, 157, 162, 166, 194–6, 199, 204
reveal 34, 37, 98–100, 181, 187, 198
revelation 4, 16, 22, 29, 35, 49–50, 52–3, 59–60, 77, 81, 85, 99, 123, 126, 152, 211
righteous, righteousness 29, 37, 146, 160, 162, 186, 198, 200, 207
royal 129, 201
ruach, rûah 26–9, 162

sacrament, sacramental 5, 47, 121–2, 131, 191, 203, 210, 213
sacrifice, sacrificial 111, 155, 159, 181, 200

salvation, salvific, save 22, 33, 39, 43, 88, 114, 129, 135–6, 138–43, 148–53, 156–7, 160, 163, 172, 174, 184, 196, 212
sanctification, sanctity 53–4, 89, 135–7, 141, 144, 149, 152–3, 157–60, 162, 166, 213
Satan 38, 89
scholastic, scholasticism 6, 96, 110, 136, 138
science, scientific 8, 48–9, 60, 91, 96
send 29, 175
servant 29, 38, 146, 159, 211
sign 122, 186, 188, 191
sin, sinfulness 6, 9, 16, 37, 39–41, 43, 51, 87, 113, 125, 143, 159, 164, 195, 199
Son of Man 35, 146
sons, sonship 39, 106–9, 113, 119, 127–9, 132, 139, 141–2, 183, 208–9
soteriology 10, 22, 59–60, 92, 128, 135–9, 141–4, 151–3, 156, 189
soul 70, 72, 141–2
spirate, spiration 97, 102, 105, 107–8, 140
spiritual, spirituality 5, 8, 19, 39–40, 47, 53, 85, 112, 143, 148, 152, 156, 158, 161, 166, 170–1, 175–6, 182, 188, 199, 207
suffer 29, 146, 172, 181–2, 186–7, 199
supper 122, 203–4, 206, 208

telic, *telos* 53, 65, 191, 196, 202, 210
temporal 48, 64, 192, 194–5, 203
tempt, temptation 38, 40, 142, 214
testimony 28, 31, 121, 143, 154
theosis, theotic 13, 22, 114, 136–42, 152, 156–7, 212, 148–50
Thomism, Thomist, Thomistic 76, 77, 101, 106, 110
throne 29, 42, 199
tradition 13–14, 31–2, 34, 70, 77, 82, 84, 86–7, 97, 101–3, 105–7, 110, 136–7, 139, 140, 149, 154, 211

transcendence, transcendent, transcendental 15, 78, 79, 157, 162, 173–3
transfiguration 69, 156
Trinitarian renaissance 6, 9–10, 22
trinitarianism 77, 80, 97, 101, 106, 124, 212
triune, triunity 25–7, 31, 50, 75, 77, 95, 97–104, 108–10, 113, 137, 151, 155, 212

unitarian 98, 132
unity 18–19, 52, 54, 62, 64, 85, 96, 101, 105, 132, 140, 171, 175–6, 186–8, 200–1, 207
universal, universality 6–7, 18, 19, 41, 171–4, 176, 188
unorthodox 31, 70, 72, 77–8, 85

virgin 36, 71

weak, weakness 38, 68, 81, 147
wedding 120, 204, 206
West, Western 6, 13, 19, 53, 96, 104–7, 115, 170
wilderness 30, 40
wisdom 28, 88–90, 102, 198
witness 15, 40, 141, 143–4, 151, 178, 181–2
Wolterstorffian 59–61, 179, 211
womb 37, 64, 71
Word 27, 35, 46, 52, 63, 74, 88, 99, 102, 108, 122, 127, 129, 183, 193
worldview 90–1, 204
worship, worshipful 9, 22, 111, 116, 131–3, 149, 151, 155, 157, 159, 163, 171, 183, 202, 212

Yahweh, YHWH 29, 111